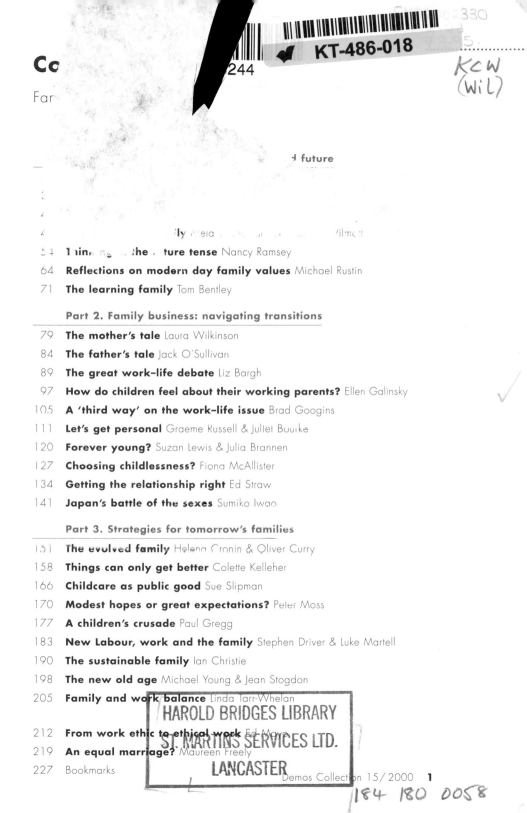

Co

Far

d future

Family Business

Demos Collection / issue 15

Contents Editor
Helen Wilkinson

Production Editor
Lindsay Nash

Editorial Team
Ian Christie
Emma Garman
Tom Bentley

Printed in Great Britain by
Redwood Books, Trowbridge, Wilts

Demos Collection is
published bi-annually by
Demos
Panton House
25 Haymarket
London SW1Y 4EN

tel: 0171 321 2200
fax: 0171 321 2342

mail@demos.co.uk
www.demos.co.uk

© Demos 2000 except
where stated otherwise
All rights reserved

ISSN 1361-1275
ISBN 1 84180 005 8

Demos is an independent think tank
committed to radical thinking on the
long-term problems facing the UK and
other advanced industrial societies.

Demos gratefully acknowledges
core funding from:
Esmée Fairbairn Charitable Trust,
Joseph Rowntree Charitable Trust,
Cable and Wireless, Northern
Foods, Pearson, Shell International,
BDO Stoy Hayward, National
Westminster Bank, the RAC, the
Inland Revenue Staff Federation, the
Lord Ashdown Charitable Settlement,
Tesco plc and Tedworth Charitable
Trust.

Helen Wilkinson and Demos
gratefully acknowledge funding from
the Tedworth Charitable Trust for this
piece of work. Thanks are also due
to the Commonwealth Fund of New
York for financing Helen Wilkinson's
Harkness Fellowship which helped
generate the ideas and contributors
for this collection.

Acknowledgements

The ideas, themes and networks gathered in this collection have a long gestation. In some ways, they represent the maturation of my thinking on gender,
work and family change for just over half a decade. In other respects, my
insights originate from way back – from my own experiences of work and
family life.

More specifically the energy and impetus for this collection comes from the
eighteen month period I spent in America between 1997 and 1999. I am
especially indebted to Ellen Galinksy, President and co-founder of the Families
and Work Institute and her staff both for their ideas, their generosity and their
support during my Harkness Fellowship. There are others gathered in this
collection – thinkers of the calibre of Arlene Skolnick and the like – who have
had a strong influence on my thinking and who now form part of my intellectual
global family. It is a delight to be able to gather their thoughts together in this
collection.

None of this would be possible without generous funding from the Todworth
Charitable Trust who have funded my work on gender, parenting and work–life
issues for quite some time. My thanks to Jamie Sainsbury in particular. I literally
could not do it without you.

On a personal level, I'd like to express my gratitude to my own extended family
– friends as well as blood relatives of course. You have been my enduring
stability. Thank you for being there. Finally, special mention must be made of my
parents, Marian and Mike, for generously giving me opportunities they never
had, and my sister Laura and her husband Fred, for bringing my nephew
Morgan into this world and for giving me my excuse to come home.

Helen Wilkinson
Contents Editor
Autumn 1999

Family Business

Helen Wilkinson

'Whatever direction public policy takes with respect to the
family, we are going to have to take the feminine/ caretaking/
family economy as seriously as we take the competitive/ market/
business economy of economic man. The caretaking economy
and the competitive economy are two sides of the same economic
reality, neither of which can function without the other'

Shirley P Burggraf, *author of* The Feminine Economy and
Economic Man

The family is our most precious business: the foundation of social
cohesion and economic growth.

Partly because of this, family values are in focus across the political
spectrum. Yet despite the rhetoric and symbolism, too little thought
has been given to the family unit as the central dimension of the
new economy. Although the need for skills and talent in this
economy is heavily debated, little attention is given to the supply of
future workers, or their social and family context. As a result, we
ignore the vital role that families play as generators of the nation's
wealth.

This leads to unsustainability. Nurturing families in the new
context – a global economy, major change in gender relations and in
social values – requires a new way of thinking about families. This
collection presents the foundation for such an approach. In this
essay, I set out its major strands and propose a range of policies that
can support tomorrow's families in ways which benefit us all.

The family reshaped

Although often debated in isolation, family life has always been profoundly affected by the wider economic and social context, and reshaped during periods of historical change. The symptoms of change – disruption, dissolution and renewal – are apparent for all to see. As Arlene Skolnick's article shows, each period of social and economic development generates a new model of family life.

The industrial era produced a distinctive pattern of family life: a rigid gender division of labour between the male breadwinner and female caregiver, the physical separation of work and home, and a particular kind of relationship between the paid and care economies.

The post-industrial era is precipitating new family forms and new sets of relationships. Families are becoming more open, democratic and flexible. Gender roles are fluid, even if they are not yet entirely equal. Children are involved in family decision-making; they are heard as well as seen.[1] Diversity has become the norm, as non-traditional families become part of the mainstream. Family networks and kinship structures are flexible and diverse, extending outwards and embracing friends as well as blood relatives.[2]

As Melanie Howard and Michael Wilmott show, the network paradigm helps to explain the new family structures. Tomorrow's families also mirror the extended families of the pre-industrial era. Michael Young and Jean Stogdon envision a 'new old age', where grandparents help ease the care burden at critical life transitions in return for nurture in old age, and become the 'new parents' in the event of family death or breakdown.[3]

Just as the physical separation of work and home in the industrial era gave birth to the traditional nuclear family, today's blurring of boundaries between work and home is accelerating the decline of hierarchy and patriarchy. Dual-earning families already define the new economy, in the same way that male breadwinners defined the industrial era. Modems, faxes, email and the Internet are enabling a shift to portfolio parenting, as well as portfolio working.

As women have entered the workforce, more and more household labour has been outsourced, contributing to the growth of the service economy and creating job opportunities in areas such as cooking, cleaning, gardening and DIY. Families increasingly resemble the micro-businesses of the new economy. They are once again becoming sites of production as well as consumption – what Alvin

1 See for example, the chapter on relationships and family life in Wilkinson H and Mulgan G, 1995, *Freedom's Children*, Demos, London. Organisations like Synergy Brand Values and Socio-Consult who track cultural change argue that emerging family values include flexibility, autonomy and interdependence.
2 Wilkinson H, 1999, 'Celebrate the new family', *New Statesman*, 9 August 1999, and also 'Family and Friends', *Big Ideas*, BBC 2, 8 August 1999.
3 The Henley Centre for Forecasting also predicts a return to the old style 'Waltons' household, as one solution to the care needs of families as they manage work and caring responsibilities in the future.

Toffler describes as 'prosumption' – just as they were in the pre-industrial era.[4]

In this sense, organisational restructuring and innovation in business – especially outsourcing to consultants and associates – is mirrored in the organisation of modern family life. As Tom Bentley argues, the commonalities between the emerging relationships, structures and functioning of late twentieth century families and the world of work are coming into view.

Trouble and strife

By all accounts, it would be easy to view these changes as leading harmoniously to a new model of family life and relationships. But the process of change is inherently fraught. The current wave of family change – and the stress and disruption that accompany it – are rooted in global economic forces and gender change. Nancy Ramsey's article offers some scenarios to help us think more flexibly about the future.

Part 2 of this collection deals with the challenge of transition – for individuals and for society at large. Laura Wilkinson and Jack O'Sullivan remind us that today's parents are pioneers, navigating new ways of working and organising family life, at a time when the supporting institutional infrastructure has yet to adapt.

It is no longer feasible – nor indeed desirable – to prop up the traditional nuclear family.[5] The transition to a new period of family life must be recognised as inevitable, and as bringing a new set of opportunities, especially for women. But on current trends, the emerging family relationships will not undergo a smooth, spontaneous transition without policies supporting their growth. The qualities and outcomes we value most in family life must be explicitly protected and nurtured.

The current pressures on family life stem from two inter-related factors. The first concerns the value we ascribe to families. The second concerns the dynamics of global capitalism.

Family values

At the most basic level, families generate social capital. They are the foundation of civil society, fostering trust, relationship skills and moral values. They are a crucible for the formation of secure attachments and intimate relationships. But this is only one side of the

4 Toffler A, 1980, *Third Wave*, Pan Books in association with Collins, London.

5 See for example, Wilkinson H, 1994, *No Turning Back: Generations and the genderquake*, Demos, London, and also Wilkinson H, 1998, 'The Family Way', in Hargreaves I and Christie I, eds, *Tomorrow's Politics*, Demos, London.

coin. Social capital enhances and generates *economic* value, and contributes to national wealth. Families enable people to feel secure, creative and productive. They underpin safe and sustainable communities, in which enterprises and business can thrive.

But families also have economic value in their own right. They are the site of reproduction – producing children to sustain the future system as workers and as consumers. They are the epicentre of the care economy, without which the paid economy cannot function. As Ed Straw reminds us, they are sites of learning,[6] acting as informal schools, colleges and skills agencies. In this sense, they are the first tier of a lifelong learning system.

This means that strong families are not just the epicentre of thriving communities and of the care economy, they are also the *hubs* of the new economy, the powerhouses of long-term economic growth. Indeed, the family's role in the emerging knowledge economy is actually more important than ever before.[7] This helps to explain why, in the prime minister's lexicon, strong families are at the centre of New Labour's communitarianism.

One reason why the economic dimension of family life has not been sufficiently recognised is that the value of unpaid work has not, until recently, been visible. Historically, the industrial era was underpinned by a settlement between men and women, paid and unpaid labour, the formal economy and the shadow world of reciprocity and mutual exchange. Women did the domestic labour, while men went out to work and were paid. The market was able to take the family as a constant, without having to factor its work into explicit calculations of price and value.

This arrangement had costs, but until recently they were privately borne, primarily by women. They help to explain the legacy of inequality that we are still grappling with: the opportunity-costs of having children, the family pay gap and the reasons why women have historically clustered in part-time, low-paid work. Mona Harrington's article argues that the current crisis is therefore as much an issue of social justice as of care.

The globalisation of economic activity, the growing time demands of paid work and the entry of women into the labour force are together helping to unravel this historical relationship between the paid and care economies. Women's unpaid work is no longer available in ways it once was. The family now has to compete in the mar-

6 For more on families as sites of learning, see Alexander T, 1997, *Family Learning: The foundation of effective education*, Demos, London.
7 Wilkinson, 1998 (note 5).

ketplace for its members' time and resources. As a result, family life is subject to unprecedented pressures.

For households, this means a crisis of time and money. As Liz Bargh shows, the conflict between the demands of the workplace and the needs of family life is a defining feature of our culture. A 'time squeeze'[8] haunts many people's lives – with low-income working families especially pressured because they are unable to buy help on the scale they need it.

This creates a crisis of care and nurture – a care deficit.[9] So far, the most common response to the new demands, and to women's increasing role in the labour market, has been to outsource household work. But there are clear limits to this approach. As Ellen Galinsky cogently argues, children need investments of time and energy. But the relentless pressure on working life and the growing insecurity of the labour market make it easy to see how families can get short shrift.

Relationships between adults also suffer. Graeme Russell and Juliet Bourke remind us that the pressure of long working hours and increased productivity on the job means that time spent with family members, and on cultivating intimate relationships, is the first casualty.[10] Time pressures also heighten conflict between couples as they seek to negotiate new roles and responsibilities. The knock-on effects include high rates of divorce and family separation. Relationship breakdown already costs the state billions of pounds. For others, the problem is finding the time to form intimate partnerships in the first place.[11]

Short-term capitalism

There is another factor that renders current changes in work and family life unsustainable. The demand for greater productivity generates direct costs for employers as well as individuals. Long working hours, job insecurity and the intensification of work affect our health, emotional and mental well-being.[12] In the end, the negative effects of long working hours impact adversely on the bottom line – through stress, ill-health, absenteeism and lost productivity. Problems at home impact adversely on poor work performance, and stress at work makes home life even more difficult, escalating the pressures in a vicious cycle. Partly as a consequence, relationship management is at a premium at work and at home, as Ed Straw's article shows.

The pressures created by the dynamic of contemporary capitalism

8 See Mulgan G and Wilkinson H, 1995, 'Well-being and time', The Time Squeeze, Demos Quarterly issue 5, Demos, London.
9 See Etzioni A, 1993, The Parenting Deficit, Demos, London and also Wilkinson, 1994 (note 5). See also Arlene Skolnick and Mona Harrington in this Collection.
10 See also Liz Bargh in this Collection.
11 See for example, working papers on Generation X in Demos's Seven Million Project and Wilkinson and Mulgan, 1995 (note 1). Liz Bargh writing in this Collection argues that the desire for work–life balance is strong among the single and childless as well as working parents.
12 See for example Job Insecurity and Work Intensification: Flexibility and the changing boundaries of work, 1999, Joseph Rowntree Foundation, York. See also Wilkinson H, 1997, Time Out: The costs and benefits of paid parental leave, Demos, London.

are also undermining the capacity of the system to sustain itself. The costs to the environment are all too evident. Ian Christie's analysis of the impact of the time squeeze on our spatial politics highlights the way in which personal choices are rapidly becoming unsustainable public problems.

The global market place is also sapping families of their energy and vitality. The most important indicator of the sustainability of the household economy is its capacity to reproduce itself, maintaining the balance between older and younger generations. The continued decline of birth rates in post-industrial societies provides stark evidence of unsustainability. In the UK we are no longer producing enough children to balance future worker–pensioner ratios. The same trends can be seen in Australia, Europe, America and Asia (with some notable exceptions like Scandinavia). In Japan, the prime minister has established a special commission to identify responses to the problem.

More often than not, these trends are discussed in cultural terms, viewed through a feminist lens. However, as Fiona McAllister shows, constraints in the economic environment are as important as social and value change in helping to explain childlessness. Part of the reason is that the opportunity costs have gone up – women lose relatively more in income and career prospects from taking time out of the labour market. Where government and employers have failed to step in and fill this gap, women have paid the economic price, with the result that more and more are opting out of the family business. Suzan Lewis and Julia Brannen argue that economic insecurity means that choices about childbearing are increasingly fraught for younger generations.

Sustainable families and the new economy

The evidence suggests that the emerging relationships and family forms of the twenty-first century will need to be fostered, nurtured and supported by government, employers and individuals if they are not to be stillborn. The challenge across the globe is to find ways in which individuals, government and business can strengthen families in all their shapes and sizes and underpin them economically during this time of transition. Governments in search of modern solutions will have to lead this process; redefining how we understand value and the processes of wealth creation, and altering the distribution of resources throughout society.

We face choices about our response to globalisation – but to make the right ones we also need a clearer understanding of the overall picture. As Peter Moss points out, the UK government may be steaming ahead on policy commitments to family friendliness, but such measures are in danger of failing unless attention is given to the broader economic context in which such measures are introduced.

At the moment, the dominant presumption – certainly in the UK and North America – is that globalisation is an inevitable and positive force.[13] For all its ambitions to radical modernisation, New Labour's unqualified acceptance of market capitalism suggest that it is yet to engage properly with the value added that families bring to our national wealth.

In fact, there are a range of possible responses to globalisation that transcend simplistic choices between modernisation and nostalgia. The globalisation of the economy is located in a broader context – of the natural environment, and the relations of gift, mutual exchange, care and trust which underpin civil society. Without a clear understanding of the broader context, and unless the conditions under which families live are moderated, the effects of individual policies will be marginal.

Any new family politics must be developed and implemented in the context of *sustainable* globalisation. As Brad Googins argues, the search is on for a Third Way between the US and traditional European models of capitalism. Finding the right model of regulation is an essential part of this search for work–life balance.

Maureen Freely and Ed Mayo's contributions in this Collection remind us that the new economy needs a new economics, one that is sensitive to the politics of gender, time, care and sustainability. Such approaches have great potential to redefine our understanding of economic categories and what we mean by work. By drawing our attention to the value of caring work, they point us towards new notions of social inclusion.

Shirley P Burggraf's article takes these arguments a step further. She apportions conventional economic value to the family economy and argues that the family accounts for more than half of the American economy's productive wealth. (Elsewhere, Burggraf concludes, it is less, primarily because countries like Britain have a national health service and family support from the state. Even so, she concludes that the family's contribution to national wealth pro-

13 See for example, Leadbeater C, 1999, *Living on Thin Air*, Viking, London. Even when Leadbeater acknowledges the fundamental role of families in generating social capital, he has almost nothing to say about how this role can be supported.

duction in those countries still comes close to 50 per cent.) Her analysis helps to explain how and why the family economy is suffering a major under-investment of resources – in time, energy and money – and points the way towards sustainable solutions.

This feminisation of economics – perhaps we should call it home economics – is a vital component in the new settlement between family life and the wider economy. This shift in thinking is already beginning to impact on international politics. All members of the United Nations are now encouraged to keep track of the value of unpaid work in a 'satellite account'.

In Japan, the Economic Planning Agency has calculated the monetary value of unpaid work to be 116 billion yen, of which 85 per cent was contributed by women in 1996, with an annual average value per person of $23,000. As Sumiko Iwao reports, findings such as this have led to an active debate about how to both achieve a balance between work and life, and promote greater gender equality.

These new perspectives help to create a basis for a new approach to family policy and household economics. They show why current trends are unsustainable and point to the need for an approach to family life that is generative, in the sense of creating solutions that add value for individuals, families, employers and communities.

Feminist perspectives have been critical in bringing home economics to the foreground, and in quantifying the economic value of the household economy and illuminating the unsustainability of industrial society, founded as it was on a fundamental inequality between men and women.

Green politics and thinking is also an important source. As Ed Mayo points out, a 'new economics' would be long term: it would identify 'defensive expenditures', such as the £9 billion spent on criminal justice in the UK, as well as taking family work seriously as a productive activity. As he puts it:

> 'it has always been possible to make economic growth and profits look good by eroding family life to promote market activity and by marginalising and disenfranchising those invested in the bulk of care. However, the extension of the market into all aspects of our lives has now corroded society's system of care, nurturing and reproduction beyond critical thresholds.'

Chilean economist Manfred Max Neef argues that industrialised countries have now passed the threshold beyond which defensive expenditures outstrip national income growth. We may be getting richer, but the good life is becoming ever more elusive.[14]

This is why the complex ecology of family life, the language of care and nurture, and the feminisation of economics is so important. It helps us to clarify the connections between economic wealth and our notions of the good life.

What flows from this new approach?

Accounting for family value

These perspectives mark a new approach to economics, which must be built into mainstream economic analysis and operationalised. In an ageing society, we need some form of generational accounting.[15] Greater transparency in the allocation of resources across the generations would certainly lead to far greater investment in children and parents.[16] At the moment, children are denied a voice in the political process. In the future, we will need new institutional mechanisms to take account of their needs – perhaps by allocating votes to parents.[17] In an era of holistic government, a Minister for Generations could be appointed to act as the custodian of future generations, counterbalancing their interests against the priorities and concerns of today's generations.[18]

Gender auditing will be a vital component of this new settlement, focusing attention in particular on changing the culture of care and encouraging a more equal sharing of responsibilities. In so far as such policies are focused on encouraging new patterns of male behaviour, we may need new institutional mechanisms to promote gender equity and stable families.

Just as we need gender and generational auditing, so too we need family accounting, as Ed Straw persuasively argues. Greater transparency here would show the real value added that families bring to the national wealth. The value of household labour has risen by half over the course of the past twenty years in the richest G8 countries (primarily because of women's enhanced economic role in the paid economy).[19] As a sector, the household economy is worth more than 22.75 per cent of G8 GDP, in comparison to 3.3 per cent for agriculture, 33.1 per cent for industry and 63.6 per cent for services.

However, without a strong commitment to recording and account-

14 For more on this see the contributions in Christie I, ed, 1998, *The Good Life*, Demos Collection issue 14, Demos, London.

15 See for example, Kotlikoff L, 1993, *Generational Accounting: Knowing who pays, and when, and for what we spend*, Free Press, New York. See also the discussion in Wilkinson and Mulgan, 1995 (note 1).

16 See note above and also the discussion in Wilkinson and Mulgan, 1995 (note 1).

17 See for example, Ringen S, 1998, *The Family in Question*, Demos, London.

18 For a broader discussion of this proposal, see Wilkinson and Mulgan, 1995 (note 1).

19 These figures are provided by the New Economics Foundation's Index of Sustainable Economic Welfare.

ing for the household and family work that is not traded in cash terms, the full value of the caring economy will not be realised. Publication of a broader set of national accounts, to set alongside the narrower measures of GDP and income per capita, is a priority. Such figures could then allow political arguments about investing resources in children and families to be explicitly made.

Investing across the new lifecycle

Alongside forms of accounting that supplement traditional measures of value, family life also needs core financial investment. As several contributors to the collection make clear, this investment must be spread appropriately across the new lifecycle. The lifecourse has been transformed and the stages of family life (adolescence, transition to adulthood, relationship formation, child-rearing, caring for the elderly, becoming old, and in turn being cared for) are fundamentally different from the linear, standard lifestages which have dominated the century.

The new settlement must reflect these new contours. As Paul Gregg argues, this partly means cushioning people against the resource shocks that come with children, and enabling them to recoup their investment or repay their debts later in life. If older generations are to make a more active contribution to family life, as Michael Young and Jean Cogden argue, then their new economic role must be reflected in pension and long-term care arrangements.

Making work pay

Any progressive agenda for families depends on stabilising families economically during a period of rapid change. The goal should be to encourage families to be self-sufficient and to encourage economic independence among men and women.

In the UK, the Labour government has made a bold attempt to develop a new strategy for families and to enhance women's financial independence. So far, the emphasis has been on making work pay. The welfare-to-work agenda, the Working Families Tax Credit, the National Minimum Wage and the National Childcare Strategy are all important steps in this direction.

However, they do not go far enough, even on the government's own terms. Welfare-to-work initiatives for lone parents, for example, have only focused on one side of the equation – getting resident parents back into the labour market by making work pay and child-care affordable. The other side – finding ways of engaging disconnected fathers, and of supporting disrupted families in the financial support and nurture of children, are only just beginning to appear on the policy agenda. There are clear lessons from the American experience. Reform of child support needs to be linked to a new generation of welfare-to-work initiatives, framed with the needs of disrupted families in mind, and linked to imaginative parenting schemes.[20]

Making care pay

To build and strengthen tomorrow's families, we must also develop policies that enable people to transfer time and resources from work into the home through the course of the lifecycle, and that take the care economy as seriously as the world of paid work.

The most urgent priority for investment is in time. In this respect, the UK government's recent extension of paid maternity leave and introduction of three months' unpaid parental leave and rights to emergency family leave are important steps. However, taken alone, they will do little to ease the pressures facing parents, or to address the gendered impact of time and caring. So long as men earn more than women, and so long as there is a scheme of paid maternity leave and parental leave is unpaid for the majority, the economic incentive will be for women rather than men to take leave.

So while the new entitlements may ameliorate some of the more extreme pressures, they do not address the structural changes required to make good the fathering deficit. To enable a real change in the culture of parenting, and to address the historical inequalities that still prevail between men and women, parental leave must be better funded and more ambitious, and it must be designed in such a way as to promote father involvement.

Most arguments against universal paid parental leave focus on cost. But many countries have introduced paid schemes without imposing onerous burdens on taxpayers or employers. My book, *Time Out*, shows that a generous scheme of paid parental leave could be introduced for less than one-tenth of the value of the married couples tax allowance at its 1997 value. If this scheme was integrated into the next generation of welfare-to-work initiatives, it could even be cost neutral to the state.[21]

20 See Wilkinson, 1998 (note 5) and also the forthcoming Demos book *Disconnected Dads?*.
21 See Wilkinson, 1997 (note 12).

In the longer run, parents should be eligible for a broader scheme of family leave which enables them to take funded time off over the course of the lifecycle according to their children's needs. (This could absorb the current British government's recent commitments to emergency family leave.) This would allow people to work flexibly, reduce their working hours, accommodate themselves to school hours, enable them to take time out for family illness and develop their own solutions to their own children's needs. A scheme of family leave should also be inclusive enough to accommodate the needs of workers looking after elderly relatives or the sick and disabled. It should be financed through social insurance, with costs being distributed between taxpayers, employers and individuals.

Enabling parents to exercise autonomy in planning their family lives, thus finding the right balance between working and caring, and thinking long term, is one of the most important responsibilities of modern government. In the longer run, this framework of support and investment must link with the emerging infrastructure of lifelong learning, as well as with wider caring responsibilities. In this sense, a new system of time rights and practical support is an essential underpinning to the new world of work.[22]

Time accounting, annualised hours and portfolio work are the reality for growing numbers of people, and forward-looking employers are already developing systems that maximise the benefits of flexibility for individuals as well as for firms. In the end, we need to integrate family leave into a time accounting scheme available to all eligible workers – including single people and those without immediate care responsibilities – who may want to make use of sabbaticals, career breaks and lifelong learning opportunities. Leave here should be self-financed, although government should offer loans repayable over the course of a lifetime. (Employers should also be encouraged and given tax incentives to offer similar schemes of support.)[23]

Time money

Enabling people to transfer time and resources from the world of work into the home during critical life transitions is a key component of any new settlement. But a society in which family life and parenting are properly valued must also embody the values of nurture and care as strongly as it does the virtues of earning and

22 For more on this, see Mulgan and Wilkinson, 1995 (note 8). See also Wilkinson, 1997 (note 12)

23 See Wilkinson, 1997 (note 12).

financial contribution. As Stephen Driver and Luke Martell argue, the tensions between New Labour's 'competing communitarianisms' – the language of social inclusion through paid work, and the notion of inclusion through one's caring role – are strong, and the government has not yet done enough to resolve them. Policies such as paid parental leave have tremendous symbolic value in this respect. The future challenge will be to ensure that the emphasis on inclusion through paid work is matched by policies that value carers' economic contribution, as well as their moral role.

When financial resources are relatively scarce, we can nevertheless value care work in imaginative ways. As Geoff Mulgan and I argued in *The Time Squeeze* in 1995,[24] new ways of recording and rewarding time are fundamental to this agenda. The New Economics Foundation have put many of these ideas into practice. Ed Mayo's article shows the potential of alternative currencies. Time and care credits, earned and exchanged through a variety of community-based activities (including childcare, out-of-school learning and teaching activities, and other unpaid forms of social contribution) would give new impetus to the diverse, entrepreneurial efforts of many parents and community groups. They are another way of boosting the mixed economy of care, and can be made much easier by Internet technologies.

Government should promote and endorse such initiatives, which should receive sympathetic tax treatment as they continue to grow. In the longer run, they could also form the basis of a new kind of personal 'satellite account', in which individuals could accrue credits and entitlements, partly based on contribution, linked to pensions and lifelong learning provision. Such a framework depends in the longer term on government, but alternative currencies can and should be operated by other sectors. Companies and community mutuals, for example, can run time banks for employees and other community members.

Building a care economy for the twenty-first century

These forms of investment and entitlement are the spine of a new system, but if people are to have genuine choices that fit their individual needs, they must also be offered other kinds of provision. A strong economy needs a robust care economy to underpin it. This means building a care economy that fits the contours of twenty-first

24 See note 8.

century society and the new patterns of work and family life.

Much more could be done by government to create positive incentives for employers to provide care. The costs of entry for direct care certainly need to be lowered. Childcare is still expensive for many working parents and too many people find themselves on the wrong side of the threshold for the working families tax credit, and struggling to afford childcare.

There are also gaping holes in the childcare framework. The Day Care Trust recently identified gaps in provision for under threes, for teenage school children and for shift workers. Colette Kelleher's article outlines next steps in the childcare agenda, and argues that we need to address the persistent mismatch between the time patterns and demands of the workplace, and the types of care available as well as developing more community-based solutions.

This does not just mean creating a mixed economy of care, including public, private and community sector provisions, it means synchronising our care arrangements with new ways of working and creating tax incentives for employers promoting these. At the moment, the National Childcare Strategy is increasing the accessibility and affordability of basic childcare, but it does not begin to create these flexible options.

The government's commitment to family-friendly employment has the potential to focus attention on new ways of working, as well as stimulating direct care provision. But much more could and should be done to build incentives for employers to innovate with new ways of working. Homeworking brings clear and measurable benefits – in terms of reduced stress, enhanced work–life synergy and positive environmental effects, reducing commuter time and traffic congestion.

It should be possible for governments to find tax incentives for promoting such innovation. In the absence of government encouragement, far-sighted employers could still innovate and encourage parents to combine flexible working arrangements with forms of direct childcare provision. A mixed economy is necessary for parents to develop options that work for them, allowing them to mix formal childcare with other alternatives (such as reducing working time, taking parental leave or accessing informal care from grandparents who in turn can benefit from vouchers).[25] The Scandinavian countries have much to teach us about the virtues of such an approach.

25 See note 5.

Community mutuals

Alongside core public and private provision, and an emphasis on new ways of working, we also need to strengthen the role of mutual exchange in the care economy. As Helena Cronin and Oliver Curry argue, families are literally 'evolved' to be the sites of reciprocity, love and mutual exchange.

Despite the rhetoric of individualism, an economy of mutual exchange already exists around the UK, evident in the community action of parents who set up after-school clubs, organise nanny shares and babysitting services, and develop support networks.[26]

These new sets of relationships are vital components of the network society and a critical dimension of the care economy. Government and employers must strengthen and support such initiatives. In particular, the role of older generations must be explicitly acknowledged and valued: according to Age Concern, a third of pre-school children are already looked after by grandparents.[27] While a reinvented extended family network can never replace the need for formal entitlement and provision, government can nurture mutuality and the gift economy.

New technologies already offer enormous potential for strengthening such activity. New communities need active support to get online. Much more could be done to facilitate the growth of the 'Internet-worked' family through cheap email and a better telephone pricing structure. Families need access to virtual communities of support. Innovative ideas for guaranteed electronic markets – trading childcare and other services– no longer look so far off.[28]

The Internet certainly offers tremendous scope for nurturing online communities and forming community mutuals with pressing needs such as this. Governments and employers could play a much greater role in encouraging the growth of parenting mutuals and clubs.[29] They could offer start-up grants for community ventures on the Internet: strengthening the networks that already exist in the physical world, such as the Kids' Club Network, as well as creating new forums for people to meet, exchange ideas, offer help and assistance. In the absence of a regulatory framework, net entrepreneurs are stepping in.[30] The challenge in the future will be to create services and support networks which benefit the less well off, as well as the time poor/cash rich clustered at the top end of the income structure.

26 See for example, Leadbeater C and Christie I, 1999, *To Our Mutual Advantage*, Demos, London.
27 Cited from Wilkinson, 1999 (note 2).
28 Rowan W, 1997, *Guaranteed Electronic Markets: The backbone of a 21st century economy?*, Demos, London.
29 See Wilkinson H and Briscoe I, 1996, *Parental Leave: The price of family values?*, Demos, London. A framework for mutuals is set out in Mulgan G with Bentley T, 1996, *Employee Mutuals: The 21st century trade union?*, Demos, London.
30 Lastminute.com already offer babysitting services as add-ons to their core business. A range of community sites such as this are currently in development with www.eTribe.co.uk. Contact: hwilkins@netcomuk.co.uk and simon@pmail.net.

Who pays?

As part of the search for sustainable solutions, governments and employers must recognise that the family is a key stakeholder in modern society, rather than a background force to be taken for granted.[30] This recognition needs to inform discussions about who pays. Linda Tarr-Whelan, writing in the American context, argues that the debate about the distribution of responsibility, and of shared investment in family life, must be clarified. In the UK too there are concerns that the government is not yet thinking strategically. Sue Slipman believes that the government is still muddled over who should pay for these initiatives and how the responsibility for children should be distributed between different stakeholders. Philosophical arguments about the public good generated by strong families have not been sufficiently articulated. In the sense that we all benefit from strong families, we are all stakeholders and must all pay the price.[31]

One implication of these shifts in thinking, which we have yet to achieve in the UK, is the recognition that it is in the national interest to invest in parenting and family life. Certainly, we need to arrive at a richer and more sophisticated definition of productivity and invest in family renewal and reproduction, just as we invest in the growth and renewal of firms.

Conclusion

Families are the hubs of the new economy. Yet they do not exist in isolation. They are part of a complex political ecology. They have an economic dimension – not just in terms of the economic context in which they are located – but in terms of the value they generate. Once, we see families in this way – as part of a complex ecology, a synergistic system – we can begin to make the right connections between economic productivity and social capital.

Beyond these connections, we must also remember that trust, love, nurture, time and psychic energy are what make families and relationships thrive. These intangibles cannot and should not be reduced to mere economic calculation, as Michael Rustin cogently argues. But in a world that commodifies our time and attention more than ever before, families must be properly valued in economic, as well as moral, terms. The home can only continue to be the haven in a heartless world, as envisaged by Karl Marx, if we take the work that

30 Campbell M, 1997, 'The Family As Stakeholder', *Business Strategy Review*, vol 8, no 2.
31 For an expansion of these arguments, see Wilkinson, 1997 (note 12).

families do seriously. This means supporting families so that we create the space and time for love and nurture to thrive.

Making these changes will be ambitious and complex. It will involve politicians making hard choices and they may be reluctant at the implications. Taking this agenda seriously means confronting the costs of investment and deciding who should pay. But it is time to translate rhetoric about family values into reality. Only then will we create the progressive, effective policy frameworks that modern families deserve.

All the thinkers in this Collection have important contributions to this project. They raise questions, as well as answers. Many caution against quick fixes or simple solutions. But running through every contribution is a central, and simple, story. The new economy cannot live on thin air alone. The family business is our most precious enterprise. We under-invest at our peril ⊙

Helen Wilkinson is an ideas entrepreneur. She sits on Demos' Advisory Council and manages its research on gender, work and family change. She is a trustee of the Kids' Clubs Network, a member of its Child Care Commission and a member of the Parental Leave Campaign. She is also co-founder of eTribe, an Internet start-up dedicated to nurturing on line communities. She can be contacted at hwilkins@netcomuk.co.uk.

Part 1

Family renewal:
past, present and future

A time of transition

Sustainable families and the new global economy

Arlene Skolnick

We are passing through one of those periods that historians will look back on as a watershed – a time of major shifts in the economic, political and social foundations of society. According to the business press and many other commentators, we have already moved into a post-industrial, globalised, information age.

Remarkably little of this discussion of the new political economy addresses the wider social impact of these shifts on individuals, families and communities. And little attention is focused on the ways in which family change affects social well-being and our economic future.

Of course, there is no shortage of worried talk about the drastic transformation of family life and women's roles in the past few decades. Public discourse across the political spectrum is based on the 'breakdown of the family' as established social fact. But talk about the family is usually totally disconnected from the discussion of technological and economic change, new modes of organisation or globalisation.

In response to moral panic over the collapse of old certainties – domestic arrangements, sexual morality, and the proper place of women – some researchers and others have attacked the 'myth of family decline'. They cite evidence showing that family life is changing, not declining; that family values remain strong; that new family forms reflect a healthy diversity; and that the 'traditional family' whose loss we mourn never existed in the first place.

While the family is more durable than the doomsayers would have it, the debate about family decline is beside the point. Neither side offers an adequate understanding of the recent upheavals of family life.

The right, however, has had a consistent and coherent account of the 'breakdown of the family': it has been caused by a broad cultural and moral decline since the 1960s, a shift towards a 'do your own thing' hedonistic individualism. The result is a disregard of traditional commitment to marriage and duties to children, aging parents and the community. While liberals and the left have countered conservative arguments, they have not agreed on a theory of family change, or whether or not there is a family 'crisis,' or whether, if there is, it is rooted in economics or moral values.

In this essay, I try to reframe the debate by putting it into historical perspective. First, I argue that today's families *are* in the midst of a difficult and still incomplete transition, in response to the same forces that are moving the world into the post-industrial, information age. The current state of family life may not be the end point of change, but rather just a troubled middle stage as families and society pass into the emerging post-industrial, global era.

Second, I argue that the current unsettled state of family life is only the latest in a series of stressful periods of transition Western families have weathered during the past two centuries. While we can't use the history of earlier domestic revolutions to predict the future, we can gain insight into the way earlier generations reconstructed family, work and community arrangements in the wake of major societal transformations.

Cultural 'earthquakes'

Some time ago, the sociologist William Ogburn coined the phrase 'cultural lag' to describe the gap between the onset of major technological change and a society's cultural, social and political response. For example, writing in 1950 Ogburn pointed out that, while economic change had altered women's roles, there had not been a corresponding change in the notion that 'a woman's place is in home'.[1]

In key respects, cultural lag is too bland a term to describe these transitional periods – they are more like cultural earthquakes, or 'great disruptions' as Francis Fukayama describes them. He links the recent troubles in family and society to the technological advances the information age. Masses of women can now enter the paid work-

1 Ogburn WF, 1950, *Social Change*, Viking, New York.

force. And the Pill and abortion have liberated men to enjoy sex without responsibility. The result, he claims, has been an epidemic of divorce and single parent families, leading in turn to rising rates of crime and other forms of social disorder and moral decay.[2]

Fukayama's overall message is reassuring: the current disorder will end – and it already is ending – because we are biologically hard-wired to rebuild damaged family structures and reweave the social fabric. Women will not leave the workforce entirely, he concedes, but biology, helped along by a few new legal constraints, will restore both sexes to their rightful places in the family. Fukayama merely offers a new twist on the conservative cultural crusade against women's new status in society.

Fukuyama brings a necessary historical perspective to the current debate over the family but, by invoking biology to explain how 'cultural lag' is overcome, he abandons history just when it could be most useful. Specifically, he ignores the enormous amount historians and others have learned about the dynamic, two-way interplay between families and socio-economic change.

In recent years, we've learned that the process of family adaptation to economic transformation unfolds through a series of stages. The first is a period of individual and family stress. Old ways of thinking and behaving – what Clifford Geertz called 'blueprints for experience' – become unsettled long before new ones take their place. Without the old norms some people feel liberated, others become uneasy; without new cultural scripts for family roles, there is no right way to behave. Increasing numbers of individuals show signs of psychological stress – personality disturbances, drinking and drug problems.

Young people in particular become a troubled and troublesome part of the population. Generation gaps open up as young people grow up and enter a world that no longer fits their parents' experience. In periods of widespread and rapid socio-economic change, parents become what Margaret Mead called 'immigrants in time'.[3]

The second stage in the transition is a period of cultural and political struggle. Private troubles become public issues. Religious leaders, journalists, politicians and others offer competing interpretations of the problem. Some call for a return to traditional ways; some call for adaptation to the new realities. Still others want to push change into radical new directions. Political and social move-

2 Fukayama F, 1999, *The Great Disruption*, Free Press, New York.
3 Mead M, 1977, *Culture and Commitment: A study of the generation gap in the 1970s*, Columbia University Press, New York.

ments spring up – moral crusades and attempts to pass new laws, create new institutions.

Finally, restabilisation occurs. Younger generations grow up and the earlier family model becomes an increasingly distant memory. Controversy gives way to a new cultural blueprint for family life; one accepts change, reconciling older values with new realities. New institutions and social arrangements are developed to deal with the problems created by change. A new 'cultural common sense' takes hold, which people come to take for granted, wondering how things could have been otherwise.

An historical perspective on family change

The early nineteenth century witnessed a cultural revolution in the Western family that illustrates this model, although the timing and exact nature of the change varied from one country to another. Until then households were economic enterprises: the labour of husbands, wives and children, and often apprentices and hired hands, was essential for family survival. A father was not only the head of household but also the owner and manager of the family business. Authority and obedience, not affection, were the guiding principles of family relations, and childhood as we think of it in modern times did not exist. Finally, the boundary between family and community was not well defined; the family was something of a public institution, open to intervention by outsiders if the household was not 'well ordered' according to the standards of the time.

With the growth of industry, commerce and cities, work moved out of the home, and fathers left the household during the working day. Mothers were in daily charge of children, and the household itself lost its central function. Young people gained a new, and for adults, troubling degree of independence. In short, the older cultural model of the family became incompatible with the daily experience of family life.

This period can justifiably be labelled a 'great disruption'. It was a turbulent period of economic stress, cultural dislocation, political unrest and religious ferment. The old work and family patterns were disrupted as the family economy gave way to a wage-based economic order. By the middle of the century, a new vision of marriage, home and family life emerged that legitimated the new structural realities. The new model redefined the roles of men, women and children.

Indeed, the ancient concepts of 'marriage', 'father', 'mother', 'child' and 'home' took on new meanings. And a new relationship between family and community was constructed.

Men and women were now thought to belong to 'separate spheres'. Men were the family providers, forced to adapt to a harsh and morally dangerous world outside the home. Women were defined as virtuous domestic beings who would create a 'haven in a heartless world'. Children were seen as tender innocents in need of maternal love and careful moral nurture. This was the era when the seemingly timeless principles of 'woman's place is in the home' and 'home sweet home' became embedded in Western culture.

In addition to a new vision of family, Western societies invented new institutions to deal with the education and welfare of children. The first public schools were part of the new 'developmental' cultural blueprint. Since that time, education has carved out an increasing share of the life course and helped to redefine both the tasks of parenthood and the stages of life course.

The doctrine of separate spheres sharpened older notions of gender difference. It both reflected and shaped further changes in the nature of work and family drawing sharp boundaries between home and work, male and female, child and adult, public and private. This imagery of the family was a middle class creation, but law and public institutions made it the 'official' version. At the same time, a persistent gap between this 'public family' and the actual families people lived in led to a persistent sense of anxiety about the institution.

Nevertheless, the 'separate spheres' model came to dominate across class and ethnic lines. Although young women had been part of the early industrial workforce, eventually women from all but the poorest families left the workplace. Poor women continued to work for money outside as well as inside the home. So did working class and immigrant children, until child labor laws were enacted.

A second era of domestic upheaval and cultural ferment occurred between the 1880s and the 1920s, the period sometimes called 'the second industrial revolution.' The automobile, the movies, the telephone and electric light became staples of modern life. It was also a time of new ideas – Freud, Einstein, the beginnings of modernism in art and literature, the first wave of feminism. In the 1920s, the first sexual revolution of the twentieth century erupted. The separate-spheres ideology was modified: marriage was now ideally based on companionship and sexual bonds. More women entered the workplace, and the issue of how to reconcile work and family became a topic of public concern. But the Great Depression and the Second World War derailed that discussion and reinforced traditional notions of gender. In many ways, the 1960s were a resumption of trends that had started in the 1920s.

From separate spheres to blurred boundaries

How does this model of change apply to our own time? Today we are stalled in the midst of another stressful and disorienting transition. The foundations of the 'separate spheres' system of gender roles have been eroding throughout the twentieth century; the economic changes of recent decades have delivered the final blows to a family pattern whose time was passing, as Ogburn noted, in the l950s. We are moving to a more symmetrical version of the family and gender roles; the realities of everyday family life have outpaced cultural images, public policy and the established arrangements of other institutions – most significantly, the workplace and the schools.

Because of the stresses of this unfinished transition, and the fear that children are not getting the care they need, there is a widespread feeling that if only women would go home again, we wouldn't have all these problems. But the move to a more symmetrical family is irreversible because it based on deeper social and economic changes. Although feminism is often blamed or credited for the gender revolution of recent decades, changes in women's lives across the twentieth century helped to set the stage for the feminist revival. It was not until the l970s, however, that the proportion of women in paid work reached critical mass.

Throughout the twentieth century, revolutions in longevity and fertility have done as much as workplace change to reshape women's lives. They have also helped to rewrite the script for the individual and family life course, and family structures. Most of the years of a long marriage are spent without children in the home; most of the parent–child relationship occurs when both are adults; more people are part of four generation 'beanpole' family; there is mass longevity, with more elderly in need of care.

In the last half-century, large numbers of ordinary citizens have gained access to education, travel and other cultural advantages once enjoyed only by the upper classes. The result is a process of 'psychological gentrification': a more informed, cosmopolitan, more psychological-minded population, more concerned, for example, with warmth and intimacy in family relationships – and more prone to distress when these are not achieved.

Finally, legal and political trends in modern democracies have undermined the legitimacy of gender and other caste-like forms of inequality, at least in principle. Shifts in women's status are challenging family systems in many parts of the world. 'There has never before been a society, so far as we know,' observes Anthony Giddens, 'in which women have even been approximately equal to men. This is truly a global revolution in everyday life, whose consequences are being felt around the world in spheres from work to politics.'[4]

Who cares? Globalisation and the problem of family

Not only must families change to negotiate the new realities, but cultural norms, public policy, the legal system and other institutions must also to adapt to the new family patterns. Today's policy-makers face two central dilemmas.

First, how can the needs of families and communities for security and stability be reconciled with a fast changing, unfettered global market economy? Second, how can enduring human needs for care and nurturance be reconciled with the passing of caste-like gender distinctions?

It is ironic that, although the new economy undermines the conditions that enable families to thrive, the psychological and social functions of the family (which used to be women's special task) are more critical than ever. To produce a workforce for a new economy that values brains and interpersonal skills over brawn, parents must invest high levels of emotion, attention, time and money in their children. And in a fast-paced and uncertain post-industrial world, the intimacy and connectedness of home and family become even more precious to adults. The functions of the family remain a vital necessity, even though family forms may vary.

Recently, the political theorist Mona Harrington has argued for a new politics of family care based on the changed realities facing families, as well the irreversible shift towards gender equality.[5] Her prescriptions are important, but I believe that this new family politics should be part of a still wider agenda for social change – what

4 Giddens A, 1998 *The Third Way: The renewal of social democracy*, Blackwell Publishers, Malden, Massachusetts.
5 Harrington M, 1999, *Care and Equality: Inventing a new family politics*, Knopf, New York

Thomas Friedman has recently called a 'politics of sustainable glob-alisation'. Like Giddens and other proponents of the Third Way, Friedman argues that the global economy needs to be tamed by a new, twenty-first century version of social democracy.[6]

There are various versions of the Third Way, but all are centrally concerned with work and economic equity – that those left behind by the new economy be given the means to adapt to it. Thus the stress on education, job training and opportunities for lifelong learning. But a politics of sustainable globalisation needs equal attention to family and care issues. In fact, families should be seen not only as humanitarian concern, but as what they are: an essential part of the economy. They create, nurture and sustain society's present and future 'human capital.'

Because it rests on pragmatic and economic grounds, the case for sustainable globalisation bolsters moral and humanitarian argu-ments for a more caring society. It argues that our self-interest in our personal security, well-being and prosperity gives us all a stake in a reasonably cohesive society, with a stable and educated workforce. We do not yet have a blueprint for public and private policies that are friendly to children and families (whatever their form) and equitable for both men and women, as well as for the caregivers. We will be grappling with these issues well into the new century. It's all too easy, looking into the future, to fall into apocalyptic pessimism or its Utopian opposite. What is difficult to imagine is a world that is 'good enough' and a plan for getting there ⊙

Arlene Skolnick is based at the Institute of Human Development, University of California, Berkeley, and is the author of Embattled Paradise: The American family in an age of uncertainty *(Basic Books).*

6 Friedman TL, 1999, *The Lexus and the Olive Tree: Understanding globalization*, Farrar, Straus, Giroux, New York.

Valuing the feminine economy

The relationship between the family and the formal economy

Shirley P Burggraf

Plato and Aristotle celebrated the public activities of men as citizens while relegating the domestic activities of women to a lower sphere. Reproduction was, according to Plato, a function on the level of the beasts and of all inferior irrational substance. Aristotle considered women to be a kind of misbegotten man, too irrational for participation in public affairs and necessarily confined to domestic duties.[1]

Separation of public–private, male–female, rational–irrational spheres of activity was maintained by leading thinkers of the Middle Ages, the Renaissance and the Enlightenment and the dichotomy still dominates the way theorists think about social problems – economic problems occur in one arena while the family operates in another.[2] Families depend on the economy for support, but the economy operates independently of the family in terms of its ability to generate income, output and productive capacity. The family's economic role in economic models is simply that of consumer. Adam Smith's *Wealth of Nations*, the first comprehensive analysis of capitalist principles, makes no mention the importance of the family or of the domestic side of life in the performance of a market economy. Like most social theorists before and after him, Smith simply continued the intellectual tradition of focusing on the public sphere of human functions while taking the private sphere for granted. Social problems at the turn of the century are now challenging these basic assumptions of Western thought since the writings of the ancient Greeks.

1 Jean Bethke Elshtain provides an extensive analysis of the way Western intellectual thought has treated women's roles in Elshtain JB, 1981, *Public Man, Private Woman: Women in social and political thought*, Princeton University Press, Princeton, New Jersey. **2** Pateman, 1988, *The Sexual Contract*, Stanford University Press, Stanford, California.

An economic system in transition

3 Cloud K, 1996, 'What Every Woman Knows: Women's preference for quality in human capital production,' paper presented to Sixth Interdisciplinary Congress on Women, Adelaide, Australia, 1996.

4 Minge-Klevana W, 1980, 'Does Labor Time Decrease with Industrialization? A survey of time-allocation studies,' *Current Anthropology*, vol 21, no 3, June, esp p279.

5 'The Real Cost of Raising Kids', *US News & World Report*, 30 March 1998, pp50-58.

6 As of 1997, 51 countries, representing 44 per cent of the world's population, had fertility rates at or below replacement, up from nineteen countries in 1975 according to Johnathan R Laing, 'Baby Bust Ahead,' in *Barron's*, 8 December 1997, p38. Although some demographers have speculated that the trend in fertility decline will level off once the effect of fertility deferral to older ages by modern couples has reached its natural limit, a recent study concludes that even with the most optimistic assumptions about the 'age effect' fertility will remain below replacement in most Western countries for the foreseeable future. Lesthaeghe R and Williams P, 1999, 'Is Low Fertility a Temporary Phenomenon in the European

When women were confined to the domestic sphere under laws of coverture, reinforced by technological conditions that made extensive gender specialisation an economic necessity for most people, omitting 'women's work' from economic models and equations caused no obvious analytical problems. It could simply be taken for granted that women would undertake society's reproductive and caretaking labour along with other domestic work. That assumption has become quite problematic, however, as women have moved into the market economy in increasing numbers and as the economic incentives for men to support families have disappeared. The current state of families in Western countries can be attributed to economic forces; likewise, the state of national economies with respect to growth, productivity, government budgets and standards of living is linked to family function.

Economic stress on families increases as economic development progresses. In poor countries, babies tend to be slung on their mothers' backs in the fields, toddlers watched over by siblings and children given a few years of schooling before being put to work by the time they reach puberty.[3] Parental costs per child are relatively low and parental paybacks from children in the form of help on farms and in small shops and in insurance for old age are significant family assets. In contrast, children in highly developed economies typically get much more one-on-one interaction with their parents and have much longer periods of dependency and schooling before becoming economically independent.[4] Economic returns from children are minimal as children generally do little substantive work at home and as the welfare state has replaced children as the major form of old-age insurance. Children in developed countries thus have become very high-cost projects for their parents with little if any economic return.

Lifetime parental costs of rearing one middle-class child in the US have been estimated recently at $1.43 million (approximately £900,000).[5] The largest component of this is the cost of parental time. Given that parental paybacks from children have virtually disappeared, the fall of fertility below replacement and the fracturing of family ties that have occurred in many countries[6] seem, in retrospect, to be inevitable. Economic ties that have traditionally bound families together – male to female and the generations to each other

– have been stretched to breaking point.

While the impact of economic forces on families is fairly obvious, the effects of family stress on macro-economic performance are harder to see, because domestic work has never been counted as part of economic output. As far as economic statistics are concerned, our grandmothers who worked from dawn to dark caring for their families did nothing valuable with their time. It's difficult to measure or even to talk about the loss of something that was never counted in the first place, but it seems illogical to assume that half of the adult population was doing nothing worthwhile before women started taking paying jobs. Much of what our grandmothers did at home is, of course, now being done in the marketplace; but family work still plays an indispensable role in reproducing the labour force.

Econometricians consistently estimate that labour generates about two-thirds of economic output in modern economies. Given that families bear most of the costs of producing workers, the family's role in wealth production has to be taken as seriously as that of other investment institutions. If families bear 90 per cent of the costs of rearing a child to productive adulthood, as has been estimated in the US,[7] then simple arithmetic (90 per cent of two-thirds) concludes that the family produces more than half of an economy's productive wealth in the form of human capital. In countries with national health insurance and more generous family support policies than in the US, direct family costs are somewhat lower, but family contribution to national wealth production probably still approaches 50 per cent.

Far from being the peripheral adjunct to a market economy that most economic models have assumed, the family is literally our major wealth producing institution; and stress on the family is arguably the greatest eminent threat to the modern standard of living.

In an economic environment in which family investment has become all costs and no returns for parents and in which both men and women have viable alternatives to making family commitments, the family and the economy are linked in ways that are unprecedented in human history. The family can no longer be taken for granted in our economic models but instead has to compete in the marketplace for the time and resources of its members, which puts the social services and production of human capital that families have traditionally provided at considerable risk.

Union?,' *Population and Development Review*, vol 25, no 2, pp211-228.

7 Burggraf SP, 1999, 'The Family Enterprise,' in *The Feminine Economy and Economic Man: Reviving the role of family in the post-industrial age*, Perseus Books, Reading, Massachusetts.

The modern dilemma

Traditional societies that enforce gender roles arbitrarily restrict individuals' choices, but they provide extensive social support for the caretaking roles. A reciprocal social contract between generations for care in periods of dependence and between marital partners for protection of caretakers is enforced by communities that put pressure on individuals to 'do the right thing' with respect to their families. In highly developed, mobile societies, however, individuals who choose family commitments are expected to go it alone with few social supports. Modern families operate in a legal environment that pays little attention to family functions in terms of maintaining even basic law and order, by which I mean keeping people from 1) doing violence to each other; 2) stealing from each other; and 3) breaking contracts with each other.

The following examples are extreme but they make the point. Involvement with the opposite sex can be a risky adventure especially for women. The statistics show that women are more likely to be killed or hurt by husbands and boyfriends than by all robbers, muggers, thieves and rapists combined. Society feels free to expropriate what families produce – and families themselves no longer have any recognisable claims on the fruits of their labours.

A clear case can be made that large socialised pension systems that depend on the next generation of workers to support the elderly but which do not recognise the contribution of the parents who have produced the workers are a form of theft from the family on a massive scale. People who don't have children, people convicted of abusing and neglecting children, deadbeat parents who don't pay child support – all have as much claim (frequently more) on the next of generation of children through many state pension systems as the most dutiful parents. The US Social Security Administration estimates the 'present value'[8] of payments to people now in the system (both workers and retirees) under current formulas to be in excess of $21 trillion,[9] which is roughly comparable to the total tangible wealth in the US economy. This is literally a transfer out of the family.

Finally, unlike other formal commitments, the marriage contract between spouses frequently carries little legal weight. Solemn promises of lifetime love and support before witnesses have little substantive content when one partner changes his or her mind. It's

8 'Present value' is a financial term. In this context it means that $21 trillion would have to be invested now at current interest rates in order to pay the future claims of people currently in the system.
9 Social Security Accountability Report for the Fiscal Year 1997, Office of Financial Policy Operation, SSA Pub no 31-231, November 1997, pp53-54.

easier in many cases to get out of the obligations of marriage than it is to get out of a car loan. Given the high risk of divorce, any marital partner who compromises career development to invest time in the marriage and family caretaking risks abandonment in mid-life with few marketable skills, a need to simultaneously care for children and earn a living, and a retirement with few assets or pension claims.

No other economic institution could be expected to function in a legal environment that is the equivalent of the old American Wild West with respect to personal protection and contract enforcement. While modern economies still depend on families to act like major investors in producing the labour force, the kind of infrastructure provided to other economic units is conspicuously missing where families are concerned. Traditional social infrastructure has broken down, and not much has been put in its place. In order for the increasingly expensive institution of family to remain economically viable, it will surely need a new social contract, which recognises the economic value of the work that families do.

A new social contract

The imbalance between the value of paid work versus the unpaid work that takes place in families must be redressed. Family involvements are becoming more expensive and riskier. Any new social contract needs to recognise that modern families require legal protection and economic support appropriate for the conditions under which they must now function.

For the past several decades, most industrial countries have experimented with family policies that have attempted to collectivise some of the costs by providing them allowances, paid parental leaves and state-funded childcare. Even countries with the most generous social programmes, however, are facing a crisis – families haven't produced enough children with sufficient productivity to pay the taxes to support the pensions and medical costs of ageing populations. Pressures on government budgets now make it impossible to expand those programmes any further or even, in many cases, to maintain them at present levels.

The basic assumption of the modern welfare state has been that the family is a peripheral institution that can be accommodated around the margins of a market economy. With the best of intentions, governments have attempted to subsidise the increasingly expensive functions of family with transfers from the market economy. Inevitably, however, the levels of subsidy cannot equal the dimensions of the problem because it simply isn't possible to collectivise the costs of something that is so expensive – no imaginable programme of taxes and transfers can come close to compensating families at the rate of $1.43 million per child. While many families would undoubtedly say that some help from the state is better than none, far more substantial measures are needed if a viable balance between family work and market work is to be sustained.

One way significant balance could be restored to the family–work equation would be to convert socialised old-age insurance programmes to private parental dividends. In the US, for example, if children's social security taxes were put into retirement trust funds for their own parents, this would make parents shareholders in their own families and restore $21 trillion of economic equity to the family balance sheet – a sum that is on the same scale as the family's economic problem. Putting substantial economic value back into the family would recognise the major investment role that families play in a tangible way that everyone including judges and lawmakers could understand. Surely part of the violence against economically dependent spouses and much of the willingness of individuals to neglect or desert marital partners is affected by a social system that tells individuals that work within the family has no economic value.

Clearly, there are many pros and cons and many details that would have to be resolved before anyone would conclude that reprivatising so much family wealth is a workable and benign proposition. Questions about the fairness and effectiveness of implementing a state-enforced parental dividend are explored extensively elsewhere.[10]

But the most obvious concerns should be briefly addressed here. The first and most obvious criticism is the distastefulness of putting a market price on the value of children to their parents. The second is an issue of generational equity. Younger generations are in effect being asked to pay twice for retirement – once for their parents and again for themselves, either by rearing their own children to generate a parental dividend for themselves or making other kinds of investments.

If we tackle cultural distaste about putting a price on children first, we can compare the current situation with the life insurance industry in the mid-nineteenth century. Prominent ministers ini-

10 See *The Feminine Economy and Economic Man* (note 7), esp ch 6 and appendix.

tially condemned life insurance as a sin and a sacrilege for putting a price on a human life.[11] As economies industrialised, however, and a worker's earning capacity replaced land as the major economic asset, a wage earner's death increasingly left widows and children to be dependent on society. The same ministers came to see life insurance as a responsible measure. Although life insurance is still banned in some places (Syria, Libya), no one in an advanced society would now confuse the value of a person's life insurance with putting a price on the value of the person as an individual. Life insurance is simply a way of using a market mechanism to take care of an important dimension of family business, a dimension made necessary by changing economic conditions in the nineteenth century. Changing conditions require new ways of thinking and new ways of doing.

The issue of 'double billing' for younger generations – by which people are required to support their parents in old age and provide for their own retirement - would in some ways represent a return to the past, and a return to economic reality in many countries. Taking care of *both* the young and the elderly is what families have always had to do. It's what any society has to do, and the two functions are inevitably tied together within the family. There isn't any way to take care of either a young generation or an old generation without the other. That basic fact of life can't be made to go away either by economic models that say families don't matter or by a welfare state that says you can expropriate large sums from families with taxes on the earnings of their children for collective old-age insurance while throwing relatively small bones to families to defray the costs of child rearing.

However unaccustomed and untraditional it may seem and however expensive it may be to construct a realistic economic infrastructure that can support the family's basic functions in the next century, the alternative is sure to be worse. To ignore the economic dimensions of family and the economic crunch that the modern family is experiencing is to abandon our most cherished and most economically productive institution to an increasingly stressful fate ☉

Shirley P Burggraf is Professor of Economics at Florida University and author of The Feminine Economy and Economic Man: Reviving the role of family in the post industrial age.

11 For an account of the early history and sociology of the life-insurance industry, see Rotman Zelizer VA, 1983, *Morals and Markets: The development of the life insurance industry in the United States,* Transaction Books, New Brunswick.

Changing the culture of care

An American perspective

Mona Harrington

The family care system in the United States has collapsed as the traditional caregiving labour force – women at home – has moved into the paid workforce. Americans have not found a way to replace nearly enough of that lost labour. Instead, the challenge of assuring good family care for everyone falls into a cultural blindspot. People and policy-makers alike recognise but do not take account of great change in women's lives and aspirations. They also recognise the need in many families for women's incomes, without quite measuring the loss of at-home caregiving time that their paid work entails. Further, American companies continue to organise work on the assumption that employers bear little if any responsibility for the wellbeing of workers' families. Work schedules, required overtime, high value placed on 'face-time', drastically limit time at home, time for children, for partners, or for workers themselves. And increasingly the country has operated on the assumption that governmental support for families should not be necessary, except in extreme circumstances.

What follows is a society-wide denial of a serious compound problem. Most obvious is a large deficit in ordinary daily care throughout the society, in different forms at different income levels. Only high income families can pay private market rates for all the good care that they need. Middle income families can pay for some, but usually must settle for less care than everyone needs. Low income families are in terrible straits with care for family members always precarious. And then there is the time problem which afflicts virtually everyone, from low-wage workers holding two or three jobs to high-powered professionals working 60 and 70 hour weeks.

The consequences are serious: children unsupervised, elders neglected, families breaking apart under the stress of trying to care for themselves with insufficient time or income or both. Then there is increasing stress upon public institutions including schools, social service agencies, police forces, and courts dealing with problems produced by overburdened, undersupported families – problems for which these institutions are not designed, staffed, or funded.

Less obvious but just as serious is the impact of epochal change in the organisation of care on those who are at the centre of that change – the country's women. By ages-old tradition women hold primary responsibility for caregiving in families. And most, continuing to accept that responsibility, try to bridge the gap between paid work and the needs of children and other family members by running tight, pressured schedules between the two. The familiar personal consequences are fatigue and chronic feelings of guilt for falling short in both roles. But there are also long-term social consequences.

Under dual demands on their lives, many women forego various kinds of workplace opportunities, which means that, in effect, they do not enjoy equal economic opportunity with their male peers. With constrained opportunity, women do not advance to leadership positions at work or in public life in numbers nearly proportionate to men, which means that they do not hold nearly equal decision-making and policy-making authority in the society. They do not hold an equal place in corporate management where decisions about executive salaries and workers' pensions are made; or in unions where bargaining priorities are set; or state legislatures where budgets for roads, sports stadiums, and early childhood education are debated; or the Congress where provisions for tax cuts, minimum wage and health insurance pass or fail; or in universities where desirable subjects for research are defined.

This means they are not in an equal position to examine, with men, the vast economic and cultural changes now disrupting old social patterns, including family care. They do not have an equal voice in the discussions that identify what is wrong, what the causes are, and what the solutions might be. That is, in a time of social trouble when present systems of family care are clearly inadequate, women – who are bearing much of the burden of those systems – have little voice in changing them.

So the care problem is also a justice problem – the need for a society that promises equality for everyone to extend it, in practice, to women. And solutions to the two problems – care and equality – are necessarily intertwined. At one level, in the province of policy design, the challenge of dealing with the linked problems does not seem overwhelming. Reform advocates, progressive think tanks, even legislators, have proposed a wealth of remedies from day care subsidies and rights to family and medical leave to a radical restructuring of work hours designed to support family care. But from the most modest to the most far-reaching, such proposals repeatedly run into blockages to anything but narrow, piecemeal responses to selected trouble-spots. Attempts to confront the care problem as a whole fall into the peculiarly American blindspot concerning work, family and women.

The force behind this cultural phenomenon is enormous resistance to the basic concept of public responsibility for social and economic problems, a virtual veneration of the private in the US – private market, private family, private individuals making private decisions. And embedded in that resistance is the idea that the private family is its own proper keeper and that public or social responsibility for family care is somehow illegitimate. These assumptions frame the national discussion of family issues in a largely accusatory mode. That is, if the family is supposed to take care of itself and is not doing well, it must be somebody's fault. Various groups place blame for lack of care on careerist women, on unmarried mothers – or worse, unmarried, non-working mothers – on deadbeat dads, on feminists, or welfare-slashing politicians. Or, more positively, experts offer advice on ingenious ways in which individuals can solve the particular problems they face as they try to 'balance work and family'.

Thus focused on wrongdoers and individuals, the discussion does not reach systemic levels. Americans do not 'see' the care problem as a whole. They do not 'see' that women remain the unacknowledged and overburdened fixers of a system that cannot be fixed piecemeal. A real fix requires really shifting the responsibilities and costs of care so that they are borne differently and fairly by employers and government and families. It requires work hours that leave time for families, and salaries, benefits, and pensions sufficient to support families. It means the creation by employers of career paths that take account of families and that apply equally to men and women. It means that the public responsibility of government must include services and subsidies that ensure family care. It means that families need to shift responsibilities for care so that they are shared by women and men.

The problem then for Americans concerned about mounting deficits in both care and equality is to challenge assumptions that block seeing the problem whole. For this the country needs a newly invigorated process of public discussion and democratic deliberation about families and care. Cultural rules that keep systemic care policies off the public agenda have to be systematically and relentlessly challenged in public forums of all kinds. These challenges must be directed to major corporations and small business, to federal, state and local legislatures, to taxpayers, to foundations and civic institutions, to law schools and business schools training future leaders, to elite policy-makers, to the media and to grass roots communities.

What people in all of these functions and places need to hear is exactly how the present systems affect children and women, parents and families in all parts of the society. Americans need to see that they are not dealing with exceptional problems facing specific populations. They need to see that the country no longer has a full caretaking labour force in place. They need to see that it no longer has an adequate capital base supporting the social institution best able to provide good daily care – the family. They need to see how much capital is necessary to support the time that attentive daily caregiving takes, and to think about where the capital should come from and where it should be invested. They need to see that women, to have a full and equal place in the society, can no longer be asked to assume most of the responsibilities and costs of the country's care.

Constructing such a complicated picture requires inventing places and ways of speaking that bring the voices of all groups – advantaged and disadvantaged – into the conversation. Then starting to solve the general problem requires building coalitions of people who do not usually see eye to eye – who have in fact serious conflicts of interest, but also a still unrecognised common interest in constructing a new care system. What's needed are coalitions of high and low income women, of city and suburban parents, of all racial and ethnic groups, people in different religious denominations, women and men – everyone affected by the collapse of family care. This is a formidable task precisely because it is so difficult to bridge class, race and gender differences with all voices being clearly heard. But only when the American blindspot is filled in by a new society-wide perception of the care question will real solutions have a chance to succeed ☉

Mona Harrington is a Fellow at the Radcliffe Institute for Advanced Study at Harvard University and the author of Care and Equality: Inventing a new family politics *(Knopf).*

The networked family

Melanie Howard & Michael Wilmott

All commentators agree that the family is changing. The debate centres around what these changes mean for society. Our view is that the family, rather than being under threat or in decline, is revealing itself to be a healthy and adaptable social institution. The best way to describe the changes that have taken place and the current evolution of relationships within the family is to consider it as a *network*.

The core family unit now effectively operates as a partnership or a team, with a more open and flexible allocation of roles which is created and maintained through increased communication and contact between family members. Thus the emerging 'networked family' reflects and manifests the reality of wider shifts in the 'network society',[1] where layers of bureaucracy have been reduced and the emphasis is on multiple roles, unpredictable life paths, economic self-sufficiency and team work. This theme of the networked family, based on original qualitative research conducted in 1998, and our own proprietary data sources, finds many echoes in the latest academic sociology – Ulrich Beck's *negotiated* family,[2] Anthony Gidden's *democratic* family,[3] and David Morgan's view that we now '*do family*' through daily practice rather than passively reside in given-structures.[4] It also has resonance with the 'flexible family' identified by Helen Wilkinson and Synergy Brand Values in work for Demos.[5]

Emotional primacy of family relationships remains

In the face of the 'individualising tendency' of demographic trends it is important to understand that the family remains a vital source

1 As described by Manuel Castells in *The Information Age, Vol 1: The rise of the network society*, Blackwell Publishers, 1998.
2 See Beck U, 1992, *The Reinvention of Politics*.
3 See Giddens A, 1998, *The Third Way: The Renewal of Social Democracy*, Polity Press, Cambridge.
4 See Morgan's essay in Silva and Smart, 1999, eds, *The New Family?*, Sage, London.
5 See Wilkinson H and Mulgan G, 1995, *Freedom's Children: Work, relationships and politics among 18-34 year olds in Britain today*, Demos, London.

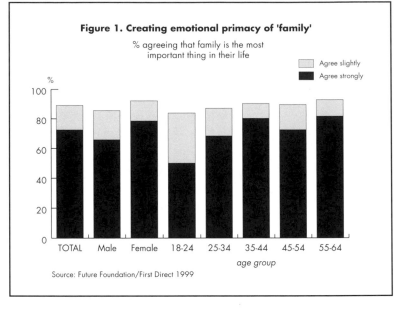

Figure 1. Creating emotional primacy of 'family'

% agreeing that family is the most important thing in their life

Source: Future Foundation/First Direct 1999

of emotional strength for most people. Recent research conducted by the Future Foundation for First Direct in a study of changing values shows that the majority of respondents (including those people living on their own) agree that family is the most important thing in their lives (see Figure 1).

Despite concerns about the family and fears that its influence is waning, our research shows that, if anything, the influence of the family (and friends) is gaining over that of more 'distant' people and institutions like government, the church and the media. And it is well-documented that family members remain the main source of support, particularly in areas such as childcare, illness and financial help.

There is a variety of different forms of family and the emergence of the 'analogue family' which includes close friends

When asked to 'map' their families there was wide variation in response (including within couples themselves – demonstrating that at one level families are individually defined). Not only does the size of the family network vary (due, of course, to different numbers of marriages and children born) but also the degree of attachment and contact. In some families, aunts and uncles would be treated as close family members while in others siblings would not.

Despite the complexity of family form, there is a pattern of sorts in the way people view their families. While parents and children often constitute the perceived 'core' of the family (sometimes alongside parents' siblings), there is also an 'outer circle', consisting of other relatives and even friends with whom the respondent has close contact. Beyond this there is a periphery of relatives with whom infrequent contact is maintained.[6] This way of describing family is prevalent despite the demographic decline in 'kin', and multi-family households.[7]

The inclusion of friends in their definition of their wider family by some couples illustrates both the flexibility and potency of the family concept. Some friends are so important a part of an individual's support network (particularly, as research shows, for emotional support) that they are considered to be family. Such friends, in this sense, are analogous to family members and create the phenomenon of what we call the 'analogue family'. The existence of these emotionally important life-long friends provides support for Ray Pahl's thesis of the 'friendly society' which posits that, increasingly, people will remain attached to friends who enable them to express important aspects of self.[8]

While such relationships have probably always existed, the more open, less rule-bound and self-definitional aspect of family networks that exists today suggests that this concept will become more important. Again, historical research highlights that people have always played within apparently rigid family structures and mores to a greater extent than we realise.[9]

Greater openness and democracy is growing within families

Our original research suggests that within the 'core' family unit – that is parents with children – there is more flexibility and democracy than in the past. Often activities are allocated on the basis of ability to carry out the task rather than pre-conceived, stereotyped views of gender roles or parent–child relations. Our quantitative study for First Direct found that women, in particular, appreciate the benefits of these changes as they acquire greater economic power through work. On the whole, modern families are more open now in the sense that there are more discussions with children on a range of

6 *The Millenial Family*, Future Foundation, 1990, p12.
7 David M, 1998, ed, *The Fragmenting Family: Does it matter?*, Institute for Economic Affairs, London, p11.
8 See his essay in Franklin J, ed, 1998, *The Politics of the Risk Society*, Polity Press, Cambridge.
9 See Pierre Bourdieu's discussion of this in his 1997 book, *Outline of a Theory of Practice*, Cambridge University Press, Cambridge.

subjects. Indeed, children expect greater participation in the family decision-making process.[10]

This openness is, on the whole, welcomed by parents who see it as the 'glue to keep the family together' and as an 'investment in the future'. There is an explicit wish in many cases to invert what were perceived to be the more 'distant' relationships of their own child-hood – they want children to be 'mates'. And this trend finds its reflection in cultural forms too – shared enjoyment of pop music, game shows and film is increasingly the norm.

There is evidence of continuing but diminishing gender inequalities

In tune with these changes, the allocation of parenting roles and domestic responsibilities between partners is changing too. However, in this area there seems to be a significant time lag between egalitarian attitudes and the genuine sharing of domestic labour, which results in time pressure on working mothers in particular. Gershuny's longitudinal study shows that the time men spend on cooking and housework has increased threefold since 1961 from fifteen minutes a day then to 45 minutes in 1995. While women, irrespective of their work status, do significantly more than that, the time they spend on these tasks has decreased. This may be due partly to the use of labour saving devices, but it is also caused by lowering standards of domestic cleanliness, eating more take-away meals and dining out more than in the past. This last point provides further evidence that 'doing family' now involves going out for leisure and shopping trips to a greater extent.

Our research about roles within family couples suggests that the allocation of tasks is slowly becoming more pragmatic reflecting either the partners' different skills (for example, a man might do more cooking if he is better at or more interested in it) or a negotiated allocation of roles rather than being strictly determined by gender roles (although these still play their part).

Indeed, adding together paid work time and unpaid work time suggests a greater symmetry does exist than some analysts accept. It also points to the degree to which long working hours effectively prevent greater male participation in the domestic sphere, regardless of their desires. Figure 2 shows that in those families where the wife spends more time in paid work her total work hours are much

10 *British Social Attitudes*, volume 15,1999, Gower Publishing, Aldershot, identifies the key measure towards a 'post-modern' society as being in agreement that 'children should learn to think for themselves'.

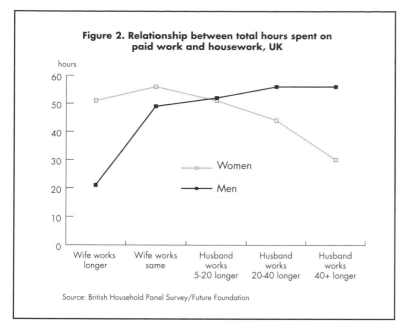

Figure 2. Relationship between total hours spent on paid work and housework, UK

hours

Source: British Household Panel Survey/Future Foundation

greater than her husband's (because she still does more housework than he does). But in those families where the husband spends significantly more time in paid work than his wife his total work hours are greater than hers (because her time spent on housework cannot match his paid work hours). In most cases in the middle, though, the husband and wife's total work hours are similar.

This is not to say that the woman's overall burden isn't greater than the man's – on average it still is. But trends point to convergence taking place some five to ten years into the new millennium as the allocation of roles in the family becomes increasingly pragmatic and individually negotiated.

There is an impetus to greater self-fulfilment as individuals for family members

As roles and responsibilities within the home slowly evolve towards a more equitable balance between the sexes, so the focus of concern for individuals increasingly turns to getting the right balance in a number of areas of their lives: between individual satisfaction and family responsibilities, and between work and non-work. Our Changing Lives[11] research illustrates how, over the past ten years, more women are balancing home with other activities in their lives –

11 *Changing Lives* is the Future Foundation's proprietary research, updating the Taylor Nelson Monitor from 1976 to 1986.

more are getting equal satisfaction from the family and out-of-home activities. This is particularly true of women with dependent children who are working full-time, two-thirds of whom say they get equal satisfaction from both. Working women claim that work is a more important part of their individual identity than men are, perhaps because it is a recent gain outside the domestic sphere for many.

This doesn't reflect a jettisoning of the family ideal (which, as we have argued, remains strong) but rather the importance for each individual (man or woman) to balance the family with other aspects of life and with work in particular. This desire to balance what were previously seen as irreconcilable opposites is characteristic of emerging values in political and social terms. Our work on social responsibility shows that while people are still keen to express their individuality (which reached its height during the Thatcher era), there is a growing concern that this should not be at the expense of participation in networks of family and community, or of greater social justice.

However, the desire for balance creates new stresses and strains in allocating the finite resources of time and energy to different areas of life. We believe that, to create a healthy environment in which individuals and families can flourish, addressing the imbalance between work and family life is one of the challenges of the twenty-first century.

The further evolution of networked families

Greater longevity and a falling birth rate are producing smaller 'core' families and hence fewer siblings – and uncles, aunts and cousins too. The result is an extended family[12] that may be numerically of similar size but is increasingly vertical rather than horizontal in form (see Figure 3 opposite).

The development of the vertical family (as Michael Young has described it) is of immense unquantified social importance – for adults, as well as for children – and will necessitate new inter-generational contracts. Grandparents are likely to be expected to assume more supervisory childcare as parents seek to isolate time for themselves or for work. Of course, geographical proximity is a prerequisite for this, as is a willingness on the part of grandparents – many of whom may be more interested in fulfilling their own interests than bowing to family duty.

Communications also look set to further promote the develop-

12 See for example, Wilkinson H, 1999, 'Celebrate the new family', *New Statesman*, 9 August 1999.

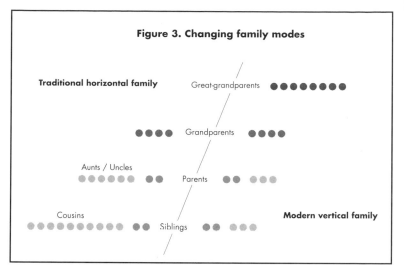

Figure 3. Changing family modes

ment of the flexible networked family. Our research confirms the degree to which communications technologies already serve an important role in maintaining family links. Over the past twenty years the telephone has increasingly been used in this way. And although some substitution has taken place (people telephoning rather than visiting) the vast majority of contacts are incremental - either in addition to face-to-face meetings or in situations where a physical meeting is impossible (for instance, overseas relatives).

Recent research conducted for BT's *Onephone* shows that the average number of calls made to family members and friends is thirteen per week per person, rising to seventeen among those with mobile phones. (This latter point confirms the thesis that more points of communication will inevitably result in more communication – nearly a fifth of mobile traffic is now between two mobiles). The same research shows that more men are using the telephone at work to make social and family, calls pointing to the way in which technology is facilitating a 'blurring' of work and social environments (see Figure 4 over).

The research also suggests a slight decline in face-to-face contact with relatives over the last decade – however it is more than supplemented by growth in telephone calls.

Already, new media are adding to family connectivity: e-mail is the most popular use of the Internet to date, rather than surfing and shopping. We expect this trend to continue, particularly affecting

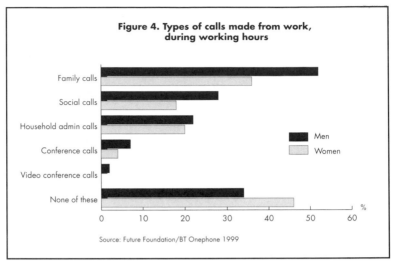

Figure 4. Types of calls made from work, during working hours

Source: Future Foundation/BT Onephone 1999

the cohesiveness of families in which divorce has taken place. Where there were 'broken homes', there may be intact networks, maintained via the telephone and e-mail.

In future, it is our assumption that, as each generation of schoolchildren becomes progressively more technologically literate, as the cost of communications technology plummets and as connectivity between gadgets increases, parental monitoring could become progressively more virtual as the child gets older, and there need be no obstacle to continuous communication among family members and their closest friends. Already the spread of mobile phones and pagers among teenagers points clearly to future developments. Constant communication will be an integral part of 'doing family' in the future and a means by which people express their emotional attachments and participation in relational networks, while fulfilling their needs as individuals.

Conclusion

It is clear that there is no one simple model of the family. To suggest there is – and that it is desirable – is an error many commentators make to the detriment of social analysis. The still popular image of a couple with children, the man out at work and the woman as housewife is outmoded, representing as it does only a quarter of couples with children and less than 10 per cent of all households. Nowadays, it is more important to recognise the new and diverse extensions of the family like the 'analogue' and 'vertically extended' families we have outlined. The flexibility and adaptability of the family is neatly captured by the concept of the networked family, which recognises that each unit will have its own unique form and method of functioning that requires active participation and communication from its members. Our analysis also suggests that the main barrier to greater satisfaction being derived from family networks comes from the conflicting pressures on parents in particular who must provide informal care through active parenting and also (usually) participate in the workplace either through choice or out of economic necessity. They may also want to derive satisfaction from work and want to participate in other activities outside the home too. Thus, the question of how to achieve better work-life balance should be at the top of the agenda for policy makers and commercial organisations alike. Exhorting families to adopt old-fashioned, outmoded and mythical practices is not the solution ⊙

Melanie Howard and Michael Wilmott are co-founders and co-directors of the Future Foundation, a commercial think tank.

Thinking in the future tense

Major trends and their implications for family, work and community

Nancy Ramsey

Today is 'the time in between'. In some cultures there is a single word for this concept. Native American and African storytellers often depict transitional periods as 'dream time'. Jungian analyst Dr Jean Bolen calls it 'liminal time'. For some, 'post-modernity' is the name that fits. In geopolitical terms we speak of it as the time between the end of the Cold War and 'the next big thing'.

Some describe these times in images. An anthropologist recently observed that we are 'hospice workers to dying systems and midwives to new ones'. Author Stewart Brand describes today as, 'a magic carpet ride which makes older generations feels as if the rug is being pulled out from under them and younger generations feel as if they are driving.'

Whatever its name or description, our experience is that *change is the only constant*. Individuals as well as systems struggle to catch up with a tumult of changes as we transition to the Knowledge and Information Age.

We feel it at work, in families, communities, recreation and spiritual centres. In governance, economics, management and the arts we work under the guise of 'managing change' while bursts of rapid, complex reordering impact our organisational process and individual lives. For most of us, the tightest pressure point in the barrage of change is between work and family, between labour and life.

We humans hold a deep need to know what we will 'get' before we 'let go' of what we have. With the degree and depth of change ongoing today, such certainty is impossible. There are few models for the challenges we are called upon to solve in the complex, evolving workplace. In each individual situation we are increasingly like jazz players, making it up as we go along, pushed into new riffs daily by the speed change.

For front line workers this pressured cycle provokes additional stress. It is not only the demand for more work completed quickly in the global 24-hour economy. It is more than the ongoing conflicts between the demands of work and the desire for life beyond the job. It is also a reaction to change itself. But change we must.

How do we learn to let go of outmoded work models and step into the breach with creative license to let enhance the skills and talents of workers struggling to meet the challenges? How do we reduce risk and enhance our ability to meet the demand for smarter faster work? How do we anticipate and learn from uncertainty while traversing transition?

First, we can polish the tools we know. Experience demonstrates that familiarity with different possibilities and appropriate coping strategies can bring insight and opportunity to an otherwise chaotic change dynamic. In everything from nuclear war gaming to sports play books, education modeling and case studies; we know that foreshadowing the future prepares us to respond appropriately in real time.

Second, we can identify key driving forces of change, probe their depth and range, and consider their relationships to each other as well as critical work challenges.

Third, we can create scenarios, stories of credible, alternative futures, which allow us to meet those forces as possible realities against which we can work through strategies and responses. By travelling these alternative pathways to the future we can consider options that provide opportunity and explore the dangers of these turbulent times.

The constant is change. The impact is stress and resistance. The challenge is learning and adaptation. The hope for the future is the cultivation of people who are able to anticipate, cope and react quickly with winning strategies. The outstanding need is for clarity on long term goals, flexibility in systems and strategies as we work our way beyond this in between time.

Seven drivers are critical to the future of work and work related issues.

Values-based groupings

Political pollsters and marketers confirm a new trend in identity groups. It cuts across but does not eliminate other, familiar, standard categories such as age, race, gender and income. It is a transnational, gender neutral, ages and races alliance united by common values.

The Global Business Network proposes five values-based global groupings: Elites, Pragmatists, Believers, Marginal I and Marginal II. Taking Believers as an example, we can see how this phenomenon is at the heart of 'culture wars' that are currently played out in and across communities and countries, often with clashes over religious definitions of values at their heart.

This trend is most visible around religious values. In every part of the world, religious groups are entering politics and even commanding governance in the name of deeply held values. For example, in America the Christian Coalition and Moral Majority are challenging local school boards for authority in education and establishing baseline positions on reproductive rights in the Republican Party. Conservative Jews in Israel are fighting to protect their special relationship with the state. In Islamic nations, religious conservatives battle the State for political control. In Northern Ireland, India and China, religions are uniting groups to action – which often translates into resisting change.

Demographics

The rate of world population growth has slowed and steadied and current UN predictions are that by 2020 the population will be 9 to 10 billion people. While a major increase above today's 6 billion it is well below earlier predictions of well above 12 billion. All indications are that this reduced rate of growth is related to word wide population control efforts, education of women and girls and women's increased ability to take personal responsibility for birthing fewer, healthier babies.

The geographic distribution of this population growth is critical, with 95 per cent of the new births expected in less economically developed areas of the world. The more economically developed countries of the global north are barely maintaining population replacement levels and in some cases, rates are falling below those levels.

Advances in medicine, biology and improved life conditions have contributed to a major increase in longevity. Future advances in biotechnology and pharmacology provide the potential for furthering the trend. In Italy, Germany and Japan the first decade of the next century will see upwards of 20 per cent population over 65 years. The greatest proportional increase in US population today is in the over 80 year old group. Every region of the world will be dealing with older populations beyond any numbers previously experienced.

But at the same time, huge youth populations will be a challenge to education and employment systems throughout the less developed world. In Iran, for example, 65 per cent of the population is under 28 years. With an ageing global north and a significant population growth in the global south the pressure of global economic migration may be profound. One corporate vice president characterised it this way: 'Diversity tomorrow will be what technology was in the 1960s. We all said technology would change our lives but we didn't *really* understand what that meant. Diversity will change our lives.'

How will societies deal with their elder's needs and how will providing family eldercare effect the workplace? Who will be their caregivers and how will it all be financed? How will we meet the need for highly educated skilled technology workers and how will we provide employment for huge numbers of unskilled labour?

Globalisation

Globalisation has become synonymous with growth, mergers, economies of scale and profitability. It has also come to mean a search for cheaper labour, expanding markets and squeezing the bottom line. As the collapse of the 'Pacific Rim miracle' and the Russian rouble meltdown have demonstrated, huge structural and cultural challenges remain to be dealt with in the economic and legal systems that underpin globalisation.

While globalisation has brought with it the growth of a new middle class in many nations, it has also perpetuated a greater economic gap between the top and bottom of the economic tier. Not all have profited equally. This inequity, together with environmental concerns, is leading non-government organisations in particular to call for more progress towards strong measures to enforce corporate responsibility and transparency as corporations challenge nations in size and influence.

The promise of expanding growth, replete with gains in equity may be before us. But in building scenarios, one must ask hard social and environmental as well as economic questions about globalisation. Is it truly irreversible? Can it continue and if it does, how must it change to accommodate to ever increasing demands for public accountability. How will new international regulatory bodies and changing economic and regional systems effect this globalisation? Can geopolitical instability disrupt economic globalisation? Is 1990s capitalism the only economic model or are we on the edge of evolving different models?

Technology

The rate and scale of technology advancement in information and communications has breached Moore's Law, the measure for decades. The speed and nature of future change have led some to hypothesize that the past progress in information technology has been to provide the new languages necessary for the biology and physics breakthroughs of the next century.

We do know that successes in key areas like the human genome project, stem cell research, nano-technology and micro-technology, energy alternatives and fields not yet invented will continue to alter our daily lives and challenge the way we work, live and relate. Technology can also challenge values such as individual privacy and personal freedom.

Are the public challenges to genetic engineering in seed and feed harbingers of a technology backlash, which could inhibit technology's progress? Could public pressure to stop funding of research in critical areas cut into the education and research partnerships, which have generated so much private growth? Is the economic imperative for growth so compelling that it is free of public influence?

The greatest changes in work for the future will spring from the Internet. Not only does it promote on line access to information resources and people, the Internet promises to be a tool for learning for an entire work life. 'E-everything' is remaking commerce from product through delivery to service.

Systems

Systems transformations in government and business organisation are underway and will continue. Information processing and connectivity demand open systems. Just as military command structures are adapting to technology driven restructuring, so too the classroom and workplace are transforming into more transparent and flexible systems. Active and passive resistance to these deep social and structural changes persists, but it is increasingly clear that information driven decision making is crucial to success in commerce and government. In the new power paradigm, access to information and knowledge rules. Will structural change follow?

Combined with the generation changes discussed earlier, this systems transformation may have profound social, emotional and economic consequences and certainly will impact any future scenario.

The increasing role of non-government organisations (NGOs) on both politics and business is challenging old orders. In local, national and international arenas, environmental and human rights organisations are placing values based pressures on systems formerly invulnerable to outside pressures. Organised NGO networks pressure corporations, governments and international institutions for environmental compliance to Kyoto agreements for example.

Another example would be the campaign for broad public disclosure of human rights abuses by police; military and para-military groups throughout the world have focused attention on formerly secure, secret power bases. From Africa to South and Central America to South Central Los Angeles open communications networks tell the dark secrets of systems and demand accountability and change. What impact will this have on governance structures? Can huge public and private organisations, governments and systems adapt sufficiently to meet the changing needs of workers and technology? Will potential technology advantages be lost in systemic intransigence and perpetuation of vested interest?

Women

The greatest transformation in the social order of the twentieth century is the change in the status of women. Every woman, man, family and society feels it. First and foremost, women are clear that being equal does not mean being the same as men. Today women see the characteristics and qualities of gender difference without attached judgment of better or worse and women no longer accept the male norm as the default for what is standard or 'right'.

In some countries women are now the majority of graduates in primary, secondary and tertiary education. Education and training are the universal 'equalisers' in the advancing information and knowledge economies. The increasing demand for skilled workers and diverse teams in international markets are opening economic and social doors for women. Will this trend continue in all economic circumstances or could old models of gender preference for men push women out of the labour force in economic downturns as it has in Korea and Russia?

A World Bank study prepared for the UN's World Conference on Women confirmed what political pollsters around the world had already identified as a gender difference in values. In asking what values governments should implement as policy, women place the highest value on health care, education, safety for themselves and their children and economic equity. Men place the highest value on balanced budgets, tax relief and military spending.

Will women assert their increasing economic power for social and political change? Will the international women's networks, which have grown over past decades, become power sources to business marketers? Will women tire of the passive institutional resistance to gender equity and abandon main line institutions to develop parallel economic, political and social structures?

Equally unclear is how evolving family structures will be influenced by the increasing demands on women for employment outside the home in an expanding global economy. How will care for elderly relatives effect women's ability to work outside the home? Will governments agree to pay for currently unpaid domestic contributions from women and men, which make a big impact on total social welfare?

Geopolitics

Challenges to traditional nation-state governance proliferate around the globe. We witness the establishment of powerful economic and judicial Transnational institutions, which both support and challenge the authorities of current states. In hot spots around the world, civil and ethnic wars rip at the fabric of existing nations. The economic strength of private corporations and wealthy individuals exceed the wealth of many nations. Rampant corruption and cronyism threaten the legitimacy of many states. While not on its last legs, this national governance form is undergoing major transformation, which can not be ignored.

Regional alliances in military and economic co-operation are also changing. NATO military action in Kosovo was a first this year. Does it indicate a new model for armed intervention in a sovereign state or was it a unique, single imperative? The European Union and World Trade Organisation are increasingly active in far-reaching international economic decision making. Will their authority prevail or weaken and how will that effect governance and independent commerce? Can nations be reconstructed from the ravages of civil war and ethnic cleansing?

Scenarios

All of these issues bear down on discussions of work. How these driving forces come together will greatly influence the future form of work, its compensation, form and role in our lives. Combining them in different credible and internally consistent ways can build scenarios, story lines that provide a framework for considering the future of work.

The follow three scenario outlines were developed in conjunction with the Work–Life Leadership Council of The Conference Board to examine the Future of Work–Life Initiatives in major corporations. Their purpose was to make connections between key driving forces and possible different futures for Work–Life Initiatives.[1]

The Big Boom: 'Transformation'

In this scenario, a global high-growth economy continues to flourish and work–life balance moves to the centre of business considerations as the pressure to hold on to skilled, steady workers increases. Options for new forms of work and individual opportunity abound as both business and society invest in people as the key to realising the potential of a strong economy and expanding technology. work–life considerations as a discrete set of issues disappear because the agenda for meeting those needs is 'mainstreamed' into business and government institutions. A stable, expanding economy has the resources to absorb the cost of providing services and the flexibility to meet changing demands. Command and control management systems give way to transitional teams and work is reconceptualised as task completion. This shifting task-oriented organisational pattern allows work across time zones, family structures and cultures. No

1 I'm grateful to the Conference Board and Families and Work Institute and my co-author Arlene Johnson for allowing me to use them here to demonstrate how we can learn from examining the future of work.

one needs to advocate flexibility because it emerges as the only way of dealing with the complexity inseparable from rapidly expanding opportunities.

The Growing Divide: 'Everyone scrambles, everyone improvises'
In this scenario a weakening economy puts strains on families and individuals as technology makes possible a fast pace, but reinforces a low paying structure with long work hours that give individuals few choices in their life style. People of all generations experience painful choices between career success and personal life. The strain this puts on families re-ignites the backlash against working women. The work–life industry thrives as companies offer multiple programs, either to attract just-in-time workers or to enrich the work environment and supports for the core elite of technology and knowledge workers. Social systems are strained by the health care needs of a large, older population who typically live into their 90s and a young population whose multiple children press the systems capabilities by their sheer numbers alone. Diminished returns from full-time employment lead many Baby Boomers to retire, leaving a young, largely inexperienced workforce that is sandwiched between childcare and elder care responsibilities. The slowed economy produces low revenues for government, hampering its capacity to meet social needs as individuals and companies search for ways to survive in difficult times.

The Big Bust: 'Back to square one'
This scenario combines the impact of a slow economy with that of a crisis in the use of new technology. The combined impact of international Y2K crises, Euro integration and a sliding American stock market make it a buyers' market for labour. IT systems failures push the global economy into recession, and weaker economies enter a depression. Trade patterns are disrupted. Many work–life arguments fall back on an advocacy theme that business must meet its social responsibility because it is the 'right thing to do'. As both small and large businesses fail, a few large multinational corporations become primary employers and set the tone for wages and working conditions. To counteract the power of these companies, sentiment builds for government intervention and legislated safety nets for families, the elderly and children. Conflicts arise among organised groups as

pressures to protect constituencies grow. In the unstable employment environment, women's role in the paid economy becomes critical to business and families and benefits tied to jobs are again a
measure for service.

Conclusion

No one of these brief scenarios will be the future, but parts of each
of them will. When drawing on these driving forces and the trends
they illustrate, we see how the complexities of change can deeply
impact the future of work. By examining and developing the scenarios and fleshing out their implications we can explore the future in
an informed way that facilitates learning and adapting as individuals and as institutions in the private and public sectors ⊙

Nancy Ramsey is an author, futurist and entrepreneur, and co-author of The
Futures for Women: Scenarios for the 21st century *(Addison Wesley).*

Reflections on modern day family values

Michael Rustin

There are three main ways to organise relations between human beings in society. The dominant way is to rely on markets for the exchange of commodities and services by individuals or institutions acting from self-interest. A second is to organise decision-making through political and democratic processes, enacted through law and implemented through law-following organisations, often bureaucracies or their professional agents. And thirdly, there are relationships that depend on gift, barter or submergence of the interests of the self with that of some larger entity. Families are one of the principal entities of this kind, but there are also friendships, churches and voluntary associations which may be founded on similar principles.

Gift relationships

Within families, gift and barter take place as a way of arranging co-operation between members of the same generation, and of different generations. Parents make many 'gifts' of their time, energy and devotion to their children. In their turn, children also make such gifts to their parents, especially when the latter become needy or infirm. The greater part of caring for the aged and for the ill who remain at home falls to family members, and especially to women. It is in families that the obligations of one generation towards another are enacted, mainly, and families remain the primary locus of identification between one generation and another.

In principle, one might expect people on the left to be sympathetic to the family as a form of life, since it represents so substantial an alternative to the commodification and individualism of social relations perpetuated by the market. Marx famously described the family as a haven in a heartless world. Socialists in Britain have also used family relationships as a metaphor for the social relations they wished to see elsewhere, through for example the appellations of 'brothers' for fellow workers, or in the idea of mutual care and responsibility that sustained the post-war project of the welfare state in Britain.

The dark side of family life

Of course, matters are not, in reality, so simple. Families have never existed in a free space, as an altruistic alternative to the regimes of political hierarchy or market exchange. Their forms of relationship and domination were and are structured by law and markets. Their members have been subject to differential opportunities and pressures to engage in market exchange. They exist within a normative order, in which the institutions of religion have had an important role.

The effects of these structures have been to impose on the family many constraining and unequal features Women and children used to be to a large degree the property of their fathers or husbands. Men until well into the last century had legal licence to control or punish them with violence. Men had a different kind of freedom to exchange their labour in the market from women, who in the middle class were confined to virtual captivity at home. Men were politically enfranchised in Britain long before women. Far from being exclusively a sphere of voluntary co-operation for mutual benefit, families were also the setting for the domination of one gender over another, and of one generation over another.

It is not surprising, therefore, that in the modern period the family has been subjected to deep critique. Women have campaigned to weaken the constraints exercised in the name of 'family values', which they saw as being largely in the interests of men. Political battles about divorce and abortion have been an important aspect of this. Both sexes, but perhaps especially women, have voted with their feet to avoid entering marriages, or to remove themselves from them when they became intolerable. Young people too have exercised their freedom to live independently of family. In Britain and North

America it has become common for young people to live in small communities of their own generation or to co-habit on university campuses or in flat-shares prior to forming permanent partnerships.

This widespread exit from the constraints of family produces consequential demands that its functions be picked up by other agencies. Women have sought a new balance between the part of their lives spent within the domain of family and the part they spend within the labour market. There are thus demands for more and earlier childcare and for public services to provide residential and domiciliary care for old and infirm people. In the sphere of higher education this tendency to 'socialisation' has recently gone into reverse, as the increasing costs of university education for students force them back into a greater dependence on their families of origin.

Families and public policy

Is the support and strengthening of the family – and of other forms of co-operation that depend on mutual identification, gift and barter a proper object of public policy?

Stein Ringen argued in a Demos pamphlet that the family is an important locus of production as well as of consumption.[1] The 'standard of living' or goods of life that citizens enjoy are substantially enhanced by labour performed in the home, or by members of families working for one another outside the home. They clean, shop, cook, drive, mend, build, garden, nurse and perform many other services for one another.

Most commodities and machines are inert and useless objects unless labour is invested in creating value out of them. Ringen points out that co-operation between family members is an efficient way of increasing the value gained from such commodities, or from the returns from labour in the market place. Cooking a meal for four does not take four times the work of cooking a meal for one. Two people do not need to occupy twice the living space of a single person, to gain equivalent benefit from it. A garden maintained by one person can be enjoyed by many. A car is driven by one person, but may comfortably transport five. Ringen argues that the measure of GNP grossly underestimates real wealth, because it does not include the value added by work undertaken in the informal family or friendship economy.

[1] Ringen S, 1998, *The Family in Question*, Demos, London. See also Ringen S, 1997, *Citizens, Families and Reform*, Oxford University Press, Oxford.

He also deploys this argument to explain the widespread dissatisfaction at the failure of rising incomes to generate an increased sense of well-being. He argues that this is not because people do not understand their own interests, or have unreasonable aspirations, but because where gains are made at the level of monetary income they are often being 'paid for' by real losses in the informal economy. Working a 50 hour week generates more money, but it means there is less time available to produce the 'goods' that are made by work in the informal sector – the 'work' of playing with the children, or taking one's aged parents out for the day. The situation must be particularly chronic in the United States, where enforced workaholism – long working hours, short holidays – is reported to be more rife than in Europe.

The schema of 'production' and 'consumption' that dominates our current view of the economy is a construction which mystifies the real economic process. This schema makes 'work' seem largely a sacrifice that we undertake to earn the money so that we can 'consume' the products of other people's work. But most consumption is in reality the location of another labour process. 'The labour of consumption' (eating, home maintenance, childcare) involves effort. Its most significant feature is that it is undertaken in a context of gift and barter relationships, not of monetary exchange. And on the other side of the production–consumption divide, much work in the market has satisfactions that are deeply missed by those not in employment. These are the satisfactions derived from co-operation, mutual recognition and the deployment of human capacities. Those who rightly demand 'jobs' as an output of economic policy are not merely asking for the means of generating income, but for the underpinnings of a whole way of life.

Ringen's argument is that just as it is proper for society to support the 'formal' economy, so governments should also be willing to support families as a site of production and as makers of well-being. He argues that our present economy undervalues the work that is done in these settings and colludes with the interests of capital in undermining and draining it of human resources, through its drive to bring all possible activities within the sphere of market exchange.

If the opportunity-cost of bringing up a child, or caring for an aged relative or friend, is high because of the superior rewards available from the market, then individuals will reduce their commitments to these tasks. If these activities are socially recognised and paid for (by child allowances, or allowances to support the care of the infirm) then individuals will be inclined to balance their commitments in different ways. Ringen's explanation of declining family size, and even more importantly of declining commitment to work within families, is that the opportunity-costs of this work in contrast to paid work have changed in ways too favourable to the latter.

This has happened, of course, in part as a positive consequence of women's new freedom to enter the labour market. Opportunity-costs have changed because women now have choices, where formerly they had few. This is in itself positive and there should be no regression to the situation where choice is not available.

But the fact that work in the market is materially rewarded is not a good reason why work outside should not be. It would be possible to ensure that many spheres of work in the informal sector, especially those involving care across the generations, are materially recognised and rewarded, on a gender-neutral basis. This is what child allowances, paid maternity leave and allowances for the care of the disabled set out to do. Paid holidays, educational leave and even provisions for retirement come into this category, if one thinks of these as settings for productive life-enhancing work undertaken in the non-monetary sector.

One of the scandals of the Blair government has been the part of the welfare-to-work legislation targeted at unemployed single mothers, which required them to retrain or re-enter the labour market as the condition for receiving benefit. This was, mistakenly, a requirement imposed irrespective of the age of their children, even though it is obvious that whereas children of four or five spend time at school, infants of up to four years of age might well not do so, either by their own or their parents' preference. The time parents spend caring for such young children is no less a form of work than the time they might spend employed at the checkout counter at the supermarket or in cooking school meals.

How far should the polity intervene legally to sanction the formation and maintenance of families? Does it matter that fewer people marry, that divorce is in effect obtainable on demand, that individuals may easily be able to shrug off any responsibility they might have for the support of their children or parents? Is there a justifiable way of giving legal and normative support to lasting relationships and obligations, while not improperly interfering with individual freedoms?

One harm inflicted by the Thatcher government was to try to enforce parental obligations for the upkeep of their teenage children aged between sixteen and eighteen, by denying the latter unemployment benefit and making them materially dependent on their parents. This imposed strains on many families of the young unemployed, both materially and in the visible withdrawal of public support for the parental function. The increased homelessness of the young, so visible in city streets in Britain, is probably in part a consequence of this punitive and counter-productive attempt to enforce family solidarity.

Ringen's solution, which is to regard marriages as binding contracts in which both partners and children have a legal and 'democratic' stake (as if the family were a miniature republic) is dubious. It imports a conception of rational self-interest and contractual exchange into a sphere whose essence is to be open-ended so far as the exact nature of mutual gifts and obligations is concerned. Here, if anywhere, is a sphere where complex forms of equality should apply.[2] Nor do government attempts to assert 'family values' seem likely to be effective. Some argue that moral guidance is one of the chief levers available to modernising governments, and this view is echoed in practice by Tony Blair and Jack Straw. In this respect, however, New Labour risks becoming authoritarian. It is moralistic in face of the symptoms of declining social solidarity but blind to its prime causes in the deregulated markets that its main policy agendas support. Tougher on crime than on its causes, in fact.

Conclusion

Most people prefer to maintain lasting ties and responsibilities for family members and for long-standing friends and neighbours, if they can do so without unacceptable costs. The task for the state therefore is to keep these costs to individuals at an acceptable level, to provide services that are supportive and respectful of personal ties, and to provide mediation services to assist in the management and negotiation of difficulties, including the facilitation of 'exit' where this is most appropriate or is deeply desired.

There are many ways in which this already happens, and where supportive conceptions of welfare have improved previously more

2 Walzer M, 1983, *Spheres of Justice*, Martin Robertson, London.

impersonal and usurping social services: encouragement of parents to stay with children in hospital, hospices that value the presence of relatives, obstetric delivery rooms that welcome fathers, counselling and mediation services provided to assist couples in marital conflict, public housing allocation policies that recognise needs for relatives to remain near to one another. A conception of 'active welfare' needs to be further encouraged, in which priority is given to the support of relationships in the family and informal spheres.

It is hard to see how democratic socialists, critical of markets as the dominant form of social relationship, and also rightly critical of the state as an all-pervasive substitute for this, can neglect the sphere of the family, and of its informal cognates of friendship and voluntary association, as an essential dimension of society. This is especially the case if we are to be sensitive to the emotional dimension of human lives. The rationalism of both liberal and socialist political traditions has tended to disregard the affective dimensions of human lives. Finding convincing ways of imagining a good society depends on working through these dilemmas ⊙

Michael Rustin is a Professor of Sociology at the University of East London. He co-edits Soundings *magazine.*

A longer version of this article is being published in Dissent *(New York).*

The learning family

Tom Bentley

When I was a young child, my newly married aunt and uncle came to live with us in the large Victorian vicarage that I grew up in. They didn't stay for very long, but that period of co-residence marked the start of a particular kind of family relationship which is the focus of growing attention. My family in many ways was the archetypal twentieth century nuclear unit: two parents, three children, strong relationships, carefully balanced career planning and a secure, supportive environment to grow up in. But it also benefited from a different kind of input. My aunt and uncle acted as *family associates*, in a way that many businesses are now drawing on the skills of people who might once have been employees.

Having decided not to have children themselves, my aunt and uncle helped to bring us up: babysitting, looking after us at weekends, taking us on visits, helping with schoolwork, generally being around. There was an implicit social contract at work. If and when they need support in old age, they can rightfully expect my brothers and I to play a part. They were not a part of the core family unit in the sense of playing a full time or unconditional role. But they did play an important part. This type of relationship, far closer to the extended household patterns characteristic of pre-modern families, is increasingly important to the functioning of post-modern families. It is an element of what Melanie Howard and Michael Wilmott have called 'network families'[1] and close to what Helen Wilkinson has defined as the re-emergence of extended families with 'supply mums and dads'.[2]

1 Wilmott M, 1999, *The millennial family*, Future Foundation, London.
2 Wilkinson H, 'Celebrate the new family', 1999, *New Statesman*, 9 August 1999, and developed in 'Family and Friends', *Big Ideas*, BBC2, 11 August 1999.

Understanding these relationships is vital in understanding the policy supports needed to underpin family life in the next two decades. Perhaps even more important, they point towards a way of analysing family and working life that helps to break down the opposition that has grown up between the two. It rests on the analysis of family and firm as *sets of relationships* which constitute an institution. Deepening our understanding of these relationships also points towards a practical, progressive way of defining social capital.

Background

We are increasingly familiar with the idea that the structures of both family and workplace are changing dramatically. For families, this has been associated primarily with the rise of divorce, lone parenthood and cohabitation. It is driven by changing gender roles, value change, female participation in the workforce and a host of other factors.[3] Whether it is seen as a form of liberation or the decline of traditional values, the debate has only just begun to develop towards serious examination of the new family structures, how they work, whether some are more effective than others. But it is striking how similar the emerging debate is to the discussion of organisational structure that has been going on among employers and business thinkers for more than a decade.

At the heart of the debate is the effect of wider economic and social conditions on organisational form. The family paradigm during the industrial era was shaped by its external environment. It consisted of smaller family units, with a strong division of labour between men and women, a relatively clear hierarchy of decision-making and a relatively clear goal: to produce and rear children, work for economic security and aim to increase its material standard of living over time, with the longer-term goal of a secure retirement. As economic production was increasingly externalised, the informal economy of care, learning and sustenance received less attention. As households became more capital intensive, containing more 'labour saving' devices, family life was characterised by consumption of goods and services using income based on the adults' earnings in that economy. This is in strong contrast to the earlier paradigm, suited to a primarily agricultural economy, in which the household was itself the unit of economic production, with extended family relationships reflecting this role.

3 See for example, Wilkinson H, 1994, *No Turning Back: Generations and the genderquake*, Demos, London, and also Wilkinson H and Mulgan G, 1995, *Freedom's Children*, Demos, London.

The new environment

We are now shifting back towards a period in which production and consumption are more closely linked, which Alvin Toffler foresaw as 'prosumption'. Economic systems are no longer characterised by single units such as firms, but by 'productive networks' – the chains of supply, demand and exchange that link together different players across a complex, increasingly international system of production and consumption. The network paradigm is increasingly prominent in many spheres partly as a result of the information economy, which uses networks to create and distribute knowledge effectively.

It is little surprise, then, that family forms are adapting to this new environment, in which working patterns are more fluid and unpredictable, relationships more contingent and networks more important. Extended households with unconventional patterns of relationship – three generations of women living together, for example, with men playing an incidental role – are becoming more common. Reconstituted families mean that the time children spend with different parents and parent figures has become less standardised. Flexible working hours mean that patterns of childcare and parenting routines are also less fixed.

Institutional comparisons

So can we learn anything from comparing families and firms as sets of relationships? The conventional wisdom is that firms are gradually becoming networks, outsourcing functions, flattening hierarchies, using horizontal division of labour, maximising flexibility and reducing fixed commitments to a minimum. At first glance, families are shifting in the same direction, with the rise of contingent relationships, flexible routines, a wider range of inputs from friends, temporary partners and older generations, and no fixed division of labour. But if you look more carefully, this generalisation only extends a certain way, in both families and firms.

While it is true that companies are shifting towards this new paradigm, and that the growth of self-employment and micro-business extends it further, it is also increasingly clear that firms need to rest on a strong institutional core that provides focus, long-term vision and integration for the activity which goes on around it. Even if fewer people are members of this core, it helps provides coherence and stability for the rest.

Strangely enough, the same is true of family life: while flexible routines and contingency go so far, without some kind of bedrock based on routines, values and priorities it is difficult to sustain a family unit in the long term. The big change is that the options for creating this core are more diverse than before, particularly in the interchangeability of male and female roles at different stages, and in the extent to which families can rely on paid service – nannies, carers, nurseries, caterers – to provide some of the core elements.

Another important question is: what defines this central core of identity? For many firms, it is their mission and values that mark them out. For families, the elements of collective identity are shifting: sharing the same surname is less common, as are fixed routines and steady working patterns. But mealtimes and food production, for some families, are taking on a new significance as a way of sustaining relationships and extending care, as is participation in family learning.[4]

What matters most?

This view of organisational life in whatever sphere of society, gives us a different vantage point from which to think about how family and working life can be supported by making organisational arrangements more effective. Central to this is the process of *customisation*: as flexibility increases, it creates the opportunity for individuals, families and firms to tailor their arrangements to specific needs, identities and circumstances. They no longer have to rely on standardised forms or expectations for their models of organisation.

But this creates a problem: in a diversified, flexible, network-based environment, where arrangements are constantly shifting to meet new needs and priorities, can anyone make judgements about the quality of family life and how well it is being supported? There is strong consensus that quality of parenting makes a huge difference to the well-being of children. There is also strong controversy over what *affects* good parenting: traditional marriage, poverty, working hours, child-rearing philosophy and so on. If the models become even more diverse, how can we ever make grounded, practical judgements about what works best under what circumstances?

A large part of the answer lies in the *quality* of relationships that constitute these organisational forms. As with firms that have changed their structure, families must be able to create relationships

4 Alexander T, 1997, *Family Learning: The foundation of effective learning,* Demos, London.

that sustain and strengthen their core, and enable them to draw on support and advice from wider networks. This means an important shift from analysing organisations in terms of their formal structure to a stronger focus on their ethos, underlying norms and patterns of communication. Day-to-day routines are still fundamentally important, since it is through these that the quality of relationships are realised in any organisation. But the crucial question is: how do the ways in which these routines are carried out contribute to the long-term strength and capacity of the relationships which they embody?

Principles of learning relationships

I have argued elsewhere that ten key qualities are essential to creating effective learning relationships in a redesigned education system.[5] The same principles apply to any organisational environment. They are:

- shared objectives
- clear and high expectations
- clear role differentiation
- regular review and evaluation
- truth seeking
- celebrating achievement
- openness
- dynamism
- voluntarism
- trust.

Although they need to be tested and further developed, these principles characterise relationships that combine the strength and durability needed for core commitment with the suppleness and dynamism needed to thrive in the current environment. They offer a framework for supporting relationships in both family and working life, without attempting prescription which may be too crude or impractical.

Social capital in practice

An important further implication is that such a framework may offer us a step towards understanding *social capital* in a helpful way. Social capital is well established as a resource in short supply, but so

5 Bentley T, 1998, *Learning Beyond the Classroom*, Routledge, London.

far it has been difficult to define or measure in ways that are actually useful. It either remains at the level of political rhetoric and academic theory, or is given concrete meaning through backward-looking references to social institutions that are usually on their way out.

To have any real purchase on policy and behaviour, the idea of social capital has to be both practical and progressive. That is, it must be convertible into lessons and principles that we can draw on in making decisions about how to behave, and it must be defined in a way that contributes to a forward-looking, rather than a backward-looking, view of community and social life. The ten principles, while only a starting point, at least offer a prospect of doing this.

Implications

If this argument is right, the move from formal structures to relationships will continue to accelerate over the next few years. It will require a corresponding shift in policy emphasis away from moral exhortation and formal responsibilities, which have characterised much of Labour's early family policy, towards designing systems of support that actually bolster people's ability to develop their own relationships. Two immediate implications stand out. The first is that, increasingly, families will need to decide on their long-term projects when they start out, rather than taking them for granted. The separation of well-being from further rises in material standards of living (apart, of course, from those who continue to live in poverty) creates an onus on partners and families to be clearer about the goals they are striving for, since the goals themselves are such an important component of success. Second, we need a new institutional form to support parents in the various tasks and demands which they have in common but are unable to share effectively because they are not properly linked into wider networks. One answer is to create parenting mutuals, which would help to organise care, homework assistance, transport and so on, creating networks of mutual support and economies of scale in many family routines[6] ⊙

Tom Bentley is Director of Demos.

6 Work on this idea has been developed at Demos in the context of working relationships. See for example the discussion in Wilkinson H and Mulgan G, 1995, *Freedom's Children*, Demos. London and also Mulgan G with Bentley T, 1996, *Employee Mutuals: The 21st century union?*, Demos, London. The virtues of collective parental clubs are also discussed in Wilkinson H and Briscoe I, 1996, *Parental Leave: The price of family values?*, Demos, London.

Part 2

Family business: navigating transitions

The mother's tale

Laura Wilkinson

In the film *Notting Hill* Hugh Grant's character, William, talks of leading 'a strange half-life'. As a mother of a then six month old baby boy I found myself thinking 'better than no life at all'. Melodramatic maybe, but it's a sentiment often felt by mothers and carers of babies and young children. As a society, we have an ambivalent attitude towards motherhood. The modern mother is either glamorised or reviled, sentimentalised or ignored. Glam mums like Madonna, Victoria Beckham (aka Posh Spice) and supermodel Cindy Crawford are so wealthy and, therefore, privileged that they may as well inhabit a different planet to the 'average' mother. Zoe Ball recently announced that she intends to give up her job in the new year in order to get healthy in preparation for a baby and to spend more time with her family. This is a luxury that most women can only dream of.

Motherhood is currently in vogue for those in the public eye but for the rest of us mere mortals I'm not so sure. Working mothers are either put on pedestals as incredible over-achievers who have got modern motherhood sussed, or they are despised and scapegoated for all sorts of social ills, from child drug abuse to male unemployment. And the mother who stays at home, whether through choice or not, is either held up as some kind of benign saint or (more commonly) overlooked completely.

On reflection, part of my problem was that when I became pregnant I was, effectively, out of the labour market, studying for a journalism qualification and taking the occasional acting job when the opportunity arose. The pregnancy was unplanned – although my husband and I now refer to it as a 'happy accident'. After the first sixteen weeks when, quite frankly, I felt like death, I was well and optimistic, planning to work from home as a freelance journalist while baby slept peacefully in the next room. Ah, the bliss of ignorance.

The reality of caring for a baby made the notion of home working faintly ridiculous. My lack of extensive journalistic experience made the prospect of nursery for Morgan while I touted for freelance contracts an economic impracticality. Without a job to return to, I decided to stay at home for a few months and search for a job that would make use of my new skills.

As a first-time stay-at-home mother the greatest difficulty for me was the invisibility. On reflection, I was almost certainly depressed. I don't mean post-natal depression in its overwhelming and debilitating clinical sense. I'm talking about low-level depression when life flatlines along and nothing seems to touch you. You neither cry a lot nor laugh a lot and you certainly don't dare to think a lot. I imagine it was because of this that the description of a half-life resonated so much with me. I suspect there are thousands of women, and a small but growing number of men, out there who know what I mean.

There is an almost total absence of social support for new parents and, if you live away from the rest of your family and have few, if any, friends with children themselves, life can be very lonely indeed. Images of popular culture fall flat when you are actually living through motherhood. Isolated, struggling with a new life which absorbs almost all of yours, the world is a very different place to the one you last inhabited – the child-free one – and your sense of self is extremely difficult to hold onto. Nothing truly prepares you for parenthood but in a society that places the responsibility for the rearing of the next generation firmly and squarely on the parents' shoulders, the lack of a support network is shameful. New parents have little more than the odd parent-and-baby group in which to find advice, exchange ideas and meet other grown ups. I felt like the incredible shrinking woman, a mature Alice in a weird and alien motherland.

My breakthrough happened, as these things always do, when I least expected it: on a sunny, Sunday afternoon in Worthing with my husband, son and sister. As we were strolling along the seafront of this 'jewel of the south coast', a Salvation Army brass band began to play. Watching the troops march down the street I was struck by the sense that, clothes and cars aside, we could have stepped back in time

50 years. Baby Morgan was bouncing up and down, excited and squeal-ing with joy, his father and my sister were bobbing to the beat of the drum and I was laughing, really laughing, for the first time in a long time. Suddenly, out of the blue, the laughter dissolved into tears.

It took some hours to work out why I'd become upset. I finally saw that part of me had felt immensely relieved to be a mother in the late 1990s, and yet part of me felt almost jealous of the simplicity of life for mothers back in the 1950s. I pondered how mind numbingly boring and stifling it must have been to be expected to stay at home with the children for years but concluded that if there was no other option and no awareness of another life then there would be fewer strains and pressures. Of course, I know that it was this restrictive and controlling culture that led to the women's movement but just for a moment I felt envious. We have so many options today but they don't come without a price.

As a result of this revelation in Worthing I resolved to get a job fast and not restrict myself by looking for career jobs. As anyone who has spent any time out of work knows, getting back into the job market is no mean feat, hence initiatives like the New Deal. Add a baby or child to the equation and things get even more complicated.

Assuming you can afford the cost of childcare (I'll come back to that later), finding it presents another problem. There is a chronic childcare gap in this country with only one (registered) place for every seven and a half children under eight years old. When I found a job, finding childcare was a nightmare. My new employers, like the majority, were unsympathetic to my domestic situation. Having been informed I was a successful applicant I was expected to begin work the following week. My son spent the first three weeks of my working life being carted between two local(ish) nurseries as a 'casual' while I scoured the childminder list. I was very lucky to have this period of grace. It was summer and parents had taken their babies on holiday, freeing up places at the nurseries.

Informed by the childminder coordinator in Hove, where I live, that there were no local vacancies, I turned to neighbouring Brighton. Uninitiated as I was to this world I was surprised to dis-cover the majority of childminders only work regular hours, and nurseries are often even less flexible. Anyone like myself who works outside of the standard nine to five day will find it even harder to get a childminder, not forgetting the additional expense (double-time after 6pm in most cases). So-called atypical working patterns (part-time, temporary, contract) are no longer atypical with 40 per cent of the workforce in work other than full-time, permanent employment. It seems that childcare provision has yet to catch up.

After a couple of hiccups I did find a delightful childminder my son and I were happy with. All this – phone calls, interviews, driving around dropping him off for 'test' times – and a job. Is this is what the glossy magazines call 'having it all'? I call it exhausting, not to mention stressful.

My primary motivation for accepting the job was to do something other than look after my son full-time. Both my husband and I are paid considerably more than the national minimum wage per hour and yet once childcare costs have been accounted for, the net increase to our household income per week amounts to a paltry £40. It would be less except for the fact that I work two 6 to 9pm shifts a week when my husband covers the bath and bedtime shifts.

This autumn the Working Families Tax Credit was introduced as part of the National Childcare Strategy. The government is investing an unprecedented £8 billion to create more and better childcare. The amount received will depend on family income and the amount spent on childcare but as a rough guide eligibility ceases at an income of £22,000 per year for a one child family and £30,000 per year for a family with more than one child.

This is a great leap forward for Britain, where parents pay more than anywhere else in Europe for their childcare. It is the most generous childcare allowance ever and the government obviously hopes uptake is high. High-profile television advertisements have been running for some months now. Although my family will not be eligible I believe that the knock-on effects of such an initiative will impact on parents nationwide. Government action will stimulate the market. If more parents go to work, outdated employers will have to buck up their ideas and offer more flexibility to all employees, not just parents. This can only be a good thing.

So far, the government appears to be focusing most of its energy on making childcare more affordable. While this is long overdue and welcome, my experience points to a more serious problem – that of availability. Parents will only be able to make use of this scheme if they can find registered childcarers. Those who leave their little ones with grandma or a friend will not be eligible, whether they pay for this care or not. I live in an urban area and finding care wasn't easy. Those who live in rural areas face an even bigger challenge.

Yet childcare alone is only part of the answer; the distribution of work is another. Before Morgan's arrival, my husband and I hoped to each work part-time, thus sharing the parenting. We felt that this would be a positive experience for both us and our child. We would enjoy rewarding paid work and share the pleasure and pain that is childrearing. But it has not worked out that way. My husband works full-time as he earns more than I do in my current post, and I work 25 hours a week only because mine is not a 'career' job, though I am looking for one. At present, we cannot afford to both work part-time as such jobs often pay less than full-time career jobs. Meanwhile, many career jobs are full time. But we are still optimistic about the future.

I do not intend to be overly downbeat and negative about raising a child. But it is a fact that modern motherhood is difficult, if indeed it were ever easy. Perhaps it is not surprising that one in five women of my generation look set to remain childless. Despite its voguish portrayal in the press, parenthood is difficult, undervalued work in our society. Deeply schizophrenic attitudes are prevalent. While celebrity mums challenge traditional images and stereotypes, the everyday experiences of bread and butter women paint a vastly different picture. Finding the balance between work and home, work and parenthood, and making it pay, both emotionally and financially, is very hard. Some mothers are more equal than others it seems.

The government is attempting to redress the balance and make life for many parents just a little bit easier. The National Childcare Strategy has three main aims: to raise the quality of childcare, make it more affordable and, finally, to make it more accessible. Financial incentives for working parents are tackling the cost of care and this is as good a place as any to begin.

I am hopeful for parenting in the twenty first century - I trust that Morgan's generation will find an easier balance. But, I have found the transition to this new phase in my life difficult. Yet despite the trials, tears, loss of freedom and torture that is sleepless nights I would not want a life without my son. As his father says, 'he's the best thing that ever happened to me' ⊙

Laura Wilkinson is a portfolio person – an actor, charitable fundraiser, freelance journalist and first time mother.

The father's tale

Jack O'Sullivan

I remember the moment when I realised that fatherhood was a radical activity – just after my daughter was born. It was immediately clear that the conventional wisdom as to what I should do next was wrong for me, my wife and our baby. I knew what was expected. I was supposed to mop my wife's brow, cut the umbilical cord and announce at the appropriate moment, Delboy-style, 'It's a baby!' Then I would be deemed to have done my duty and I would be despatched to light a fat cigar, head for the pub and 'wet the baby's head'. Or perhaps the more acceptable version would be that after a gruelling night in the labour ward, I would head home for some well-earned kip, so I could be on top form next day, with balloons blown and bunting waving, to welcome mother and child back into the family home.

But neither option appealed to me. I wanted to stay. It seemed so unfair that I should be sent home just when the fun was starting. After all, I'd been present for the conception, supported my wife through morning sickness, shared the ups and downs of her pregnancy. We'd gone to ante-natal classes together and I'd accompanied her on various hospital appointments. I'd felt the baby hiccuping inside my wife and collected a fistful of radar-like photographs showing the baby at various stages of foetal development. So, why, I asked myself, should I have to miss the baby's first night?

I knew why. A labour ward is, understandably, a female place. The midwives were all women and the patients were unmistakably so, as several walked slowly by, faces pained, hands gripping the small of their backs. Easier, thought I, to find a bed in a convent than to lay my head down here. But both my wife and I were determined that I should stay. The first night was easy. Our baby was born around midnight. Her mother was exhausted after a long labour and was in no condition to breastfeed until the following day. No one pushed me out. A sympathetic midwife let me give our daughter a bottlefeed rather than doing it herself and then showed me how to bathe her and change her nappy. Then, as dawn broke, the three of us were left alone amid the debris of the labour room, each of us stunned by what had happened.

I will always cherish that time, that sense of being with our daughter right from the beginning, when her head was still distended by a difficult delivery, her body still bloody and her hands still cold and rubbery. That experience and determination to stay mean that I don't consider myself an appendage to herself and her mother, a secondary parent, a semi-adequate male. I feel confident and at ease with her.

Had I not been committed to staying, I would perhaps have left at that point. But mother and baby were in hospital for another couple of days and I remained, bringing my wife her meals, taking our daughter to the nursery to bathe her, changing her nappies, listening as a steady stream of doctors, midwives, a dietician and a paediatrician dropped by, dispensing advice. Had I just been confined to visiting hours, I would have missed all this. A few eyebrows were raised, but most people accepted what I was doing in the intended spirit.

We had booked an amenity room so I tried to stay there out of the way, sleeping in a chair. It was obvious that at night, my wife, recovering from a gruelling physical ordeal, was not fit enough either to walk or wind the baby after night feeds and that the midwives were too busy to help as much as they would have liked. A blind eye was turned.

I was turfed out on the fourth final night and my wife had a sleepless night with little support. But I felt lucky. When all men are allowed to stay with their children after birth in, say, 30 years, I will not be thinking then that it is great for the young generation. I will not feel resentful of their good fortune.

The experience taught me several lessons. I realised there is generally plenty of goodwill towards fathers but that change will be slow until we take the initiative and ask for what we want. We are not victims. But we find it hard to ask for what we need and make the personal political. The place where I find it most difficult to live my ideals is at work. I must work to support my family and – if I am honest – because so much of my identity remains tied up in work. But so often work slowly kills us off as caring fathers.

I remember one episode that demonstrated to me the difficulties. Soon after our daughter was born, my wife said that she and the baby would come into the office canteen for lunch. It seemed a great idea. Why not do it every week? Why, I wondered, did my colleagues not do so given that they too had young families? However, putting down the phone I suddenly had second thoughts.

Would I feel comfortable entertaining our child in the office canteen? I would be bumping into bosses and colleagues while pushing a pram in my suit and tie. Who would I be pretending to be then – father or employee? What if our child roared and needed her nappy changed? I pictured heads turned in judgement and disdain at New Man gone mad. I realised that I was scared of revealing my domesticity, a separate side of myself, to the unsympathetic gaze of work colleagues. All that softness and babyness would have left me vulnerable, uncontrolled. At work you are meant to be professional and unflappable, cool and unemotional. As it happened, my wife rang back and said she could not come. I think I might have bottled out anyway. Instead I ate quickly and returned to my desk. If I cut down on lunch time, I thought, maybe I would get home for bath time.

I imagine that these are the types of issues lots of dads have turned over in their minds. But I cannot be sure, because it is so hard for us to get together for a chat. I can count on one hand the occasions when the fathers from my ante-natal class got together for a dads' night out in the first couple of years. Some of our partners, particularly those not back at work, met weekly, chatting in front rooms, trying to stop the children sticking their fingers in electric sockets. But there wasn't much chance, apart from first birthday parties, for the men to get to know one another personally. When we were at home, at night or at weekends, the nuclear family tended to close in on itself. On the rare occasions we met, it always seemed sad we could not praise each other's kids in the way the mothers did. We didn't know the children well enough.

Yet the great potential for paternal radicalism always becomes clear when I am down in the park with the other dads on a Saturday morning. I am surprised to find myself in what is virtually a semi-political meeting. There are no banners, no marching. But chatting to other fathers is like witnessing the slow gestation of a political programme. It is an unusual occasion for most of us: just dads together with their kids. Before long aspiration and frustration pour out: aspiration to be good fathers, frustration with the world, with the demands of work. And then, just as quickly, the moment passes. We return home. The collectivity fragments.

These experiences have made me wonder what sort of a political programme we might fashion if we were able to stay together a little longer. Of course, we would want employment ministers to tackle long hours. We would certainly want Alistair Darling, a father of two, to champion more than today's laughably short paternity leave. Surely Alan Milburn could challenge healthcare professionals who hold clinics while we are at work, who politely throw us out of hospital once our babies are born and health visitors who look through us if they ever see us at all. David Blunkett could act on evidence showing stunning interest among boys in everything about father-hood. He could grill Ofsted about why schools provide such awful preparation for the task.

But work is the big issue. Will Tony Blair ever grasp the nettle and embolden millions of fathers by encouraging us to leave work on time and be with our children? Will he ever tackle the contradiction in Labour policy and recognise that better fathering means less working? These are not outrageous demands. They just seem radical because fathers have been so absent from the family policy-making process. We have been cast a few crumbs. It is planned that unmarried fathers who sign the birth register should acquire parental responsibility. Hardly a revolution. Nor is the promise of three months unpaid parental leave after childbirth: this is not much use to men at an expensive stage in life. I am delighted that ministers are gradually seeing the need to hear the views of fathers and have backed Fathers Direct, the new independent information service. But progress is very slow.

But the worst of it is not government policies. It is that the tone of discourse on the subject is so demoralising to those doing their best as fathers. Does Tony Blair realise the damage he does every time he takes out his big stick and tells fathers (particularly the teenage variety) that he is going to make them pay for their children?

The prime minister is of course right to say that fatherhood brings with it financial responsibilities. But the tone is all wrong. It reinforces contemporary prejudices against fathers, particularly younger ones, as irresponsible sperm-chuckers. Additionally, the punitive language makes responsible fatherhood sound miserable, like a prison sentence. Where, I always wonder, when listening to the prime minister on this subject, is the aspirational tone that so characterises his attitudes in other areas? Dads – like all parents – need leadership that offers less moralising and more in the way of encouragement.

I have not so far touched on the relationship between fathers and mothers. Deliberately so. For too long, the politicisation of fatherhood has been seen as a challenge to motherhood. It isn't. In the main it is a challenge to the modern work and political culture, which so fiercely constrains the possibilities and aspirations of fatherhood. The shift towards active fatherhood and more domestic involvement is being greeted warmly by most women, particularly the partners of the men involved, who already have too much on their plate. Of course, some women will feel threatened that there is some hidden mysogynist agenda. It needs to be made clear that more fathering does not mean any less of a role for mothers. We need to be sensitive to women's fears.

I love being a dad. The constancy of the lifelong relationship it has created rehumanises me daily. Becoming a father has also served as a rich source of identity whose clarity is valuable during a time of confusion for men. It has turned me into a radical against the demands of work, empowering me in a way that no trade union ever could. At last, as a middle-class lefty I have stopped looking around for other people's battles to fight. I know my job is to fight to make sure that children get the fathers they deserve and so clearly desire ⊙

Jack O'Sullivan is a co-founder of Fathers Direct, the new independent information service for fathers. He is also an associate editor of the Independent. *He can be reached at j.osullivan@independent.co.uk*

The great work–life debate

Must success cost us so much?

Liz Bargh

We are frequently told UK productivity is low; UK working hours are long. Why? Does this make sense? What is going wrong?

Male respondent aged 31-35

Throughout the 1990s, British industry has faced major change. Re-engineering, downsizing, globalisation and increased competitiveness for both markets and skilled labour have driven employers to reduce costs, increase productivity and generally attempt to achieve more with less. At the same time the labour force has changed. More women, particularly women with young children, have entered the labour market. The population is ageing – leading to the emergence of a 'sandwich generation' of workers with caring responsibilities for both dependent children and elderly parents. Thus a greater proportion of the workforce has to combine their work with caring responsibilities.

In June 1997, a MORI survey conducted on behalf of Ceridian Performance Partners (formerly Work Family Directions) among full-time workers throughout Britain found that half were concerned about having too little time with their family. Contrary to popular myth this concern was marginally higher among men than women, and it was particularly high for those with young children, the highest earners, those working in large companies and those in the professions. Nine out of ten of those interviewed singled out the ability to balance work with their personal life as a key factor in determining their commitment to their employer.

Yet it is not only those with family or caring responsibilities who feel the strain of working long hours. For many young professional men and women the challenge is finding time to build relationships outside the workplace. For many the ability to combine work and a good personal life is simply not a reality. And those without personal commitments are just as keen to have a life outside work as those with domestic or family responsibilities. A long hours culture is detrimental to all.

The findings of the MORI survey were an early indication that work–life balance is an issue for British workers. This led WFD to follow-up with a bigger survey conducted in association with the journal *Management Today* among general subscribers to the journal as well as members of the Institute of Management. Close to 6,000 people took part in this survey representing organisations of every size and area of activity throughout the UK and beyond.

The primary objective of this second survey was to establish a picture of the attitudes, perceptions and experiences of British managers with regard to the impact of work on their personal lives and on the lives of the people they manage.

The Great Work–Life Debate survey

The picture that emerged was of a workforce where only four in ten managers are reasonably sure that they have got their life in balance. Many managers appear to be sacrificing their personal life, and that of those close to them, for their work. The survey found a majority of respondents working long, not always justifiable hours under increasingly higher levels of pressure and who admit that in many cases they are pushing their staff too hard. Many organisations appear to be at best unenlightened as to the potentially damaging effects of this imbalance on their businesses (let alone their staff); at worst, they have chosen to ignore the situation.

Long hours

Many of the respondents worked considerably longer hours than the national average. Well over half the male respondents (58 per cent) routinely work more than 46 hours per week and over a quarter work typically work more than 51 hours per week. Women tend to work fewer hours – 60 per cent of the female respondents worked less than 45 hours per week and a third worked less than 40 hours per week.

A great majority felt that the hours they work are justifiable. But this has to be taken in the context of the amount of control people feel able to exercise over their work time. While two-thirds of all those responding felt they have reasonable control over the hours they work, at least a third of the respondents felt they only have partial control. This view was most prevalent among those in less senior roles and those working for larger organisations.

Ideally a majority of respondents would like to work differently. Well over half would choose to work a compressed week – longer hours over four days – and the majority would take the Friday as their extra day. A further 15 per cent would choose other alternative working patterns.

Managers are feeling an increasing pressure to perform at work to the detriment of their personal lives. And this pressure appears to extend downwards. Over two-thirds of managers responding to the Great Work–Life Debate survey said that they are expected to ask ever more from their staff. This is particularly true in the public sector where 77 per cent of managers felt that this is the case (compared with 65 per cent in the private sector). Only a third of those responding would deny that they push their staff too hard in order to meet targets.

Flexible working arrangements can enhance a person's ability to manage their home and work commitments more effectively and give that individual a greater sense of control over their working arrangements. Accordingly respondents were asked their views on the extent to which flexible work or part-time work might affect their efficiency. Half felt they would be just as effective if they worked flexibly. But nearly 40 per cent of directors and senior managers disagreed, believing that flexible working would impair their efficiency. On the other hand, only a quarter of women respondents felt their efficiency would be impaired if they worked flexibility

Staff turnover

A third of all those responding to the survey reported that the sheer pressure of work is becoming a prime cause of staff turnover in their organisation. And this was particularly true in the public sector where this figure soared to 43 per cent, compared with 29 per cent in the private sector. It was also seen as a problem more by those working large organisations, where 41 per cent believed it to be a prime cause of turnover, compared with organisations with less than 500 employees, where only 25 per cent believed this to be the case.

Inefficiency

But are the hours that people are being asked to work necessary? Around two-thirds of the respondents felt that in their organisations long hours are often confused with commitment. Again this view was particularly prevalent among respondents from larger organisations – 75 per cent held this view compared with 52 per cent of those working for smaller employers. And middle managers (73 per cent) were far more likely to agree than directors or senior managers (59 per cent).

Around four out of ten of all those responding felt that in their organisation working long hours has more to do with inefficiency than with the workload involved. Once again, there were differences in perception between middle managers and their bosses. Forty-seven per cent of middle managers subscribed to this view compared with 36 per cent of senior managers and directors. Similarly those working in larger organisations were more likely to hold this view than those in smaller organisations (46 per cent and 36 per cent respectively).

Window dressing

Only a third of all respondents felt that their organisation does all it can to help staff maintain a healthy work–life balance. Indeed four out of ten definitely did not agree. There was also a considerable degree of scepticism regarding their employer's commitment to work–life balance. Just over a third believed that in their organisation the work–life balance ethic is no more than window dressing, and again this view was held more strongly by middle managers (46 per cent) than by senior managers and directors (30 per cent).

Sacrifice

Almost 84 per cent of the sample – over 4500 people – felt they had sacrificed something important at home for the sake of their career. The respondents presented a litany of regrets, lost moments and even personal tragedies. Broadly categorised the two largest sacrifices were missing children growing up – around a quarter of all respondents cited this – and putting work before family, again cited by a quarter of the sample. But the answers revealed a far-ranging scale of personal regrets, from simply missing a school event through to missing the birth of children, divorce, the postponement of a parent's funeral and not being with partners during serious illness or even death. A worrying proportion of women (10 per cent) cited having either postponed or forgone the opportunity to have children for the sake of their jobs. They were also twice as likely as men to have had difficulty in forming relationships because of their work.

The price of success

Work–life balance is not only important for individuals. It also impacts on productivity and achieving business objectives. As the UK's workforce struggles to get the balance right in their personal lives, businesses are constantly challenged to get more from less. In order to understand more fully the impact on organisations, crucially on the retention and motivation of key staff, Ceridian Performance Partners teamed up again with *Management Today* in May 1999 to conduct a further survey – The Price of Success.

Once again the survey tool was a questionnaire sent out with the journal to members of the Institute of Management, together with an invitation to general subscribers to participate. Nearly 2,000 managers, representing the full industrial, commercial and public service spectrum, responded. The primary objective of this survey was to build up a picture of just what it is that attracts people to an organisation, what makes them stay and, crucially, what might make them leave.

The findings of this latest survey must be a cause of concern for both private and public sector employers in Britain. Despite the fact that around two-thirds of those responding are mostly happy in their work, at least four in ten will look for a new job during the next twelve months. This figure rises to half for the women and public sector employees who took part in the survey.

Above all else the feature that attracts people to a new job is professional challenge, and this is particularly true for women. Over three-quarters of the women responding rated professional challenge as very important to them. Having their contribution recognised is almost as important, rated highly by 68 per cent of women and 53 per cent of men. The third most important attraction is the ability to balance work and personal life, ahead of both job security and money and rewards. The latter is seen as important by well over half, but only a quarter ranked this as a prime motivator for a new job.

Once in the job, 40 per cent reported that improved work–life balance and personal contribution were worse than expected. And for a third of the respondents the culture of the organisation failed to live up to expectations.

Pressure at work

Stress at work is endemic – only one in six of those responding rarely or never feel stressed at work. And this is particularly true for women – two-thirds said they frequently feel stressed at work, compared with half the men. For many of today's managers the relentless pace and pressure at work is squeezing them to the point that event their lives are not their own. Worryingly, an alarmingly high number of them are now finding that their health is at risk. The picture shows a group of people for whom the personal price of success is beginning to go into an inflationary spiral that no remuneration package, however attractive, can keep up with.

Some, like the former CEO of a privatised public service, take drastic steps to redress the balance:

> 'I found my life balance had become so very out of balance (long hours – 60 to 70 per week – no time to enjoy the money, no time for personal or family activities) ... and I had become so unhappy that I resigned to take a year off ... Making the decision to throw away a big salary and status was terrifying, but has proved to be the right decision. I am now much happier than I have been for years.'

The picture that emerges is of a whole section of the country's workforce living under siege. Long hours, prolonged absences from home, a perceived lack of support and a seemingly insurmountable workload are all taking their toll. Only four out of ten respondents felt that suggestions for new ways of working are taken seriously in their organisation and a similar proportion believe that staff are not respected. Close to half are finding it increasingly difficult to recruit staff and a third say that retention is a problem

Lack of trust

Particularly depressing is the apparent lack of trust of their employers felt by a significant proportion of the sample. Some 30 per cent
of respondents reported that they do not trust their employer and
approaching a third more are not so sure. This mistrust is strongest
in larger organisations and in the public sector. Furthermore nearly
40 per cent of respondents felt that their organisation does not
respect its staff. Again this view is most prevalent in larger organisations and the public sector. Not surprisingly the perceived levels of
staff morale are extremely low. Only a fifth of respondents reported
high morale in their organisation. Once again this particularly
applies in large organisations.

Personal health and well being

Clearly the stresses experienced in the workplace are impacting on
manager's personal lives. Overall around 30 per cent say that their
health is suffering because of their work. This figure increases to
nearly 40 per cent in the case of women and 36 per cent for those
working in the public sector. A quarter of men and third of women
reported that their sex life is suffering because of their work – fewer
than half were confident that it is not. Over half the women respondents and nearly half the men said they have no time to build relationships outside work, and just over half of the respondents said
that they don't have enough time for outside leisure activities. This
was particularly the case for women – around 61 per cent say they
have too little time for leisure pursuits.

A brighter future?

Work–life imbalance, long hours, unsympathetic corporate culture
and sheer weight of workload are the main concerns of today's managers. The picture is of tensions between work and family, tensions
that are damaging individuals, their families and the organisations
that employ them. Ultimately it is our society that suffers. But there
is some cause for optimism – around 40 per cent of those surveyed
believe that things will get better over the next five years, compared
with a third who see no change on the horizon.

However, until they do get better the message from the surveys is
that those in small and medium enterprises fare best. They feel less
stressed and have a greater sense of control over their working lives.

They are less likely to believe that long hours are a result of ineffi-ciencies and more likely to trust their employer. Not surprisingly, they show greater loyalty and are less likely to consider leaving their present employer within the next year. Large organisations and the public sector must look to their smaller counterparts if things are to improve ⊙

Liz Bargh is Associate Director of Ceridian Performance Partners.

How do children feel about their working parents?

Ellen Galinsky

Whenever I mention that I am studying how kids see their working parents, the response is electric. People are fascinated. Parents want to know what I have found, but inevitably they are nervous, too. Sometimes they say, 'I wonder what other people's children would say. I'm not sure that I'm ready to hear what mine have to say!'

Why has a comprehensive, in-depth study of children's attitudes about working parents never been conducted? Because we have been afraid to ask, afraid to know. Until now.

Now I feel the time is right for us to listen to children. Their answers are illuminating, not frightening. They help us see that our assumptions are often at odds with reality. Ultimately, this information will help us be better parents—and better employees, too. In fact, adding children's voices to our national conversation about work and family life will change the way we think about them forever.

Are working mothers good or bad for children?

In the five years that I have spent studying children's – and parents' – views for my book, *Ask the Children*, it became clear to me that many of the debates we've been having about work and family life miss the mark. Take the debate about whether having a working mother is 'good or bad' for children. Numerous observational studies have found that you can't tell very much about a child's development simply because his or her mother works, yet the debate still rages.

One way of addressing this issue in terms of children's perspectives is to see whether children of mothers who are not employed and children of working mothers differ in the way they feel they are being parented. In my *Ask the Children* study, I had a nationally representative group of more than 1,000 children in grades three through twelve (ages seven to eighteen) evaluate their parents in a number of areas strongly linked to children's healthy development, school readiness and school success. Note that this is merely a research technique to obtain children's views accurately. I don't think that your children should 'grade' you, or mine 'grade' me.

These parenting competencies I looked at include:

- making the child feel important and loved
- responding to the child's cues and clues
- accepting the child for who he or she is, but expecting success
- promoting strong values
- using constructive discipline
- providing routines and rituals to make life predictable
- being involved in the child's education
- being there for the child by attending events that are important in his or her life as well as when the child is sick.

Which of these skills earned parents the highest – and lowest – marks? Children in the seventh through the twelfth grades give mothers the highest grades for being there when the child is sick (81 per cent give their mothers an A). Mothers receive the lowest marks for controlling their tempers when their children make them angry (only 29 per cent give their mothers an A). Fathers are given the highest marks for raising their child with good values (69 per cent give their fathers an A) and the lowest for knowing what is really going in their child's life (only 31 per cent give their fathers an A).

It was a surprise to many that having a mother who works is *not* predictive of how children assess their mothers' parenting skills. Never once. Neither is having a mother who works part time or full time.

It might seem counter-intuitive that children whose mothers are at home caring for them full time are not seen as more supportive. But a mother who is employed can 'be there' for her child or not, just as mothers who are not employed can be.

It was clear that many children appreciate the efforts of working parents from the in-person interviews we conducted as part of this study. One fourteen year old son of working parents commented: 'As hard as it may be, you're doing a good job, and keep up the good work.' A fifteen year old girl whose father works full time and whose mother does not said: 'Your children may not like you working now, but it will pay off later on.'

My study, along with others, shows that the impact of parental employment on children depends on a number of factors, including whether the parent is doing what he or she thinks is right. Studies find that it is who the mother is as a person – what her values and ethics are, how she practices these ethics and how she connects to her children – that matters most. Thus, the public debate that sets mothers-at-home and mothers who work against each other is the wrong debate. In fact, from my point of view it misses the real issue: that mothers – and fathers – are not valued and supported enough as parents. We need to emphasise values and strong and caring relationships between parents and children if we want children to prosper.

Is it quality time or quantity time?

Another debate that misses the mark is the quality time versus quantity time debate. I looked at this issue several ways. For example, I asked the children, 'If you were granted *one* wish to change the way that your mother's or your father's work affects your life, what would that wish be?' I also asked a representative group of more than 600 parents to guess what their child's response would be.

Taken together, 56 per cent of parents assume that their children would wish something about *time*: that their parents stop working, work less time, work a different schedule, be at home when the children come home from school, and so forth.

Children's views tell another story. Only 10 per cent of children select as their 'one wish' that their mothers would spend more time with them, and 15.5 per cent say the same thing about their fathers. What then do children then wish for? The largest proportion wish that their parents would be less stressed and tired: 34 per cent make this wish for their mothers and 27.5 per cent for their fathers.

Does this mean that time is unimportant to children? Not at all! Why else would children wish that their parents were less stressed and tired? As one teenager put it: 'When parents are tired and stressed, their children are tired and stressed.' Children are making this wish so that the time they spend with their parents is better.

Another way that I looked at the issue of time was by asking children and parents if they have enough time together, too much time, or too little. Overall, 50 per cent of employed parents with children from birth to eighteen years old say they feel that they have too little time with their child – fathers even more so than mothers (56 per cent and 44 per cent respectively).

Again, children's views differ. Sixty-seven per cent of children in the third through twelfth grades feel they have enough time with their employed mothers and 60 per cent feel they have enough time with their employed fathers. In terms of not having enough time, 28 per cent feel they have too little time with their employed mothers and 35 per cent with their employed fathers.

My findings illustrate why it is so important to ask the children rather than to rely on our own assumptions. The issue of time with children has typically been framed in the public debate as a mothers' issue. But when we ask children, we see that fathers and older children need to be central to this discussion as well. Teenagers are more likely than their younger counterparts to want more time with their fathers. Thirty-nine per cent of children aged thirteen to eighteen feel they have too little time with their fathers, compared with 29 per cent of children aged eight to twelve. Also, perhaps surprisingly, children with employed mothers and those with mothers at home do not differ on whether they feel they have too little time with their mother.

But does this mean that the quality of time is more important to children than the quantity, as some commentators have assumed upon hearing these findings? No. In fact, I found that the quantity of time with mothers and fathers does matter a great deal. Children who spend more time with their mothers and fathers on workdays and non-workdays see their parents more positively, feel that their parents are more successful at managing work and family responsibilities, and see their parents as putting their families first. 'The more time you spend with your kids, the stronger the bond between you. If you can't find the time, make the time,' says a twelve year old boy whose divorced parents both work full time.

To move beyond simply cataloguing the number of hours children and parents spend together, I looked at what parents and children do while they are together, such as eating a meal, playing a game or sport or exercising, doing homework together or watching TV. For all these activities, the same patterns holds: the more frequently parents and children engaged in them together, the more positive the assessment parents got from their children.

Thus, spending time together can't really be separated from what happens in that time. Those children who feel that their interactions with parents feel rushed and hurried also see their parents less positively. More than two in five (44.5 per cent) children feel that their time with their mother is rushed, while 37 per cent feel their time with their father is rushed. Some mentioned mornings as particularly hectic times for their families. One twelve year old girl said of her mother: 'She's rushing and telling me to rush ... And my backpack weighs a ton, so if she walks me to school, it's like running down the street. I'm like, "wait up."'

Predictably, children are more likely to see their parents positively if their time together is calmer. For example: of children aged eight to eighteen who rate their time with their mothers as very calm, 86 per cent give their mothers an A for making them feel important and loved, compared with 63 per cent of those who rate their time with their mothers as very rushed. And 80 per cent of children who feel their time with their fathers is very calm give them an A for 'appreciating me for who I am', compared with only 50.5 per cent of those who rate their time with their fathers as very rushed.

The flip side of feeling rushed and distracted with children is *focus*. In one-on-one interviews, we asked parents to describe moments when they felt particularly successful at home. Over and over, we heard the word 'focus.' The mother of a twelve year old says: 'It's the time you spend with your children [when] you are really focused on them that's good; not a distracted time.'

Of children in the seventh through twelfth grades, 62 per cent say that mothers find it 'very easy' and 52 per cent say that fathers find it very easy to focus on them when they are together. And children are very attuned to the times when their parents are truly focused on them: 'They're not just saying normal things like "uh huh ... uh hmmm". They seem to be very intent on what I'm saying, they're not just looking away,' said a ten year old boy. In contrast to the idyllic and often exhausting notion of 'quality time', focusing can involve grappling with tough issues as well as having fun together.

Every analysis we conducted revealed that when children feel that their mothers and fathers can focus on them, they are much more likely to feel that their parents manage their work and family responsibilities more successfully and put their families before their work. And they give their parents much higher marks for all of the parenting skills we examined.

Surprise answers from children

Among the surprises in my study is the finding that children learn more about work from their mothers than their fathers. In fact, 66 per cent of children say that they know a lot about their mothers' work compared with 54 per cent who say they know a lot about their fathers' work.

Another surprise is that children don't think we like our work as much as we do. Only about two in five children think their parents like their work a lot, compared with 62.5 per cent of parents who say they do. That's probably because many of us have said to our kids, 'I have to go to work.' Or 'I wish I didn't have to leave.'

We seem to talk *around* children rather than *with* them about our jobs. In fact, many children play detective to figure out what is going on in our jobs that upsets or elates us. They study our moods at the end of the workday. One of the children we interviewed says you can tell if your parents are in a bad mood 'because you get a short and simple answer. If they had a bad day, they won't talk. Or they will just go off by themselves.'

Some children even call their parents at work to get a reading on how they are feeling. Children told us that knowing about their parents' mood helps them figure out whether to clean up the house before their parents come home! Other children look for 'mood clues' in the way that their parents open the door and walk into the house, and they adjust their behavior accordingly.

Of course, children would try to read our moods whether we were at home all day with them or at work. The point is that that children are getting haphazard rather than intentional information about our lives at work. This study finds that such information frames how children feel about their place in the world of work in the future. For example, when children feel their parents like their work and when they hear about the good things about their parents' work more often, they are more likely to want to manage work and family life they way their parents do.

Changing the work–family debate

If I were granted a wish from the findings of the study, I would wish that asking the children will change the work–family debates that we've been locked in. It isn't that working mothers are good or bad for children. It depends on the person. And it isn't quality time *or* quantity time – *both* are important.

It is also clear that the language we have been using to describe everyday realities of employed parents and their children is out of synch with what really matters. So if I were granted another wish for this study, it would be that we change the language we've been using. Changing the language is one way to change the debate. For example, to move beyond the debate about whether mothers should work or not, we should talk about values, about caring and intentional parenting. And to move beyond the quality/quantity time conundrum, I suggest we use 'focused time' and 'hang-around time' to help inform our understanding of what children need. These are the words that parents and children use when they are feeling successful.

We also need to replace the notion of 'balancing' work and family life. Balancing implies an *either/or* situation – a scale where if one side is up, the other side is down. It is thus a win–lose seesaw. Yet the research conducted for this book reveals that if work life is 'up' or family life is 'up,' the other side is very likely to be up as well. This is not a 'zero sum game' in which giving to one side necessarily takes away from the other.

I suggest the phrase 'navigating' work and family life. I make this suggestion after developing and testing a theory of how work affects how we parent. There is a flow between work and home, a dynamic inter-relationship in which positive – or negative – aspects of one area can spill over, enhancing or impairing the other. It is our priorities as parents that set the course. If we know where we want to go, we will be more likely to get there.

So I have a final wish for this study. I hope that we will continue to 'ask the children'. When parents and children talk together about work–family issues, reasonable changes can be made. Children will tell us how some things could be better.

Yes, they will still try to push our guilt buttons. Yes, they will still read our moods and plead their case for what they want because kids will be kids. But we are the adults, and we set the tone for our relationships with our children. I repeat the wisdom of a twelve year old child: 'Listen. Listen to what your kids say, because you know, sometimes it's very important. And sometimes a kid can have a great idea and it could even affect you.' So let's ask the children ⊙

Ellen Galinsky is the co-founder and President of the New York based Families and Work Institute. She is the author of Ask the Children: What America's children really think about working parents *(William Morrow).*

A 'third way' on the work–life issue

Brad Googins

The surging tide of globalisation has now swept onto the shores of virtually every sector of the globe, leaving in its wake a scarred and markedly different social, economic and political landscape. As McDonalds, Hitachi and Daimler-Chrysler remake the rules by which commerce and consumers operate, they have also created a strong undertow in the lives of citizens everywhere. Most of the prevailing norms and values that have served to define private and family life have been turned upside-down, as have assumptions about the nature and characteristics of family and community life.

In virtually every community and workplace across the globe, the problem of balancing work and family life has become a prime concern. Citizens in Asia, America and Europe are experiencing unprecedented levels of stress at home and at work. Part of the problem is that many of the traditional models that adequately served a previous era clash with the demands of the global economy, which requires flexible and adaptable individuals.

In the West, two major camps seem to be emerging which frame the worlds of work and home in the era of globalisation. The two approaches that are emerging in North America and in Europe provide strikingly different responses and supports to work–life issues.

In much of Europe, for example, traditional government-supported social benefits are under siege in light of global competition and the increasing dominance of private sector markets. Structural unemployment and the search for social cohesion defines a new work–life agenda.

In America, the corporate sector has aggressively assumed a dominant role in responding to work–life issues, the like of which has not been seen since the early industrial welfare capitalism that created company towns at the end of the nineteenth century. The participation of government and institutions in the civil sector have become all but mute in the new world of corporate work–life. America Inc represents the purest form of the new global capitalism with almost no role for the public sector and a general disparagement of any government role outside of defence and mandated social security.

The free market model that best describes the North American experience differs considerably from the social benefits model reflected in much of Europe. Both models reflect the unique social, economic and political contexts of their societies, but they also push much of the traditional work and family arrangements aside in order to adapt to the quickly moving forces of globalisation.

It is difficult to predict which model (or combination of the two) will dominate in the twenty-first century. Each model upholds a different vision of how society should be organised around social and economic principles, and how the needs of homes and families should be met. However, there is little awareness, discussion or debate of the trade-offs that are explicitly and implicitly contained in each model.

It might be fruitful to briefly examine these two approaches.

The North American approach

In the United States and Canada over the past two decades a corporate approach to work and family life has evolved that reflects unique North American social values and ideology and also the driving forces of a new form of global capitalism. This model is corporate driven and does not assume any explicit social policy and governmental role.

In this approach, employee and family issues are addressed and financed by business. Responses are defined and implemented at the workplace. Driven primarily by the need to attract and retain employees, and employees with young children specifically, this corporate model has given rise over the past decade to 'family friendly companies'. These in turn have spawned a quickly growing group of independent entrepreneurial businesses which provide corporate programmes and services to large businesses in the forms of information and referral programmes, on-site child care centres and consultation.

This corporate model reflects the new employee contract, in which the traditional values of life-time employment and benefits have given way to an environment in which employees and employers act independently of each other as free agents.

In the past decade, the corporate-based model of work–life has quickly come to dominate how North America defines its response to work and home issues of its citizens, and reflects the prevailing values of a relatively unbridled market based economy and society with a minimal role for government.

There are weaknesses to this approach. For the most part, only large corporations have responded to the needs of their employees. Employers have tended to focus on the needs of employees with young children, while insufficient attention has been given to the role of community structures and public policies in aiding working parents.

The European approach

The European approach differs sharply from that of North America in that government tends to play a significantly larger role in responding to work and home issues. Although there is great variation among European countries in the role of government and the nature and extent of social benefits (one cannot lump, for example, Britain and Sweden in how they construct their work–life responses), there are nevertheless a number of commonalities that differentiate it from the North American approach.

On the European continent corporations have played a minimal role in shaping responses to work and home issues and a much more active public sector is evident. European Union membership has placed social issues such as working conditions and vacation time on the political and social agenda. In some countries such as France, universally available pre-school education has been established. In Germany, unions have developed a powerful voice in setting policy through dialogue and negotiations with the government. In Scandinavian countries, an even more active government role provides a rich array of benefits for ensuring family well-being.

This approach reflects a public sector involvement that defines citizenship as grounded in social policy, not through participation in the private workplace as is the case in the North American approach.

More recently, long embedded social benefits in many European countries have come under closer scrutiny and, in some cases, under siege as global competitiveness threatens the existing system. As Europe becomes more unified through the Common Market, and gears itself to compete in the global marketplace, the needs of work and home will inevitably be caught between the economic and social forces that are at the heart of globalisation.

Globalisation and work–life

Globalisation has brought with it a new world of 24-hour operations, technological advances with largely untested consequences for family and community life, and a forced re-examination of how all societies are going to restructure and reinvent themselves to cope with this new set of social, political and economic realities.

Because there are few guidelines for this new set of realities, countries across the globe rely on their existing institutional structures and prevailing policies and cultural norms. But the question remains: in light of globalisation, will the unique differences in social policies, responses to working parents and trade-offs between work life and home life be left to each country or society? Or will there be greater homogenisation because of globalisation, with the North American model holding sway?

Political reform has been manifest in most European countries over the past few years, aimed in large part at maintaining a competitive economy within quickly changing global environments. The post-war capitalism that relies primarily on free markets and private sector dominance has become the standard, and the power of markets and shareholders has all but drowned out the needs and rights of other stakeholders such as employees and communities. Consequently, much of what has been set in place throughout Europe is increasingly subject to rigorous examination and debate, particularly by the business sector which is being pushed hard to follow in North America's footsteps.

Lest we think all is rosy in the North American model, it is important to recognise the significant strain between the inadequacies of the family-friendly corporation and the increasing indices of stress at work and at home. Far from addressing growing work–family stress, these problems are even more pronounced in a society that continues to experience unparalleled growth and prosperity.

As North America takes the lead in exporting globalisation and the opening up of markets, it may also be exporting a model of work–life that is open to legitimate criticism within its own borders, and most certainly clashes with traditional values of most other countries around the world. Can we expect longer working hours in Europe at the very time the movement towards social cohesion is attempting to reduce chronic unemployment through shorter work hours? Will the 'time famine' and briefer vacations become the norm as the need for economic competitiveness overshadows all other needs?

Although there is increased discussion of the Third Way in Europe, there remains very little vigorous dialogue on the growing issues of family and community life. Proponents of a more balanced approach such as the Inclusive Society or Triple Bottom Line approaches are labouring against the powerful tides of globalisation, and the prevailing themes of free market economies. In North America there is in effect no voice other than the corporate one on these issues. Government has been marginalised, unions have been fighting for their own survival and community-based interest groups have for the most part been mute. Consequently the interests of families and communities have been swept along with the prevailing tides of economic growth, and few effective voices or vehicles have been organised to represent their interests.

Future directions

In the global society, the economic sector will continue to fuel growth unless the other sectors play their role. Issues such as those represented in the work–life arena are played out in a delicate set of relationships between government, businesses and community or civil society. Each of these three sectors are critical for healthy and sustainable life at work and at home. However each of these three sectors is also in the midst of dramatic transformation based on the social, political, technological and economic forces that are reshaping our lives.

The time has come to establish a new forum in which the issues of families and communities and sustainable development can be discussed within a global context. Existing forums are local and nationally based and suffer from the provincialism that any one sector represents in a world constructed on global dimensions. However, although the starting points are quite different – based on existing values, norms, social policies and the mix of public, private and civil sectors – they do represent a starting point on which the long overdue discussion of work–life in a global environment should take place.

There are virtually no networks that cut across these global boundaries to discuss similarities of issues amidst the markedly different social, political and cultural structures. Almost no cross-national research has been developed to better understand where the commonalties lie. Even the few conferences that have been created on this subject have been much too narrow and timid in exploring the global dimensions.

In this sense, there is a clear opportunity for politicians, policy-makers and researchers to facilitate dialogue and research. There is a growing need to better understand the interface between the sectors of business, government and civil society. Each of these sectors is critical in creating sustainable growth and healthy environments. Without the full participation of each, and without an adequate understanding of what roles they can and should play, one sector will dominate and the others will not realise their potential. History demonstrates quite accurately that when one sector dominates, the good of all suffers. Only when all three sectors have understood their contribution and have learned to interact with the others for the good of all can we expect that work–life will be adequately addressed ⊙

Brad Googins is Executive Director & Associate Professor of the Center for Corporate Community Relations at the Carroll School of Management, Boston College.

Let's get personal

Missing the intimate relationships connection

Graeme Russell & Juliet Bourke

Work–family research and the debates that flow from it have moved into the mainstream in recent years. But a highly critical aspect of personal and family life that is missing from current analyses[1] and much discussion is the potential impact workplace demands have on intimate relationships, and the possible reciprocal positive workplace impact of satisfying intimate relationships.

Should organisations be concerned about the quality of intimate relationships?

If the responses of organisations to the work and family needs of employees is any indication, the 'intimate relationship issue' has a low priority. The emphasis tends to be much more on addressing the work–family needs of employees through 'flexible work options' and 'dependent care arrangements'.[2] Many organisations, of course, would argue that they are addressing relationship issues by providing Employee Assistance Programs (EAPs).[3] EAPs are by their very nature confidential and therefore there are limited opportunities for any data from the analyses of problems or services provided to contribute to changes in workplace practices and expectations. Further, in my experience of providing consulting services to organisations over the past ten years, I have found that very few have shown an interest in incorporating an analysis of the quality of marital and intimate relationships into work and family strategies.

Recently I conducted a senior management seminar on work and family (with the primary focus on addressing the business argu-

1 See, for example, Bond JT, Galinsky E and Swanberg JE, 1998, *The 1997 National Study of the Changing Workforce*, Families and Work Institute, New York.
2 See Bankert E and Litchfield L, 1998, *Business Week's Work and Family Corporate Rankings*, Boston College, Boston.
3 Ninety-seven per cent of companies in the Bankert and Litchfield study reported that they did provide EAPs.

ments) in an organisation. As part of the early discussion with the group it emerged that one manager worked on a fly-in, fly-out basis (leaving home early Monday morning, working in a remote mining plant and returning home on Friday afternoon). He had two children, an eighteen year old and a sixteen year old. The eighteen year old was doing her final school exams and he was having the usual adolescent challenges with the sixteen year old. He was struggling with parenting issues as well as with his relationship with his spouse. I asked him: 'Does the corporation have any concern about the difficulties you currently have with your family relationships?' His emphatic response was, 'no'.

I asked the entire group whether an organisation should have any concern or responsibility in reducing the exposure of employees to relationship risks. What followed was a very heated debate. I was challenged by several managers who argued that this was really a matter of personal values and that if a person experienced relationship difficulties because of their job, they should resign and find another job ('if it is too hot in the kitchen, get out'). This is not a corporation's problem and they should not have to be concerned about it. All managers, agreed, however, that it was a corporate responsibility to eliminate or reduce environmental risks (for example, ensuring the air is not polluted) and to ensure that employees are not exposed to occupational health and safety risks. But personal and family relationships were not considered to be a concern for an organisation's business outcomes.

In another organisation, however, the response was quite different. In this case, I was preparing to present a 'Diversity' workshop to a group of senior managers. In a preliminary briefing session to determine what the key issues were for this group, family lifestyle and the balance between work and family was raised as a key concern. When asked what they considered to be the issues for this group, one senior manager said: 'We need to do something about relationships at the top. Take a look at our senior management team. They are all men and I think there are only two who have not been divorced or are not currently separated from their families. This can't be good for decision-making and job effectiveness.'

Note, however, that the concern here was for the impact that the quality of family relationships have on workplace productivity, not on how workplace practices and expectations might have contributed to the relationship difficulties.

Given the acceptance of the links between productivity and personal relationships, however, it was an easy step to take to include these issues on the management agenda within a broader framework. This covered the exploration of reciprocal effects and a critical analysis of the ways in which work demands impact on relationships. Taking this even further, though, to change current practices and expectations was much more difficult.

My belief is that the quality of intimate relationships *do matter* to individuals, to families and to the community and that they *should matter* to the workplace. Providing better opportunities for people both to establish and maintain intimate relationships is likely to have a positive impact on personal and family well-being and on a person's effectiveness at the workplace.

The nature of close relationships and their impact on well being

In a recent comprehensive review, Cramer points out that close or intimate relationships (involving passion, mutual trust and commitment) are a major part of the lives of most people.[4] He reports findings from a UK study[5] which show that 77 per cent of people either live with a spouse or partner, or have a continuing close relationship with someone they don't live with. Critically, after reviewing the available research Cramer concludes that: 'There is growing evidence from longitudinal studies that the presence of supportiveness of a close relationship is related to living longer and being less psychologically distressed.'[6] Further, Barnett has found that for full-time employed men and women in dual-earner couples, having higher quality marital relationships can 'buffer' the negative effects of job demands on psychological distress.[7]

Research shows that intimacy – being sensitive to the other's needs and getting to know one another – grows from spending time together, talking to each other and listening. Intimacy develops from the everydayness of life and from comparing experiences at the end of the day. This leads to an involvement of each in the life of the other and a sense of being important and heard. It does not depend on sessions of soul-searching but feeling free enough to speak about the little things that hurt or excite, and knowing there is a receptive ear to listen.

4 Cramer D, 1998, *Close Relationships: The study of love and friendship*, Arnold, London, 1

5 By Jowell, Witherspoon and Brook, 1987; sample size: 1416 adults.

6 See note 4, p58.

7 Barnett RC, 1994, 'Home-to-work spillover revisited: a study of full-time employed women in dual-earner couples', *Journal of Marriage and Family*, no 56, pp647-656.

Generally, research shows that there are four key indicators of the quality of close/spousal relationships:[8]

- the extent to which there is consensus on key relationship issues (for example, philosophy of life, recreation, friends)
- the level of satisfaction with the relationship
- the level of relationship cohesiveness (for example, how often something is calmly discussed, how often there is a stimulating exchange of ideas, how often there is shared laughter)
- agreement and satisfaction with the expression of affection.

Findings from many studies conducted over the past 30 years tend to support this conceptualisation. For example, Cramer reviews evidence concerning views about factors that either 'wreck a marriage' or 'make for a happy marriage'. The five most commonly mentioned factors (by both women and men) for each question were:

- *wreck a marriage:* 'neglect and bad communication'; 'selfishness and intolerance'; 'infidelity and jealousy'; 'poverty, money disagreements'; and 'conflicting personalities, no common interests'
- *make a happy marriage:* 'give and take, consideration'; 'comradeship, doing things together'; 'discussing things, understanding'; 'mutual trust and help'; and 'love and affection'.

Cramer concludes that research consistently shows that the following factors predict marital compatibility: being loving, sexually satisfied, communicative and emotionally stable.[9] In one of the more comprehensive studies it was found that those who were maritally satisfied had more problem-solving communication, more and better leisure time together, more affective communication, less conflict over childrearing, less sexual dissatisfaction and fewer financial disagreements.[10] These are all factors that are likely to be linked to workplace demands and expectations.

The impact of workplace demands and expectations on intimate relationships

In a recent study I conducted in a large organisation (sample size 3,977) employees were asked which family demands impact on their

8 Spanier GB, 1976, 'Measuring dyadic adjustment: new scales for assessing the quality of marriage and similar dyads', Journal of Marriage and the Family, no 38, pp15-28.
9 See note 4.
10 See note 4, pp71-72.

work and which work demands impact on their family life (and what the specific impact is). The five most commonly mentioned family demands were: time pressures (47 per cent); lack of time for social and recreational activities (33 per cent); financial difficulties (33 per cent); problems juggling work and family commitments with spouse; and difficulties in their relationship with their spouse (15 per cent). The five most commonly mentioned work demands were: coming home from work feeling stressed (53 per cent); having to change work hours at short notice (34 per cent); difficulties in relationships with co-workers (33 per cent); coming home late from work (27 per cent); and pressures from work deadlines (25 per cent).

These work demands were reported to have a significant impact on the following aspects of family life: generally poor quality family relationships (45 per cent), not being able to plan family life (19 per cent), not enough time for spouse (17 per cent), not enough time for self (7 per cent) and a high level of conflict with spouse (6 per cent). Even though some of these figures might look small, it is important to keep in mind that 6 per cent of the workforce is approximately 240 employees.

The findings also indicated that relationship issues are even more critical for senior managers. Forty per cent of this group regularly go home stressed; 42 per cent say that their work has a negative impact on their partner relationship; and 48 per cent say it has a negative impact on their family life. The spouses of senior male managers have very different views about the work and family priorities of the manager, and about the impact his work has on family life and on their relationship.

I will illustrate this through the findings from one corporation where I surveyed 142 male managers and 73 of their partners. There was a huge gap between what senior male managers thought was happening in their family life and what their partners thought was happening. Nearly 80 per cent of partners compared with only 50 per cent of male managers agreed that: 'Work demands of employees frequently mean they spend less time together than they would like.' Intimacy in relationships is also a key issue, and partners are much more concerned about this than the managers. Intimacy in relationships develops by having the space and the time just to relax and talk openly and frequently. In this study 45 per cent of the female partners compared with 30 per cent of the senior male managers agreed

11 MacEwen KE and
Barling J, 1988, 'Inter-
role conflict, family support and marital adjust-
ment of employed moth-
ers: a short-term longitudinal study', *Journal of
Organizational
Behavior*, no 9, pp241-
250.
12 Kinnunen U, Gerris
J and Vermulst A,
1996, 'Work experi-
ences and family func-
tioning among
employed fathers with
children of school age',
Family Relations, no
45, pp449-455.
13 MacEwen K E and
Barling J, 1994, 'Daily
consequences of work
interface with family
and family interface
with work', *Work and
Stress*, no 8, pp244-
254.
14 Bedeian A,
Mossholder K and
Touliatos J, 1987,
'Individual propensities
for emotional support-
iveness within a dual
career context: work
and non-work reac-
tions', *International
Journal of Manpower*,
vol 7, no 4, pp7-12.
15 Adams G A, King L
A and King D W,
1996, 'Relationships of
job and family involve-
ment, family social sup-
port and work–family
conflict with job and life
satisfaction', *Journal of
Applied Psychology*,
no 4, pp411-420.
16 White L and Keith
B, 1990, 'The effect of
shift work on the quality
and stability of marital
relations', *Journal of
Marriage and the
Family*, no 52, pp453-
462.

that the demands of the management job made it difficult for them to spend time talking and relaxing together.

One of the groups being given increased attention are younger males (under 35) who have young children (usually below school age) and who also have partners in the paid workforce who are pursuing careers. It is estimated that that dual worker couples constitute up to 40 per cent of the workforce now and this number is likely to grow in the future. Survey findings indicate that men in these relationships are feeling more stress and are keener to change the corporate world to enable them to achieve a better balance between their work and personal life. In a recent survey I conducted, 63 per cent of this group of young men said that they would refuse a job or promotion if it had a negative impact on their family life or on their partner's career, or they would refuse a transfer for those same reasons. Other data I have collected suggests that 20 per cent of these men have actually made employment or career decisions based on the perceived impact on family relationships. Family and partner issues matter to young men and corporations need to take account of this.

Academic research has shown that work–family conflict and job stress are associated with lower levels of marital satisfaction for women[11] and men,[12] and withdrawal from marital interactions by both women and men.[13] Bedeian, Mossholder and Touliatos have found that the impact of job factors on home and family life is lower when higher levels of emotional support are provided by partners in dual-career relationships.[14] Adams, King and King have also found that higher levels of family emotional and instrumental support are associated with lower levels of work–family interference.[15] Working unsociable hours in shift work has also been found to have an impact on intimate relationships. In a large-scale longitudinal study, shift work was found to reduce marital quality and increase the probability of divorce (while the effects are significant, they are relatively small).[16] Moreover, findings indicated that shift work has an impact on all aspects of marital quality: marital happiness, marital interaction, disagreements, marital problems and sexual problems.

Some current workplace demands can be expected to have similar negative impact on the capacity of employees (both women and men) either to establish or maintain quality intimate relationships. Two work demands that are especially likely to have this impact are: extended working hours and working at unsocial times. Bittman and

Rice conclude that:

> 'The study of time diaries provides support for those who
> argue that changes in working time are affecting the time
> available for other activities. Since the 1970s, working times
> have become more dispersed, with higher rates of unemploy-
> ment, fewer days of work, but longer working days. Standard
> working hours are now less typical for both men and women
> workers. Work at unsociable times (outside the hours of nine
> to five on weekdays) has also increased over the course of
> this period.'[17]

Other work demands (especially for those who work in global or
national organisations) that could have a negative impact on intimate relationships include:

- *Constant short-term travel.* For some employees this means being
  away for short periods of time (between five and ten days) on a
  reasonably constant basis, for example, every three to four weeks.
  Many corporations require employees to travel on personal time –
  on weekends or during early morning or evening – to ensure they
  are available during regular business hours at their destination.
- *Overseas assignments for up to twelve months.* Corporations usually
  have policies that enable family members to relocate with
  employees if the assignment is to be over twelve months. Yet
  some continue to design assignments that make it difficult for
  the maintenance of intimate relationships (for example, assignments of eleven months or assignments to foreign countries that
  also involve considerable short-term travel).
- *Expectations about 24 hour accessibility.* For many employees this
  means staying back at the office to participate in global video-
  conferences (that are often based on US time zones, for example,
  9am US East Coast time would be 9pm Perth, Australia time).
  Expectations about availability for telephone conferences and
  responding to e-mails from home have also increased.

Each of these work demands has a potential to have a negative
impact on the all aspects of relationships noted above. They also
make it less likely that those in dual career relationships are able to

17 Bittman M and Rice J, 1999, 'Are working hours becoming more unsociable?', *Social Policy Research Centre Newsletter*, no 74.

provide the continuing day-to-day personal support that can benefit their well-being. Effective communication and resolution of conflicts and differences are also made much more difficult. As Gottman argues: 'If there is one lesson I have learned from my years of research it is that a lasting marriage results from a couple's ability to resolve the conflicts that are inevitable in any relationship.'[18]

How can organisations respond?

There are several possible ways for organisations to respond. They can, for example:

- include questions about relationships in surveys to assess: the impact work demands have on relationships, current relationship difficulties and their possible impact on work performance
- conduct surveys with partners of employees to assess the same kinds of issues
- conduct focus groups with employees and their partners.

How might this work in practice? In one organisation, I conducted a three-hour workshop with senior managers and their partners as part of a strategic planning process. The workshop investigated the impact of work–life and relationship on the managers and their partners and on the business outcomes for the organisation. There was some reluctance to include this as part of the process – as the chief executive officer said: 'This is high risk stuff, it had better work!'

In fact, it was a highly successful session with partners arguing strongly that the time was too short and that they would have preferred to have continued discussing the issues rather than go on a planned social outing.

Conclusion

What can be done? Companies and organisations need to include intimate relationship issues in business analyses of work and life initiatives – to consider the possible impact on productivity and employee retention (especially for dual career couples). They also need to include discussions about the importance of intimate relationships in management training that involves work–life issues. Traditionally such training has focused much more on enabling

18 Gottman J, 1997, *Why Marriages Succeed or Fail, and How You Can Make Yours Last,* Bloomsbury, London, p28.

managers to achieve personal work–life balance and on general issues concerning dependent care responsibilities.

Relocation and short-term assignment policies and practices need to reflect a greater consideration of intimate relationship issues. Specific strategies need to be developed to facilitate the maintenance of intimate relationships for couples who are relocated or separated because of work. Currently, employees evaluate organisations positively in terms of addressing their financial and dependent care issues when relocating or while on assignment, but say they fail to take account of their intimate relationship needs. Travel policies could also be reviewed to reduce the expectations of employees travelling on personal time. Some organisations have already put such policies in place. These include business travel only on regular work days, two days leave following travel that has involved personal time and adjustment to different time zones.

Organisations also need to take a lifecycle approach to relationship issues. The concerns of younger employees might include being able to establish relationships and to spend the time to fufil their commitment to a long-term relationship (for example, in the case of a newly married couple). A common report from younger employees is that work–family strategies tend to focus more on dependent care issues and fail to take account of their relationship needs (for some, there is an even higher expectation of travel and working longer hours).

More generally, organisations could broaden their approaches to work–family issues by including the consideration of intimate relationship at every stage. What is needed is an approach that includes an *intimate relationship impact analysis* for current and future work demands and expectations ☺

Graeme Russell is based at the Department of Psychology at Macquarie University in New South Wales, Australia.

Juliet Bourke is co-director of Work+Life Strategies, Sydney, Austalia.

Forever young?

Generation X's views on gender, work and family issues

Suzan Lewis & Julia Brannen

'Youth is wasted on the young', Oscar Wilde famously lamented. If by youth he meant a relatively brief and defined period in which to dream, hope and plan for the future, a time of freedom from responsibility and care, then he might have changed his dictum. For the period lasts much longer nowadays. Young people spend longer periods in education and training than earlier generations. Many choose to travel for extended periods before looking for work. It takes longer, if not for ever, to find a secure job. Long-term relationships and children are often postponed, perhaps indefinitely. There is more time to enjoy youth but, paradoxically, the extension of youth can also diminish its attractiveness, since it becomes more difficult to move on to the next phase of life. Part of the sweetness of being young may lie in the anticipation and confidence of knowing it is possible, albeit improbable, to realise one's dreams, hopes and plans in the future. With the demise of 'jobs for life' and the rise of globalised and flexible labour markets it is becoming increasingly difficult for young people to map out their futures as the twenty-first century draws near.

In a recent five country study funded by the European Union, we worked with colleagues in Ireland, Portugal, Sweden and Norway to explore the ways in which groups of Generation Xers between the ages of eighteen and 30 talked about their current lives and their future work and family aspirations.[1] Our findings (based on interviews and focus group analysis) illustrate some of the dilemmas young Europeans experience in the context of the rapid changes

1 For further details see Lewis S, Smithson J, Brannen J, Das Dores Guerreiro M, Kugelberg C, Nilsen A and O'Connor P, 1998, *Futures on Hold: Young Europeans talk about combining work and family*, Work Life Research centre and IOD Research Group, Manchester.

which have characterised the end of the century. Those taking part in our study came from diverse backgrounds and expressed a range of views. Nevertheless, they share the experience of being young, albeit from different vantage points, at a point in history when old certainties about work, gender and family life are giving way to new realities. While young Europeans seek 'to blaze their own trails', as one young man put it, new freedoms and opportunities come with new constraints and costs. Young people face a range of stresses and strains as they contemplate their futures, for which the past offers little guidance.

Youth and young adulthood are usually regarded as times for preparing for the future and this preparation is particularly urgent in Britain today as government sets about reducing its sphere of responsibility and support and encourages independence and self-sufficiency in its citizens. For this generation economic, occupational and other uncertainties make planning increasingly difficult. All workers are expected to take risks: to be mobile, flexible and entrepreneurial, moving readily from job to job or project to project. While some young people, especially those with highly marketable skills, may thrive in this climate, others are more vulnerable to the effects of precarious employment.

In our study, whatever the occupation of the young person, jobs were widely experienced as insecure. Many of the young people were in temporary work or had short- or fixed-term contracts but even those in 'permanent 'jobs did not expect to remain in the same job in the long term, nor did they think that the nature of their jobs would remain the same. They expected neither security nor stability, reflecting a realistic acceptance of change, but also often a mistrust of employers. Whether they regarded the lack of job permanence as a threat or a challenge, they all faced some essential dilemmas about how to make plans for the future in this short-term labour market.

In this changing context young people are redefining work commitment within shorter time frames. Their relations with their employers are shaped by a changing psychological contract which focuses on a short-term 'give and take'. For example, the expectation of rewards for long service are replaced by short-term support for employability. Instead of permanent work, they speak of 'a secure kind of job – secure in that you have a contract every few years instead of every six months'. Some are willing to make trade-offs, settling for insecurity or poor conditions in exchange for flexible hours and a reasonable workload . Others feel they have no choice but to comply with the long, inflexible hours that many employers expect. Their notions of career are changing: 'I don't have a career as such. Just a series of short-term jobs'.

Labour market flexibility and job insecurity are also changing the way Generation X think about time. Young people live in what has been termed the extended present[2] or the 'long now'. Especially via new technology, everyday time is experienced as a constant sense of busyness, of never being unavailable, and is accompanied by an intolerance of waiting.[3] Accordingly, when changes happen so fast the future arrives before its time, as it were. The future is taken into the here and now and loses its meaning. People are unable to think in terms of the future, much less plan for it. Young people want to enjoy and make the most of this extended present, with all the consumerism and apparent lifestyle choices on offer. They talk about 'having a life before settling down', as though life is something that excludes responsibility and care of others and as if (not unjustifiably!) adulthood is dull, boring and predictable.

Yet most also have a notion that they will, at some point in the future, 'settle down' and for most this is envisaged in terms of the ideals of satisfying work, a relatively secure income, a partner and perhaps children – a future surprisingly similar to previous generations. But most say they will not have children without some economic stability and, even with current funds to do so, taking out a mortgage to buy a home is seen as risky. Shorter time horizons and shrinking definitions of security make it difficult to plan for the future. As Richard Sennett has pointed out, it is difficult pursue long-term goals in a short-term society.[4]

For those in work there is a feeling moreover that it is difficult to 'have a life' in the extended present. As fewer people are taken on in the workplace, the long hours culture takes hold and the pace of work intensifies. Young people seek a work–life balance now as well as in the future. As young working women and men try to project their futures, they question whether it would be possible to work in the ways they do currently and also manage to raise a family. A young woman who admits to working an average of 55 hours a week realises that 'to try and tie down any kind of life around that would be impossible.'

2 Nowotny H, 1994, *Time: The modern and postmodern experience*, Polity Press, Cambridge.
3 Daly K, 1996, *Families and Time: Keeping pace in a hurried culture*, Sage, Thousand Islands, California.
4 Sennett R, 1998, *The Corrosion Of Character: The personal consequences of work in the new capitalism*, Norton, London.

It is not just work that is seen as problematic. There are also fewer expectations of long lasting relationships. Young women expect to be self-sufficient and not dependent on men, with those from all social backgrounds valuing education, training and experience as a basis for independence. As a young woman student in an FE college put it: 'who's saying he [a man] is going to be there for you, the rest of your life, whereas if you get this education, you've got more qualifications. You can get a better job'. Most young men do not expect to become sole providers for families, although working class men in all the countries and a group of British Asian men in our study were more attached than others to a traditional gender pattern.

When we asked about differences between women's and men's experiences the first response was usually to say that differences are disappearing, that 'we are all equal now'. Within their extended present both women and men feel that they have the same opportunities, especially in the workplace. But on deeper questioning, and particularly when pushed to think beyond the present, many differences and tensions emerge. Young women are much more likely than the men to have thought seriously about future work and family scenarios. Women at the older end of the age range are conscious that their biological clocks are ticking away as they wait for a time of stability and security before embarking on a family of their own. British women mostly talk about a preference for less than full-time work if they have children, but many say they would also like their partners to work reduced hours. Some young British men talk about wanting flexibility to spend time with children if they become fathers, while others talk about mothers and fathers managing the childcare between them. Few believe that this will be possible in practice.

Young women have more clearly formulated ideas about how they would ideally balance work and family and more awareness of the likely problems. But they struggle with notions of difference and inequality. Do they want to be 'like men' or to have different, but equally valued, career and family trajectories? These dilemmas are particularly acute in Britain where mothers of young children (especially lone mothers) are increasingly expected to be in paid work, but state support for childcare and generous paid parental leaves, which make equality more of a possibility in the Scandinavian countries, are largely absent. While the discussions among Swedish and Norwegian participants in our study are by no means free of gender dilemmas, they suggest a much greater likelihood of equality than elsewhere.

There is considerable consensus that old gender expectations are too restricting for the women and most of the men of Generation X, but they have not quite worked out what should replace them. Clear rules about gender roles and relationships no longer apply. Instead there are guidelines which have to be negotiated.[5] This generation talks of endless 'choice' and 'lifestyle options', but their stories also tell of risk and uncertainty. Women especially have more opportunities than previous generations but at the same time many young men as well as young women feel ambivalent about, for example, role reversal and lone parenthood. One young woman considering the pros and cons of having a househusband explains 'we are still victims of our upbringing'. In particular, the issue of combining paid work with parenthood carries with it a residue of strong normative undertones about 'the right and proper thing to do'.

Thus while young people stress personal preferences and options, their views of the future conditions under which they expect to combine employment and parenthood make reference to social norms and moral values, especially about the way children 'should be' brought up. Without some degree of job certainty and support for childcare and given a strong moral climate of parental responsibility, especially in Britain, childrearing may appear a very risky business indeed.

The key issues for Generation X are how to manage the risks to which they are exposed without supportive structures in place. Job insecurity stems from employers' reliance on short-term and episodic labour whereby employer risk is transferred from capital to labour. At the same time, in order to reduce public spending and support, the state is attempting to shift risk onto individuals and families to provide for their own welfare. Today's young people, as they contemplate their future life course, have to confront and manage these risks without access to the tried and tested experiences of the parent generation who grew up in quite a different world.

Given the climate of flexibility and risk in Britain and the short history of public support for working parents and their young children, British young people not surprisingly hold low expectations of non-family support for combining paid work and parenthood in the

5 Finch J, 1989, *Family Obligations and Social Change*, Polity Press, Cambridge.

future. Their expectations contrast markedly with those of young people in Sweden and Norway where the state is more active in supporting the reconciliation of work and family in gender equitable ways. In Britain, young people talk much more of individual responsibility and expect little from the state. Their expectations of employers are low too. They adopt the employers' short-term perspective and expect little in the way of support unless they too can see a business case for this, that is, a bottom line benefit to the organisation. Nor do they feel trade unions have much to offer. In the flexible labour market, concerns about getting another contract or having a contract renewed are the ones that dominate.

Our study has inevitably raised more questions than it has answered. The future of organisations, families and communities depend on Generation X and the generations that follow. What are the implications then of their inability to envisage their own futures? We end by raising some issues for the different stakeholders which address the critical importance of the way we live in and think about time present and time future.

To government, we suggest that it should continue to give thought to the means for supporting young citizens as they confront the challenges of the extended present, with its complex opportunities and demands. Even more critically, it should consider how to find ways of sustaining the increasing multiplicity of different pathways through the life course that will encompass changing forms of work, family and care at different moments and in a variety of sequences. If learning is to be lifelong, other policies concerning work and family should adopt this radical perspective also.

To employers, we suggest that if they wish to attract and maintain a highly skilled workforce in the long term, they will have to think long term, beyond the extended present. It is important to recognise the short termism that often lies at the heart of the business case for family friendly or work-life policies, a case that young people themselves appear to be internalising, thereby diminishing their own self-worth.

Indeed we suggest that whether we talk of 'family friendly' or 'work–life' policies these are part of the old order – 'benefits' offered as incentives to a permanent, core workforce – notably the rising new workforce of mothers. Under the new order everyone will want to 'have a life' beyond work and will have responsibilities to fulfil.

Work–life policies and practices will not just be optional extras which people take up at their own risk. In a rapidly changing world, such policies and practices will need to be an intrinsic part of managing both the present and the future. Under the new order, it will become more, not less, urgent to sustain human resources, children, families and communities.

Most importantly, all parties need to ensure, before they set about finding ways of helping young people to envisage and prepare for the future, that there is a future for young people that is worth envisaging and striving for ☉

Suzan Lewis is Reader in Psychology at the Manchester Metropolitan University and a director of the 'virtual' Work–Life Research Centre.

Julia Brannen in Professor of Sociology at the Institute of Education, University of London, and a director of the 'virtual' Work–Life Research Centre.

Choosing childlessness?

Fiona McAllister

The decision not to become a parent is a life choice rarely discussed, and any debate usually centres around the assumption that not having children is connected to the decision to pursue a career. However, recent research suggests that such a view may be simplistic: rising rates of childlessness may in fact reflect *constraints* in the environment related to choosing parenthood, as well as *opportunities* to choose childlessness positively.

Changing times

Studies into this subject from the 1970s and early 1980s focus on childlessness as a reflection of the transformations in women's lives and their liberation from domestic roles. In the 1990s, women's behaviour has been a major impetus behind research: with 20 per cent of the current British cohorts predicted to remain childless, the place of choice in low fertility societies, and its implications for the future of social care (particularly of the elderly) have become critical issues.

Historically, women who have remained childless have come disproportionately from highly educated backgrounds, and have enjoyed economic independence – either as self-supporting single women or as married women with relatively high status jobs. However, there is no straightforward relationship between rates of female participation in the workforce and fertility trends in particular countries.[1] For instance, in Italy, fertility rates are among the lowest in Europe, alongside relatively low rates of female employment. Moreover, fertility rates and rates of childlessness in particular

1 European Commission, 1994, *The Demographic Situation in the European Union*, Office of Official Publication of the European Communities, Luxemborg.

countries are not statistically correlated,[2] so that in Britain our fertility rates are higher than those of Italy, but our levels of childlessness are higher too. Within countries throughout Europe, low fertility is characterised by different balances in the proportions of women having no children, one child, and multi-child families.

While the association between higher educational qualifications and childlessness remains, in Britain the threshold at which qualifications make a difference to expectations is actually quite low: twice as many women born in the 1950s with at least GCE O levels expect to remain childless compared to those with no qualifications.[3] Women who have no qualifications are the least likely to expect to remain childless, and the most likely to bear children early. For the majority, relatively late motherhood has become commonplace – in 1997 the average age of mothers at first birth in England and Wales reached almost 27, a 40-year peak. Most mothers of young children are now employed, albeit frequently in part-time and relatively low-status jobs, whereas of women without dependent children only about one quarter worked part time, according to the 1995 report on the British Social Attitudes Survey.

Thus an 'either/or' model of choice between motherhood and the labour market appears to apply to – or be practiced by – relatively few women in contemporary Britain. Furthermore, the expectation of childlessness is far outstripped by its eventuality: General Household Survey data shows that while 10 per cent of sixteen to 22 year old women born between 1970 and 1974 expect to have no children, population estimates predict that double that number will in fact remain childless.[4] This indicates that an early preference for childlessness is still quite uncommon, and that intentions about having children may vary over time. Shaw has shown that older women are more likely to expect childlessness, whilst women at the start of their childbearing years are more likely to anticipate having two children[5] – perhaps conforming to an ideal family size, rather than assessing their individual options in detail. Increasing educational and employment opportunities may mean that more women delay thinking seriously about whether they want children, rather than ruling them out from the start.

Women born in the 1920s in Britain had rates of eventual childlessness matching the 20 per cent predicted for women today. However, the role of choice is different now, with no shortage of

2 Coleman D, 1998, 'Reproduction and survival in an unknown world: what drives today's industrial populations, and to what future?', The Hofstee Lecture, 7 May 1998, The Trippenhuis, Amsterdam. See also Colman D, 1993, 'Britain in Europe: international and regional comparisons of fertility levels and trends', in Bhrolchain N, ed, New Perspectives on Fertility in Britain, OPCS, London.

3 ONS Birth Statistics, 1996, HMSO, London.

4 McAllister F and Clarke L, 1998, Choosing Childlessness, Family and Parenthood: Policy and practice series, Family Policy Studies Centre and Joseph Rowntree Foundation, London.

5 Shaw C, 1989, 'Recent trends in family size and family building', Population Trends 58, 19-22.

men of marriageable age, and less punitive reactions to births outside of marriage. The trend towards later childbearing through-out Europe has in fact been accompanied by increasing rates of child-lessness. It is important to note that women can have difficulty con-ceiving at in their thirties and forties, so that higher rates of even-tual childlessness may include growing cases of involuntary, as well as voluntary, childlessness.[6]

Choosing childlessness – a modern myth?

The Family Policy Studies Centre's recent in-depth study indicates that for many women and their partners, not having children is a complex process: an outcome of many different decisions or life events, which was not necessarily predicated on the desire to pursue occupational success above domestic life.

In consultation with the National Centre for Social Research, we were able to recruit interviewees from the annual British Social Attitudes Survey (BSAS) population. We focused on women aged 35 to 49 – women who were likely to have been exposed to opportunities to have children but had not done so. We obtained a group of 34 women who were eligible for interview and willing to participate in the study. Eleven of their partners (either cohabiting or married) also took part.

Respondents were asked in a variety of ways whether, when and how they had decided not to have children, and about the context of that decision. On the basis of respondents' accounts, a 'continuum of childlessness' was developed, reflecting differences in the context for, and the motivations behind, the choice of childlessness. Those who had resolved early and permanently not to have children were described as 'certain'. Different shades of wavering over the possibil-ity of children were encapsulated in groups named 'certain now' (had wavered over having children in the past, but now firmly decided not to have children), 'accepting' (had expected to have chil-dren but now accepted childlessness and its advantages) and 'ambiva-lent' (included both those who had put off any decision and still had not firmly ruled out children, and those who felt they had never made a decision either way). Another category (decision 'taken for me') arose from the experience of a small number of respondents, and suggested the existence of a genuinely intermediate set of expe-riences, 'between' voluntary and involuntary childlessness.

6 Beets G, 1995, 'Does the increasing age at first birth lead to increases in involuntary childlessness?', paper presented at the *European Population Conference*, Milan Italy. (Available from the author, Netherlands Interdisciplinary Demographic Institute, PO Box 11650, 2502 AR, The Hague, Netherlands.)

Seeing the choice of childlessness as a *process* which may have many twists and turns cautions against viewing the decision as a one-off moment which defines subsequent experience. The evidence, in terms of employment decisions and choices about fertility, suggests that influence in both directions is possible. People decide about work based on their attitudes to having children, and vice versa. Commitment to work, like commitment to childlessness, can change over time.

Most of the women interviewed did not see themselves as 'career women' or as ambitious. Those who did attached provisos: to a certain extent; not to the exclusion of other things; up until a year ago; in my twenties; only because of circumstances. The men in the study were not markedly careerist either.

Women who were 'certain' in their choice of childlessness did not often identify themselves as career women, in spite of an early and permanent commitment to childlessness. They valued work chiefly as a means of supporting themselves in their life outside.

The 'accepting' group seemed distinctive, in that all reported having decided on a career at an early age, while also anticipating that they would have children. Later on, a new partnership could transform work–home balances. The women in this category who had formed stable partnerships later in life, often reduced their commitment to work in this context. Resolving finally not to have children can perhaps be seen as 'giving permission to retreat' from the workforce, as much as to become more involved – a point not often made in the literature on interactions between employment and fertility.

Around one-third of those interviewed had already taken, or planned to take, early retirement. The popularity of early retirement among respondents (which reflects trends in the older population as a whole) again contradicts an 'either/or' picture of work and having children.

A widespread aversion to risk and poverty meant that financial planning and provision for retirement plans was paramount. The desire for financial security and independence was further reflected in respondents' perceptions of parenthood. Having children often represented an unacceptable cost, while positive childless identities were connected with *freedom and individual responsibility for the future*.

Although money was not put forward as the reason for choosing childlessness, the advantage of sustained earnings meant that childless women living alone, and those in partnerships, compared their finances – especially in relation to housing – favourably with their parents' circumstances.

The presence of a partner and the stability of partnerships were important factors in the process of choosing childlessness. Late marriage and remarriages often involved men with children from previous relationships, who were thus not eligible to participate in the study. Choosing a partner who had already had children may provide a scenario where ambivalence about, or resistance to, having children is unlikely to be challenged.

Unmarried women in the study did not see single parenthood as a viable option, both because of lack of economic security, and because of the lack of a partner to share in finding a balance between employment and family life. Those with a stable relationship preferred an egalitarian division of labour in the home, although not everyone felt that this had been achieved. Women who were 'certain' in their choice of childlessness all reported sharing household tasks with their partners, and few women overall reported having sole responsibility for housekeeping chores. Men in the study also highlighted the benefits of egalitarian partnerships and viewed parenthood as *incompatible* with these values.

For respondents as a whole, perceptions of parenthood were marked by negative views of 'responsibility', 'commitment' and 'sacrifice'. Important among the disadvantages of parental responsibility was its association with traditional roles in marriage – women become primary carers, while men are more able to maintain employment and leisure activities apart from family life. Not having children meant fewer compromises.

That there were few positive perceptions of parents balancing work and family life reflects both how difficult it is in practice for men and women combine employment and childcare, and the low status of parenthood as an activity in its own right. The voluntary childless people in this study emerged as thoughtful and responsible about what parenting might mean, not as radical opponents of conventional morality and family life. They find it variously undesirable, difficult or impossible to incorporate it into their lives. Far from being a 'selfish' generation who aim to 'have it all', they saw themselves as making considerable effort to maintain a reasonable quality of life without children.

7 Morell CM, 1994, *Unwomanly Conduct: The challenges of intentional childlessness,* Routledge, London, p61.

8 Marshall H, 1993, *Not Having Children,* Oxford University Press, Melbourne, p148.

9 Veevers JE, 1983, 'Voluntary childlessness: a critical review of the research', in Macklin ED and Rubin RH, eds, *Contemporary Families and Alternative Lifestyles: A handbook of research and theory,* Sage, Beverley Hills, p92.

10 Macintosh CA, 1987, 'Recent pronatalist policies in western Europe', in Davis K, Bernstram MS and Ricardo-Campbell R, eds, *Below Replacement Fertility in Industrial Societies,* Cambridge University Press, Cambridge; Bane MJ and Jargowsky PA, 1988, 'The links between government policy and family structure: what matters and what doesn't', in Cherlin AJ, ed, *The Changing American Family and Public Policy,* The Urban Institute Press, Washington DC; McDonald P, 1997, *Gender Equity, Social Institutions and the Future of Fertility,* Working Papers in Demography 69, Australian National University, Canberra.

Previous studies of choosing childlessness have also drawn attention to the non-radical views of voluntary childless people concerning the balance of parenthood and a reasonable standard of living – and living together. Morrell argues that talking about 'choice' in relation to childlessness is misleading. She asserts that, 'Such a notion emphasises personal decisions and distracts attention away from social relations of power. The insistent focus is on the internal as opposed to the institutional and sociopolitical'.[7] This line of argument says it is vital to account for the fact that parenting does not have equal status with labour market activity, and that the status divide is a 'gendered' one.

Marshall also sees childless couples as non-conformists operating within an ideology of parenthood, rather than radical opponents of childbearing and family life. 'They [the couples] decide not to have children because they in fact accept fully the prevailing ideas about what parenthood represents'.[8]

These perspectives on the process of childlessness bring us back to Veevers' critical question: 'On the issue of childbearing, are the persons involved getting what they want?',[9] a question which cannot be ignored from a social policy perspective.

Policy implications?

In the literature on the relationship between fertility levels and public policy, there is a general consensus that effective policy is unusually difficult to design.[10] The relationship between policy support for additional children and national fertility behaviour is by no means clear. France and former West Germany have both provided considerable financial incentives for parenthood (for example, favourable tax rates for couples with children; increased child allowance for third children; generous maternity leave; state subsidised childcare services) and yet their birth rates have dropped – the rates in France are comparable to Britain while those in Germany are lower. At what point might voluntary childlessness warrant policy interventions?

The ageing population of Western countries, characterised by below replacement-level fertility and decreased mortality, shifts the balance of social investment away from young families and towards older people. Voluntarily childless people may actually find funding old age easier than do parents, because of their greater chance of unbroken careers and relatively constant expenses. Weighed against this advantage is the fact that they cannot count on any care being provided by children. The UK still has one of the higher fertility rates in Europe, so the case for intervention on population grounds is unclear.

Public policy could respond to desire for greater equity in parenthood through more flexible employment. Younger people support more flexible and gender-neutral experiences. For example, in the 1992 British Social Attitudes Survey, two-thirds of eighteen to 34 year olds disagreed that a husband's job is to earn money and a wife's to look after the home and family, compared with one-third of 45 to 54 year olds and one in eight people aged 60 or over.[11] Britain has less state-subsidised childcare than other European countries, and there is no tax relief for employer-provided schemes. More affordable childcare options would help parents bear – and share – the costs of family life more easily.

There is also an argument for policy intervention in terms of information and health education about fertility levels.[12] A continuing trend of delaying parenthood means that women (and men) need to be well-informed about the declining chances of conception in their thirties, just as they are regularly reminded of the costs and implications of teenage pregnancies and unplanned childbearing.

Adults who value equality in relationships, a stable domestic environment, a reasonable job and economic security may find it increasingly hard to make the decision to become parents. Cliquet has drawn attention to the high expectations in societies of young people, who are supposed to acquire education, occupational success, a secure home and having children in a tight time span.[13] With the added pressure of a finite period of fertility in women, it is not surprising that increasing childlessness is one outcome.

Many non-parents do not see having and rearing children as a choice that is as well promoted and esteemed as choices about the world of paid work. Unless we find ways to recognise parenthood as a valuable contribution to society and make it more compatible with thriving in work, then we should expect that more people will choose to stay childless ⊙

Fiona McAllister is a freelance researcher based in London. She has worked as a family sociologist throughout the 1990s.[14]

11 Kiernan K, 1992, 'Men and women at work and at home', in Jowell R, Brook L, Prior G and Taylor B, eds, *British Social Attitudes: the 9th report*, Dartmouth, Aldershot.

12 Beets, 1995 (note 6); Bouwens A, Beets GCN and Schippers JJ, 1996, *Societal Causes and Effects of Delayed Parenthood*, report written on behalf of the Commission of the European Union, University of Utrecht Economic Institute, Utrecht.

13 Cliquet RL, 1997, 'Below replacement level fertility and gender politics', paper presented at the *European Sociobiology Society*, Alfred USA. Brussels: CBGS (Centrum voor Bevolkings en Gezinsstudie) Document 1997-2.

14 The research presented here was funded by the Joseph Rowntree Foundation (JRF) while the author was employed at the Family Policy Studies Centre (FPSC) in London. Material presented here has previously appeared in the 1998 publication, *Choosing Childlessness* (see note 4) and the author thanks them for permitting reproduction here. The views expressed are those of the author.

Getting the relationship right

How home and workplace can learn from each other

Ed Straw

Several years ago, I was talking over dinner to a consulting project team about Relate, the relationship counselling charity. There was much interest. The next day I took a chance and sent six copies each of two Relate relationship guides. Within an hour of their receipt there was a complaint: why had I not sent a copy for *every* member of the team?

The error was corrected and I reflected on the value of these guides. Everyone (and my conclusion then and now is *everyone*) wants to and would benefit from improving his or her relationship. The skills to do this are well understood by the specialists but hard to access. These skills are particularly important for partners working away from home. And equally important when one is at work. To get things done, a consultant relies very much on the relationship she or he builds with the client's staff. Organisations want to work with consultants with whom they have a good relationship. Successful management consultancies use relationship management as their primary selling tool.

For recruiters seeking people to join today's fast-changing organisations, the more scarce commodities are not intelligence and a strong education, but the inter-personal skills that oil the internal machinery and provide successful service externally. These are skills learned at home and sometimes at school. In what follows I consider how home life skills can make a positive contribution to life at work.

The family as a skills agency

There is a wall between family skills and organisational skills. In terms of the mental models people bring to running families and to running organisations these skills are kept separate, compartmentalised. I can think of three reasons why this might be so.

First, home is a private space in which the organisation has no locus. This is commendable, especially as the electronic reach of the workplace requisitions yet more disposable time. But it also stems from a culture which believes that what goes on at home is for its residents only.

Second, the people most driven to get to the top usually put their family (rarely deliberately) a long way second to their careers. Such leaders and managers may be uncomfortable with the open airing of relationship and parenting skills entailed in acknowledging the exchange between work and family life.

Third, large organisations are difficult enough to run at a time of rapid change without taking on responsibility for the home lives of employees.

Synergy is an oft-used word in business, usually in relation to mergers. In the future, the trail-blazing organisations will acknowledge and harness *home–work synergy* To my knowledge (and I hope I'm wrong) few organisations appreciate the relevance of relationship skills to the emerging links between home and work. But they would gain a great deal from taking seriously a mission statement along the lines of 'To build enduring relationship at work and at home, and with customers, suppliers and the community'. This would be a mission that would pervade and enhance its market purpose.

For the skills learned at home are often of a *higher order* than those learned at work. Accounting is undoubtedly more complex than washing-up. But teaching a child to wash-up is in some ways more complex than teaching a student accounting. The most difficult job the prime minister does is parenting, not running the government. Setting boundaries, being consistent with them, being authoritative and not authoritarian, using positive reinforcement in preference to negative enforcement, motivating people with warmth, love and values are skills learned and practised as a parent; and are vital to good management. Dealing with dissatisfied customers is a doddle compared with handling truculent teenagers. The communication and conflict-resolution skills learned in successful families are far more extensive than those learned in leading organisations. People who have made use of counselling and psychotherapy for personal reasons can find their performance at work improving significantly. What led to aggravation or to feeling kept down or to conflict at home has the same drivers and consequences at work.

The point is startlingly obvious particularly as it needs saying so loudly: organisations and families comprise people; and people need to be able to relate to others to fulfil themselves in both spheres.

Home–work interaction is largely unmeasured – a difficult task but one worth attempting. Consider the French bus drivers recently in the news. Because of a shortage of native drivers, they were recruited to work in Britain. Of their first few months' experience, they said that they had learned to speak English and to drive on the left, quite easily. But they observed that on the job there was no time to talk, in sharp contrast to their workstyle in France.

Now, what might be the consequence of this tight management style showing little appreciation of the business value of everyday humanity? In the long run, low job satisfaction, taking out work frustrations at home, sickness and even depression may result. Who bears these costs? The bus company, in terms of increased staff turnover and the days lost to sickness. The family, in terms of lower contentment and happiness. The state, for the medical bills and benefit costs from unemployment and divorce, and the crime costs if the parenting suffers too. But these costs are never accounted for as a whole.

We need some notion of 'accounting for families' if the full social costs and benefits of different management styles are to be understood. Rather than accounting vertically within each organisational silo, the accounting would run horizontally across the silos and would follow the family. This would then provide an understanding of the full consequences of an action or style in one place on another. Thus, the parenting and relationship skills learned by a family would have their incremental value in the workplace estimated and added to their outputs. Lack of parenting skills, resulting in under-attainment at school with excess costs to their education system and to future employers, would show up in the negative column of the families' accounts. The value of relationship skills learned at work with home benefits would register positively in the accounts – and so on.

This somewhat mechanistic approach is not a tool to reduce public expenditure by issuing a set of accounts and a bill to family members on death. Its purpose would be to raise our understanding of home–work synergy and to strengthen our capacities for change.

Business and the family

The best commercial organisations are inadvertently providing more training and development in relationship skills than any other source. The list is endless. Coaching, mentoring and influencing skills; self-awareness through role plays, video and 360 degree feedback; psychometric tests, from the Belbin assessment of team roles to Myers-Briggs, a Jungian-based personality profile; situational leadership, distinguishing directive and non-directive styles dependent upon the circumstance; frank customer satisfaction surveys; consultative selling skills; staff satisfaction surveys with open feedback on management performance. All these enable us to learn about how others see us and would like to see us; and give us tools to relate to others better. Some even explore our psyches at a limited level and surface some of the positive and negative emotional-drivers acquired in childhood. The psychologist has returned to the work place. 'Soft skills' in relationship management have become a key source of organisational effectiveness.

All this is driven not by altruism but by hard-nosed competitive pressures. Relationship skills at work matter. Good practice is transferable to the home from work (although some of the benefit may be lost as some of the value is in creating a common psychological language among a work team – a benefit lost with an untrained partner). 'Situational leadership', for example, is as applicable to parenting as it is to managing. A child about to run into the path of a car needs to be directed strongly not to do this – it is usually termed 'shouting'. Placing a child in an environment where she or he can learn (a progressive education model) appropriate to learning to cook. But learning by doing represents too great a risk with regard to the effect of being hit by a car.

Similarly, poor practice in one domain may be carried over into the other. A manager who finds from his '360 degree feedback' that although he values his staff he never tells them so, is likely to be doing the same with his children. A salesman bent on finding fault in a customer company's equipment as a reason to buy new, may carry this habitual criticism into his home relationships. And, classically, the leader who finds that staff would value clearer boundaries being set, could usefully take this message on with her children.

Best practice in the workplace has other things to teach us in the home. 'Change management' is now a well-researched and practised approach to implementing successful changes. We know the cycle many people go through when confronted with a significant alteration to their work – denial, frustration, anger, depression, private and public checking out. We've learned that change has to be managed: a clear and consistent vision; listening to feedback on progress; communication, communication and communication; involvement; continuous leadership and commitment; project management; all contributing towards building organisational resilience.

How much of this could be applied to fundamental changes in the home? For example, to the arrival of the first child – a major change issue if ever there was one and often the time an adult relationship starts on a downward spiral. First, as a society, we could recognise 'first child' as a joyous event heralding a new life *and* a major and potentially very difficult change. We could be prepared for the cycle of emotional reaction and better understand our present feelings. We could view the satisfactory introduction of the first child to the family as a project - with a beginning, middle and an end, and one requiring something more than laissez-faire, tolerance and hope as a plan. Above all, we could recognise the importance of building personal emotional resilience to change.

The hard, but ultimately fulfilling, work inherent in a good long-term relationship is another work-to-home opportunity for sharing knowledge. Organisations do, at least, know why they exist – to provide something in a manner satisfactory to the owners, staff and customers. But why does a marriage exist? The term marriage here is used as short-hand for all long–term committed couple relationships. What is a marriage? It is certainly not a legal document, a ceremony, a public avowal, or a party, although these may be a good way to start. But to start what?

Reflecting on the traumatic end for the play-off participants at this year's British Open, a golfing friend said that the reason he loved the game was because 'it taught you about yourself'. That's also a reason for loving marriage. A marriage is the best opportunity for psychic growth. At the moment you know for sure that what your partner says hurts because it is true. At that moment, you have a marriage. At the moment you recognise that conflict in a relationship is an opportunity for learning, when pride and defensiveness have been put aside, when you enjoy being wrong, you have a marriage. The purpose of marriage is the development of the self.

Understanding the purpose of marriage is but part of the considerable agenda many families are wrestling with. The family, as we have known it, is at sea. Negotiating the fluidity has become a weekly task. The agenda on which in our various ways we are all working, wittingly and unwittingly, is long: from understanding marriage, running a long-term relationship successfully, defining the new settlement between male and female roles, providing a sufficiently good environment for child-rearing, opening-up the nuclear family, managing that most difficult and complex family form – the blended or step-family, to working out the trade-offs between career and parenting, a life-long relationship versus serial monogamy, and mass consumerism versus inner peace.

Tomorrow's organisations

In some ways, the family is *ahead* of the organisation in experimenting with new relationships and forms. But organisational life is as much in need of reform as is family life. Today, we look back at Victorian medicine and wince at its barbarity. In 50 years time, we will look back at today's organisational life and wince at its chaos and stress. Organisations really are at a very rudimentary stage of development contrary to the self-image of the 'masters of the universe' in the high-tech, high stress services sector.

Most of us put up with an extraordinary amount of nonsense for the sake of doing our jobs. The extremes are well-reported: the Stroud aerospace company refusing, on pain of dismissal, its employees an eclipse-viewing break in exchange for their lunch break, being the latest. But it is the mainstream organisation we should focus on, where the combination of corporate politics, semi-competence, neglect of the impact on other people of a decision, ignorance of what is possible, management under pressure to show action, and management roles as cul-de-sacs, produces the overload, lack of control over one's life, lack of respect, separation and even abuse which is the common experience for too much of their working lives for the majority. None of this is the inevitable consequence of the vibrant productivity of market economics. It is simply that we have as far to go in getting organisational life right as we do with family life. Successful and happy organisations exist just as such families do. But they are not the norms.

Too often, we find organisations which are punitive, conformist, bureaucratic, rigid, stuck in the past, chaotic or insensitive, or the dysfunctional exposition of the person at the top. The cause may be lost in history, may be a management system which rewards and preserves the status quo, or weak governance allowing the political system for the acquisition of power to dominate.

The new openness

Both the family and the organisation have suffered from being closed systems. This has limited the scope for learning. Not being wrong (and having nothing to learn) is valued very highly in most families and in many organisations. The closed system and ignorance as a dominant value have together created more unhappiness and under-performance than anything else.

Fortunately, the appetite for change is increasing apace. It is interesting to note how modern and refreshing the new UK government appeared in 1997 by comparison with its dysfunctional predecessor, but just two years on how old-fashioned it is starting to look to a public that has rejected hierarchy and authority and is seeking to create its own codes.

The future could be very bright. It may be a very rare time to be alive: when we define for ourselves the moral and other codes by which we live our home and work lives; when home–work synergy is recognised, valued and exploited; and when we are no longer prey to those whose dominant need is power over others ⊙

Ed Straw is chairman of Relate, the relationship and counselling service; board member of the National Family and Parenting Institute; and management consultancy partner at Price Waterhouse & Coopers.

Japan's battle of the sexes

The search for common ground

Sumiko Iwao

Today, many younger Japanese women feel that the distribution of time and energy spent by men and women on paid and unpaid work is off-balance and unfair. In the past, the main burden of unpaid work related to the home – housework and parenting – has fallen on women, regardless of whether or not they are also involved in paid work. Young Japanese women today are in revolt – unless there is a more equitable redistribution, more and more young women look set to postpone the joys associated with marriage and having children. Personal choices are becoming public problems. Already, the birth rate is low enough in Japan for the government to belatedly propose various ways of creating a social and economic climate that induces single people to want to marry and have children.

The good old days

When men were the sole breadwinners for the family, they were excused from unpaid work at home, including looking after themselves. They depended on their wives for their daily needs. Women, on the other hand, thought their place was in the home and were economically dependent upon their husbands; they focused their responsibilities on unpaid work and looked after family and home. Both men and women depended on each other for survival and an asymmetrical equilibrium was maintained.

When women did not participate in paid work, a husband's earnings were handed over to his wife more or less intact; these she spent as she thought fit for the family and he, in turn, was given a monthly allowance by his wife.

This traditional pattern is somewhat different to the pattern in Europe where typically it was the stay-at-home wife who received a housekeeping allowance. In Japan, the traditional wife was responsible for managing daily family expenses with the husband's income, and if it was not sufficient, she was expected to use her talents to make ends meet, for example, by earning extra money herself or by bringing her belonging to a pawn shop. (Thus, Japanese women traditionally became very keen on 'saving for rainy days,' manifested in Japan's high savings rate.) As long as men brought their salary home, they had the freedom to spend long hours outside of the home and consequently not participate in unpaid work at home. Many Japanese women, on the other hand, enjoyed the autonomy given to them by the 'absent husband' and welcomed the situation by saying 'good husbands are healthy and absent'.

Such a division of life's spheres by gender typically works until men retire and invade the sphere run by women. As a result, women's autonomy and freedom is curbed, which can sometimes become intolerable to emotionally independent women. These women are then likely to seek divorce rather than face life with man who has not developed the skills to participate in unpaid work and leisure pursuits. Therefore, it is necessary to consider the balance between paid and unpaid work and leisure/cultural activities over the entire life course rather than only during the employed period.

Stressful transition to a new style family

But there is another problem – the new patterns of family life are generating more stress and strain. With more women participating in both paid and unpaid work, life styles and financial arrangements in the family are changing. However, even to this day, families where the husband is the major breadwinner more or less follow the traditional pattern of the wife holding the purse strings. With double income families, however, where the incomes are of more or less equal size, both husband and wife equally share both earning and spending responsibilities.

Not only has the financial relationship between husband and wife changed today, so has the attitude toward marriage. Marriage, once considered a necessity, has more and more become one of life's options, especially with young single women. Rather than husband

and wife playing different roles as in the past, young women today hope to share both economic and family responsibilities with their spouses – an equal partnership is what they want.

But there are a range of problems – men's attitudes have been slower to catch up in the domestic sphere and workplace cultures have been slow to shift leaving women with a double burden. Just as in many other countries today, an increasing number of Japanese women are employed. About 40 percent of the employed paid workers now are women; of them, 57 per cent are married and 33 per cent are single. Many of the paid working women who are married with families are carrying a double burden of paid and unpaid work, while men and working women who can relegate unpaid work to others (such as their wives, mothers or paid help) are carrying only the single burden of paid work. If women with a double burden have to compete with men and women who are carrying one burden, it is clearly unfair. They also have difficulties at work. Many workplaces still expect their employees to place work before family, which makes it impossible to keep work-family balance. If one wants to keep a balance among work/family/leisure activities, time is never sufficient and stress is great. Some women have sought to balance paid and unpaid work by being part-time workers, which now makes up 36.5 percent of employed women, but these women still are carrying a double burden because they do the vast majority of unpaid work at home.

Japanese men for their part are also hampered from playing a greater role at home. The long working hours culture in Japan is well known – many men feel they must stay at their workplace for long hours, thus putting the workplace before the family, where most unpaid work is performed. The workplace culture interferes with their ability to achieve a better balance between paid and unpaid work. In addition, the long commuting hours that many men (and increasingly full time working women) must put in to reach their workplace further prevents them from participating in unpaid work at home; this adds to the existing imbalance in paid/unpaid work and cultural pursuits.

The amount of time both men and women spend on paid work and on unpaid work has been researched and illustrates the problem. According to a survey conducted by the NHK (Japan's public broadcasting station), Japanese men, on average, spend seven hours daily on paid work and only thirty-one minutes on unpaid work. Japanese women, by contrast, spend three hours and forty-one minutes on paid work and four hours and forty-one minutes on unpaid work – or housework – daily.[1]

Private choices become public problems

Today's young single women live in an information age. They can easily imagine what sort of life is waiting for them after marriage and after childbirth. They know that even with good intentions to share unpaid work more evenly, their future husbands are unlikely to be able to carry out what they intended. Demands from the workplace will always have priority. At the same time, today's young women believe companionship with their spouse is most important for a good marriage; otherwise, they don't feel that marriage offers enough rewards to justify the plunge. They are children of affluence and know the taste of overseas vacations and expensive restaurants, but they also know that their regular paid employment is necessary for such luxuries. Thus, there is some reluctance or hesitation to marry and have children.

The trends show this clearly. In 1975, the average age for a first marriage in Japan was 25.9 for men and 23 for women, but it went up to 28.5 for men and 26.3 for women in 1995. Also in that year, the percentage of single women 25 to 29 years old reached 48 per cent, and for those 30 to 34 year old it reached 20 per cent. Women know that if they quit paid work on the birth of a child, the opportunity costs for them are very high. Thus, their hesitation to marry or have children is quite understandable, yet the declining birthrate, which affects the country as a whole, cannot be ignored by policymakers.

Though the choice is entirely a private matter, the resultant postponement of marriage (as these figures imply) has a wide social and economic impact. For example, unless more women marry earlier, a decline in birthrate is expected (children born out of wedlock are still quite rare in Japan). Japan's population will reach its peak in the year 2007, then start declining. A birthrate of about 2.08 is needed to maintain the population at its current size. However, at the current birthrate of 1.38, Japan's population will be less than half its present size within 100 years. The lower birthrate has serious economic as well as socio-cultural implications. Labour shortages, shrinking markets, and the difficulty of maintaining public pension schemes

1 NHK Broadcasting Culture Research Institute, 1995, *International Comparison of Time Use Survey*, Oozora-sha, Tokyo.

and children's culture (some children's books are no longer available due to shrinking markets) are some such implications. These trends are all the more worrying because Japan has been becoming an aged society at a faster rate than any other nation in the world.

Japan's work–life agenda

In responding to this challenge, the Japanese government has put great efforts into providing life-long learning opportunities in addition to various courses offered by business organizations. Right now, middle-aged or older women, who tend to have more free time than men, are the major recipient of such opportunities. But the government needs to do much more. Indeed, to really tackle this problem, the Japanese government must find a way of satisfying women's desires to maintain paid work, while getting men to share unpaid work more equitably as a good companion.

The Japanese government has made two fundamental efforts to create a work–family balance for men and women, as well as providing an environment that is attractive enough for people to want to marry and have children.

Promoting gender equality

The first initiative was the passage in June 1999 of the Basic Law for Building a Gender-Neutral Society, which states that both men and women be given equal opportunity to find both paid and unpaid work. Now they are working on specific measures to implement this law based on recommendations from the Council for Gender Equality.

There have already been some important initiatives. The economic value of unpaid work has been quantified. In 1996, the Japanese Economic Planning Agency calculated the monetary value of unpaid work for Japan to be 116 billion yen ($1,392,000) of which 85 per cent (98 billion yen) were contributed by women. The Agency estimated that, on average, the unpaid work carried out by one woman has an annual average monetary value of $23,000.[2] By putting a price on the economic value of unpaid work, the Japanese government has made women's traditional work visible, and has valued it.

They have also tried to tackle the other issue – namely how to bring about a shift in male responsibility. Earlier this year, the Japanese Ministry of Health and Welfare produced a poster that captured an unusual amount of public attention compared with other

2 Japanese Economic Planning Agency, 1998, *Monetary Value of Unpaid Work for 1996.*

government-run campaigns. The poster features a popular male dancer holding his baby boy; the mother is a nationally admired young pop singer. The caption reads: 'We don't call a man who does not take care of his children a father. Just 17 minutes a day is the average time Japanese fathers spend for childcare'. The poster was produced to urge men to share household responsibilities so that women alone do not shoulder the full load of childcare and house work. Its explicit objective was to achieve a better balance for both men and women between paid work and unpaid work related to the family. Some male politicians in the National Diet were obviously irritated by this poster. They summoned the ministry's staffs for an explanation. They seemed to think that they were qualified to be fathers simply by being the breadwinners in the family. Thankfully the government no longer seems to subscribe to this view.

Tackling the low birthrate

The other key policy initiative focuses on measures to reverse the declining birthrate. In addition to parental leave and the expansion of services at day care centres, the prime minister has also formed a task force for solving the problems of the declining birthrate. The task force submitted a report to the prime minister in December 1998 with over one hundred concrete suggestions for reforming work styles and making family life more attractive. For example, more efficient work styles are encouraged so that workers can leave the office early enough to participate in unpaid work at home. Another example is the setting up of 'consultation service stations' to help parents with problems they might face in raising children. Parents who came from small families with only one or no siblings may not have experienced even holding a small child until they themselves became parents and are scared of failing to produce 'perfect' children. They have more than enough information about the serious difficulties that face parents and children, which makes them hesitate to have children.

Clearly, many interrelated problems are reflected in the declining birthrate. Government, as well as politicians and the business community—which are primarily composed of and run by men—are finally and slowly realising the importance of those problems that they have neglected, and they cannot solve them without women's cooperation. Lower birthrates clearly imply a dwindling market for the business community, and a dwindling economy overall. It is this business case for pursuing gender equity which is bringing about government and business action. Looking to the future, I believe that the great challenge for Japanese society in the twenty-first century will be about achieving genuine synergy between paid and unpaid work, between the sexes and across the generations. Long term economic prosperity clearly depends on much greater gender equality and a far better work–life balance, and both are the keys to solving the problems of an ageing population, low birth rate and the negative effects of workplace culture on women, men and family life ☉

Sumiko Iwao is Professor, Musashi Institute of Technology, Yokohama, Japan. She chairs the Council for Gender Equality and the Japanese prime minister's taskforce for solving the problems of the declining birth rate.

Part 3

Strategies for tomorrow's families

The evolved family

Helena Cronin & Oliver Curry

There is a strange lack of humanity in the government's most recent pronouncements on the family. They deal with dramas – parenting, divorce, under-age pregnancy. Yet real people are missing. In their place are stock characters from doctrinaire sociology: robotic actors, mindlessly performing 'roles' or activating 'relationship skills'. Confined to the pages of textbooks, notions so misguided could be dismissed as harmless socio-babble. But now they appear increasingly to be influencing policy. This should alarm anyone with an interest in social justice: policies based on such shallow assessments of the human condition, however politically correct their credentials, will inevitably leave serious problems untreated.

Assumptions about human nature play a role in all political theorising. They are usually implicit – and often wrong. Darwinian theory offers the prospect of at last getting them right. For human nature is our evolved nature, the evolved psychology of our species; and in the past decade or so evolutionary theory has begun to reveal that psychology.[1] An understanding of our motivations and desires is vital for anyone, including government, that wants to change people's behaviour.

But, if human nature is the result of evolution, aren't we stuck with it? Surely there is little that policy-makers can achieve. Not at all. Human nature is fixed; but the behaviour that it generates is richly varied, the result of our evolved minds reacting to different circumstances. In particular, we are designed by natural selection to respond appropriately to the ever-shifting sands of social conditions.

1 Pinker S, 1998, *How the Mind Works*, Penguin, Harmondsworth. For a brief introduction that deals with specific topics relevant to policy, see *Matters of Life and Death: The worldview from evolutionary psychology*, Demos Quarterly issue 10, Demos, London.

So it is mistaken to think that biology is relevant only to what is constant in society. On the contrary, very rapid social change can be brought about by evolved minds responding in predictable ways to changing environments. Change the environment and you change the behaviour. Thus the task for the policy-maker is to work out which aspects of our environment need to be altered in order to achieve the desired ends.

Why do families break up?

'Why can't fathers be more like mothers?' goes the fashionable cry. But for an evolutionary biologist the striking question is the opposite: Why do males invest so much in their children – a commitment so profound that it puts all other mammals, including our closest primate cousins, to shame? After all, in the evolution of our species, women had little choice but to invest nine months hard labour, nutrient-rich milk and unceasing vigilance. But men could get away with the briefest of encounters. Why then do they contribute so much more? Because in our species offspring are so dependent that providing resources and protection pays. Thus, although fathers don't put in the intimate care that mothers do, they nevertheless make a hefty investment. And natural selection has favoured them with the appropriate emotional dispositions – love, solicitude, commitment – for becoming good fathers under the right conditions.

But what are the right conditions? And how might they have changed in recent years? Given that the difference between a family and a broken family is generally the presence of the father – there is, after all, no Child Support Agency chasing absent mothers – the answers to these questions are of crucial importance to a government that has set itself the goal of 'supporting families'.[2]

Inequality among men

2 *Supporting Families Consultation Document*, available at http://www.home office.gov.uk/vcu/ suppfam.htm. See also Curry O and Cronin H, 1999, *Response to the Government's 'Supporting Families' Consultation Document*, Darwin@LSE, London.

Darwinian analysis suggests that a potent cause of family breakdown is likely to be a marked inequality among men. For increasing inequality (particularly in a winner-take-all economy) creates increasing numbers of relatively high-status and low-status men; and that gives rise to two conditions under which fathers become more likely to abandon their families.

First, men who lack access to resources – because of low pay or unemployment – find it difficult to be adequate providers and adequate husbands. Families break down in such circumstances because fathers have become liabilities rather than assets to the domestic economy. And sometimes they jump before they are pushed. Study after study of what the sexes find attractive in a partner – including the largest study ever conducted, spanning 37 diverse cultures – has shown that (unlike men) women in all cultures put a high value on economic prospects in a mate and that a husband's failure to provide resources is a major cause of divorce.[3]

Second, men towards the top of the social ladder can seize opportunities to start new families. This needn't involve abandoning the existing one. In societies that practise polygyny – common in traditional societies – rich men acquire multiple wives (while poor men are consigned to monogamy or celibacy). But in our society, some rich men practise serial monogamy – which is effective polygyny straining at the leash of institutionalised monogamy – and leave single mothers in their wake.

Women's independence

Darwinian theory also suggests that the standing of men relative to women is important; and that, too, is liable to be affected by such factors as unemployment. The 37 culture study also found (as have many other studies) that women prefer to marry men of higher status than themselves and that they find cues to higher status (including income) attractive. In sharp contrast, in none of these cultures, do men prefer to 'marry up', whatever their own social or financial circumstances.

Other studies have shown that the higher the economic power of the husband relative to the wife, the less likely that the marriage will break up; the divorce rate among American couples in which the woman earns more than her husband is 50 percent higher than among couples in which the husband is the higher earner, irrespective of the financial standing of the couple. Several studies, from Cameroon to California (most recently among female graduates leaving university), have found that women who are successful educationally, professionally and financially prefer men that are even more successful; indeed, they put an even higher priority on resources and status in a mate than do less successful women.[4]

Thus, however valuable the promotion of women at work as an end in itself, the government should be aware that there might be a

3 Buss DM, 1994, *The Evolution of Desire: Strategies of human mating*, Basic Books, New York.
4 See note 3.

conflict between its stated policy goals of 'enhancing financial independence especially in women' and achieving 'fewer broken relationships between parents'. This is because, as women become better off relative to men, the incidence and success of marriage is likely to decrease in line with the decrease in the pool of desirable male partners. The Ally McBeals will find that fewer men meet their exacting standards for a love match, while the dearth of dependable men will leave the mother on the housing estate with little choice but to turn to social security or take that part-time job at the call-centre.

Changes in male–male inequality and male–female relations have put monogamy under pressure, reducing marriage rates and increasing divorce. But why aren't families just happily reconstituting themselves? Why are they so dogged by problems that the government is hurrying to the rescue?

Why blood is thicker than water

If the government is to win its game of Happy Families, it needs to understand the rules – most fundamentally, why blood is thicker than water. Evolutionary theory provides a meticulously precise account. Family psychology was forged in the context of a shared genetic inheritance. To the blind forces of natural selection, altruism towards kin is just one way of replicating genes: help those who share your genes and you help the genes. But from this cold genetic reckoning arose our most cherished family values. For evolution equipped us with an elaborate physical, cognitive and deeply emotional repertoire – such as maternal devotion and brotherly love – dedicated to lavishing altruism on our kin as on no others. That is why it has been found that working mothers would rather leave their offspring with kin, particularly grandparents, than with strangers (albeit professionals),[5] and why our priorities in rescuing people from a burning house, leaving money in our wills or choosing who to turn to for advice neatly track our genetic closeness.[6]

This is of course not to suggest that altruism is confined to the family. It also flows between unrelated individuals, such as friends. But friendship operates according to its own rules and is quite distinct from kinship: whereas maternal love is largely unconditional, even the closest of friendships can founder if it becomes one-way. Thus these two kinds of altruism are not interchangeable and do not result in the same level of support or personal sacrifice. As family

5 Research summary: 'Women's attitudes to combining paid work and family life', available at http://www.cabinet-office.gov.uk/womens- unit/1999/research/attitudes.htm.
6 Buss DM, 1999, *Evolutionary Psychology: The new science of the mind*, Allyn and Bacon, Boston, Massachusetts, pp230-40.

relations become disrupted (by factors such as divorce, migration or working far from home) a growing cohort of people take on family commitments without being family members. But the government cannot realistically expect these reconstituted 'families' to generate the same care or social cohesion.

Step-parents epitomise the distinction between kin and non-kin. These are people who have chosen a mate but acquired children as part of the package. And they don't find that simply being placed *in loco parentis* automatically evokes heartfelt parental devotion or its emotional rewards. A wealth of evidence shows that, on average, compared to their genetic counterparts, step-parents and children view the relationship as less loving and less dependable emotionally and materially; that step-parents withhold investment and look forward to the children leaving home; and that step-children do indeed leave earlier. One chilling consequence of this predictable difference in feelings is an enormous differential in the risk of violence. Children are up to 100 times more likely to be killed by a step-parent than by a genetic parent. Even after taking into account confounding factors (including poverty, mother's age and personalities of people who remarry) the presence of a step-parent in the home is the single most powerful risk factor for severe child maltreatment yet discovered.[7]

Step-parents know that they are not kin. But even the suspicion that one is not kin can undermine families. Men can never be entirely sure that 'their' children really are their own; and they are not inclined to invest in other males' children. With estimates of misattributed 'fatherhood' running high in some urban areas (up to 25 per cent in some American cities[8]), uncertainty of paternity could be a major factor contributing to the numbers of absent 'fathers' and to family patterns in general. One cross-cultural study of 186 pre-industrial societies (current and historical), for example, found that where confidence of paternity is high, men invest far more (wealth, position, personal involvement) than where it is low.[9] And there are societies in which confidence of paternity is so low that – as Darwinian theory accurately predicts – the 'avunculate' system is the norm: a man will invest not in his wife's children but in his sister's (his nieces and nephews), for they are likely to be his closest relatives in the next generation.[10] What's more, as Darwinian theory again predicts and as studies in Western societies have shown, uncertainty of

7 Daly M and Wilson M, 1998, *The Truth about Cinderella: A Darwinian view of parental love,* Weidenfeld & Nicolson, London.
8 Betzig L, 1993, 'Where are the bastard's daddies?', *Behavioural and Brain Sciences,* no 285, p16
9 Gaulin S J and Schlegel A, 1980, 'Paternal confidence and paternal investment: A cross-cultural test of a sociobiological hypothesis', *Ethology and Sociobiology* no 1, pp301-9.
10 Alexander R, 1979, *Darwinism and Human Affairs,* Pitman, London, p172.

paternity leads to a sex difference in the altruism of grandparents. As expected, most grandparental investment comes from the mother's mother and least from the father's father, with mother's father and father's mother intermediate. (This is not merely because women invest more than men; maternal grandfathers, for example, invest more than paternal grandmothers.[11])

Which factors raise and lower confidence of paternity? And in what ways have these factors varied in recent years? The answers are far from clear. Could it be increased inequality among males or enforced absence from home (unsociable hours or long commuting) or increased sexual freedom for women or contraception and abortion? The government could perhaps set the new National Family and Parenting Institute the task of investigating some of these many unknowns.

Large levers

The government has claimed that there are no 'large levers' that it can pull to affect family formation.[12] But from the government's own reports one can see that unemployment, and in particular male unemployment, is a major contributing factor to marital instability and family break-up.[13] A Darwinian analysis supports this conclusion, and shows how – by increasing inequality among males and lowering the standing of men relative to women – unemployment can lead to absent fathers and lone mothers.

A government committed to supporting the family could count the impact on men's desirability as marriage partners as one of the social costs of unemployment, and make the reduction of male to male inequality a higher priority.

Equally important, the government could recognise that achieving sexual equality between men and women does not entail treating them as identical. Contrary to fashionable 'gender' thinking, women – like men – have their own distinct evolved psychology. If the government genuinely wants to extend the scope of women's choices then it should allow for the fact that their priorities are not always identical to those of men.[14] Rather than taking male standards as the universal measure, or expecting the sexes to adopt the same working 'roles', the government should design family-friendly employment practices that reflect the different preferences of women and men. For example, as revealed in the government's recent survey of

11 See note 6.
12 *Supporting Families Consultation Document,* op cit.
13 Simons J, ed, 1999, *High Divorce Rates: The state of evidence on reasons and remedies,* vols 1 and 2, One Plus One Marriage and Partnership Research, Lord Chancellor's Department Research Programme, London.
14 Browne KR, 1995, 'Sex and temperament in modern society: a Darwinian view of the glass ceiling and the gender gap', *Arizona Law Review,* vol 37, no 4, pp1088-9; see also Browne KR, 1998, *Divided Labours: An evolutionary view of women at work,* Weidenfeld & Nicolson, London.

women's attitudes, women choose and are happier with a different balance of work and family.[15] Following the birth of the first child, for instance, women work less, men work more – an arrangement that both mothers and fathers endorse. Indeed a recent study found – no doubt contrary to the expectations of its authors – that of all parents in the 1990s '[t]he most contented groups [describing themselves as "highly contented"] appeared to be mothers and fathers in the "traditional" single earner families in which only the father was in employment'. The unhappiest mothers and fathers were those in families without an earner, followed by families where mothers were the sole earners.[16]

Information, information, information

The government seems convinced that if it throws sufficient 'information' at problems – divorce, teenage pregnancy, domestic violence, child abuse and so on – they will go away. When this approach fails, its answer is all too often to throw even more information, earlier, harder, faster. But the government should be tackling the causes of family breakdown. There is no evidence that interfering with the symptoms – re-educating the poor with new 'parenting' 'roles', purveying marriage guidance, instituting prenuptial agreements or redesigning marriage ceremonies – will have any effect on marriage and divorce rates. Parasitic counsellors and well-meaning commentators who peddle 'advice', 'information' and other such 'talking cures' are helping to perpetuate the myth that the problems created by inequality and disadvantage can be erased in a few therapy sessions. They are allowing the government to duck its real responsibilities ⊙

Helena Cronin is Co-Director of the Centre for Philosophy at LSE and runs the Darwin@LSE programme.

Oliver Curry works at LSE on evolutionary theory and politics and co-edits Darwinism Today, *a series of short books on evolutionary topics.*

15 See note 5.
16 Ferri E and Smith K, 1996, *Parenting in the 1990s,* Family Policy Studies Centre, London, p22.

Things can only get better

Services and support for families in tune with the times

Colette Kelleher

Family life in Britain at the end of the twentieth century is in a state of flux. Change is manifest in the home, community and in the workplace. In my own life as a working mother with two children, my family too is in a state of flux. I have not inherited a blueprint from my own parents, who actually ran a family business, on how to manage the day to day demands of my family and work responsibilities. As the Director of what is essentially a small business, I also grapple with the challenges of not just talking about, but also trying to practise, the art of being a 'family friendly' employer in a climate of scarce and uncertain resources. In both my home and in my work, I am in uncharted territory, often making it up as I go along.

Changing patterns of family life

There are profound changes going on in family life in Britain. The 'breadwinner dad and stay-at-home mum' model is now the minority form: 62 per cent of couples with dependent children are now in work.[1] More mothers are in the workforce than ever before, leaving their homes and communities every day to go to work. The biggest increase in participation is among women with young children. Two-thirds of mothers now return to work after maternity leave, a 50 per cent increase since 1988.[2]

However, these figures mask a huge divide between work rich and work poor households: between women in couples with a working partner, and households with no paid work including one-parent families. These divisions in access to work, exacerbated by lack of

1 Office for National Statistics, 1998, *Social Trends 28*, The Stationery Office, London.
2 Labour Market Trends, 1999, *Women in the Labour Market: results from the spring 1998 Labour Force Survey*, The Stationery Office, London.

affordable childcare and family-friendly employment, have huge long-term implications for child poverty and the social exclusion of many families in Britain.

In part because of the changes in participation in work, parental relationships are also being redefined. It is easy to make a case that there is a 'crisis' in fatherhood: there are many more families without fathers than ever before. But the other side of the coin is significant: in many households fathers are getting *more* involved with their children than ever before. Nowadays they are often present at the birth, some are able to take leave around the time of the birth, they change nappies, push buggies and get up in the night to take care of a crying child.[3] In my own experience, there is simply no comparison between the involvement of the father of my children in their rearing with my own father's involvement in looking after my brothers, sisters and myself.

However, even among dual-earner families the balance of responsibility for children remains with mothers. Many more mothers than fathers work part-time. British men work the longest hours in the European Union.[4] Fathers view providing an income for the family as the central aspect of fathering, with other aspects viewed as additional. The Daycare Trust's recent MORI survey of parents revealed important differences between men and women. Women say that not having access to adequate childcare means that they are more likely to be unable to take a full-time job. Conversely, men particularly complained about working long hours.[5] The expectations of society means that the emotional burden still remains with mothers: who is the school more likely to call if a child is sick, who remembers to buy the birthday card and present for your child's best friend, who arranges the childcare?

The pattern is that of frustrations arising from the imbalance of demands on *both* women and men in families. It is what we might term the 'extra shift' syndrome – problems stemming from an overload of conflicting demands on top of what one sees as one's key working role. For many men, the 'first shift' is the performance of full-time breadwinning; the second shift is the pressure at work to put in longer hours in order to survive and thrive in the 'flexible' workplace, and also to live up to legitimate demands for greater involvement in childcare and household management, as well as for the emotional care of one's partner. For many women, the first shift

3 JRF, 1999, *Fathers, Work and Family Life*, Joseph Rowntree Foundation, York.
4 *Labour Force Survey*, spring 1996, Office for National Statistics, London.
5 MORI/Daycare Trust, 1999, *Childcare and Family Friendly Policies*, MORI/ Daycare Trust, London.

is the juggling of childcare and part-time or full-time work; the second shift is the bulk of the work of household management and maintaining family ties and friendships. What is new is that men are joining women – who have long been used to it – in the stress-laden work of juggling the different 'shifts', and neither women nor men have found ways of reconciling the demands of work and home. It is not so much a question of 'having it all' as of being able to do justice to each part of the portfolio of 'shifts'.

The role of extended families is also changing, with families living further away and less able to rely on their families than before. However this should not be over exaggerated. The recent audits of childcare in every local authority area in England carried out at the end of 1998 indicated that there is still an enormous reliance on *informal* childcare in certain communities and areas. It is not known whether this reliance is of necessity because of cost, availability or the cultural appropriateness of local childcare services or if it is the first choice of families; or if dependency on childcare provided by family and friends is sustainable given the trends towards a more mobile and flexible workforce and the participation of more women in work.

In general, we have grown up accustomed to physical and psychological separation between the worlds of home and work. My own experience of being reared in a family business meant that there was no separation between work and home. My experience may becoming more common. Advances in telecommunications may mean that for people in some jobs this separation of home and work may be overcome to varying degrees.

There are changes in community life too, with environmental changes having a profound effect on the family. Children are being driven to school rather than walking. Mayer Hillman's famous study of school children showed a marked decline in children's personal independence over a twenty year period. Whereas three quarters of junior school children were allowed to cross the road on their own in 1971, by 1990 the proportion had fallen to half.[6] In urban areas cars and traffic are preventing children from playing outside and in the countryside dangerous pesticides and chemicals are keeping children indoors and isolated. Scare stories in the media about 'stranger danger' are also creating a climate of fear among parents, too anxious to let their children stray beyond their gaze.

6 Hillman M, 1993, *Children, Transport and the Quality of Life,* Policy Studies Institute, London.

Families at the end of the twentieth century are under more pressure as consumers than ever before. Children are targeted by advertisers with a never-ending supply of 'must have' products tied up with the latest Disney film release or 'celebration'. You have no sooner forked out for the back to school essentials, when you are assailed with Halloween, quickly followed by Christmas and, no doubt this year, Millennium gimmicks. Having the latest designer clothes, football strip, computer game, sports wear or trip to the expensive theme park are now part of the shared experience of our children. They are also an indication of the status and income of the parents.

No parent wants to deny their children or admit to not being able to afford to participate in popular culture, but the range and frequency of the demands from our children for new products is infinite and insatiable. We pay through the nose for often expensive but ultimately empty experiences. Parents may need to question if it is for these disposal consumables for their children that they are working so hard. Parents at the end of the twentieth century may also need training to say 'No' to our children's demands for such things.

Political and corporate responses

How have government and the corporate world responded to families in this state of flux, conflicting loyalties and tension? In the last couple of years there has been an enormous shift in policy by government. There has been a recognition that women as well as men with children work; that current childcare facilities are inadequate; that the state has a role in making sure the services are properly planned – in pump priming the development of new services, in ensuring that services meet certain standards and in helping parents on low and middle income pay for childcare. A massive investment is being made to make the National Childcare Strategy a reality. This government recognises the connection between the availability of childcare, the ability to work, social inclusion and tackling child poverty. This is nothing short of a sea change. The Conservative government's view was largely that childcare was the private responsibility of parents, with a residual role for the state. Given that there is often a 'bad childcare' story in the media with the blame being firmly placed on heartless working mothers, the previous government's distance from the issue was also convenient.

This government is also introducing more help for families to strike a balance between work and family responsibilities. Maternity rights have been enhanced, a new right to unpaid parental leave is being introduced as well as for time off for child emergencies.[7] A National Family and Parenting Institute has been set up to help parents with the demands of this all important role. The Sure Start programme, running in 250 communities, will help families with young children. Car-free 'Home Zones' are being designated to give children more autonomy and safe places to play in their communities. Services to support children in rural areas are being included in the Early Years Development and Childcare plans.

The changes being brought about by this government should help mothers and fathers to share more equally the responsibility for their children. They should help to level the playing field for one-parent families to successfully combine work and family commitments. They should give children access to appropriate services and more freedom of movement in their communities.

The new government family agenda also affects employers. Some of the top employers already have 'family friendly' measures in place, but what about the majority of employers which do not? What contribution do we expect the corporate world and indeed small and medium sized companies to make to achieve a satisfactory work life balance in the twenty-first century?

Two MORI surveys commissioned by Daycare Trust for National Childcare Week in 1998 and 1999 give an interesting insight into employer activity in helping families balance work and family life.[8] The 1998 survey of the UK's top 500 companies revealed some double standards about support for families in the workplace. Encouragingly, 75 per cent of employers agreed that there is a recognised business case for companies to introduce family-friendly policies, and a surprising 73 per cent felt that employers have a moral responsibility to provide family friendly policies. Sixty-five per cent agreed that their company should do more to help working parents. But these same companies also revealed that only 5 per cent currently provide a workplace nursery, 2 per cent have reserved nursery places and 3 per cent have after school clubs for all of their employees children. Only 9 per cent are likely to introduce a contribution to nursery costs for employees. Daycare Trust's follow up MORI survey of parents in

7 Callender C et al, 1997, *Maternity Rights and Benefits in Britain*, DSS Research Series No 67, DSS, London. **8** MORI/Daycare Trust, 1998, *The Family and the Workplace*, MORI/ Daycare Trust, London; see also note 5.

1999 reinforced the 1998 findings. Only 8 per cent of parents had employers who help them with childcare but 80 per cent said that their employer should provide more help with childcare. Both employers and parents want an active government to encourage employers to do more to support working families.

Future challenges

Clear progress has been made by the government in closing the childcare gap and in helping parents balance work and family responsibilities, but are they enough for families in a state of flux? The National Childcare Strategy, the Employment Relations Act and other measures are steps in the right direction. But only time will tell whether the new measures and services are in tune with the times and give children and parents what they need.

The already massive investment in the childcare sector may not be enough. The expansion of childcare services for children aged up to three years is still being left to market forces even though the biggest growth in workforce participation is among mothers with children in this age group and this is the age band where quality is most vital. Policies for maternity and parental leave policies along with the National Childcare Strategy have not yet been 'joined up' by government. Unpaid parental leave may end up as a perk for those on higher income. The childcare tax credit in Working Families Tax Credit may not be taken up and the benefits may not get passed on to the currently badly paid, largely unqualified female workforce.

The government's spending priorities may mean that the additional investment for childcare for children under three, paid parental leave or investing in a qualified, well paid childcare workforce may not be available against the competing demands from health and education for scarce government resources. The local Early Years Development and Childcare Partnerships may not be up to the challenge of working across sectors to plan, expand and improve childcare services for children aged up to fourteen years in their areas. Schools may keep their doors shut. Employers may not make their contribution to sharing the costs of childcare and parental leave with government and parents but only come 'kicking and screaming' to the table under duress of statutory regulation for minimum family friendly measures. A backlash against family-friendly measures from employees without children may materialise.

Looking to the future, I do worry about the negative scenarios, but in general, I believe that we are much nearer to more positive outcomes. These include:

- a range of quality, affordable early years and childcare services for children aged up to fourteen years in every neighbourhood, with schools having a new role acting as a lynchpin in the community life of families and as a base for local services for supporting families and facilitating exchange and reciprocity among families;
- early excellence centres, after school clubs and holiday play schemes in every community – for every child who needs them, offering learning through play, art, sport and music and providing stimulation and risk – places for friendship and fun;
- safe communities for children to play, reclaiming the streets, parks and fields – with the needs of car owners coming second to the needs of children, with parents valuing such 'low cost' measures over the containment and consumerism of theme parks;
- a well paid, qualified, stable early years and childcare workforce – with the development of an early years specialism for teachers;
- a robust regulatory regime enforcing the highest standards for childcare and early years services for children aged up to fourteen years;
- a changed work culture with paid maternity, parental and other leave policies as well as the expectation of reasonable working hours instead of the long hours culture. Employers to join with government and parents to finance childcare and parental leave. Coherence and consistency between maternity, parental leave and the National Childcare Strategy;
- continuing dialogue between men, women and society about a fair sharing of the responsibility for caring for children and others.

All this is achievable and necessary for families in flux; the essential ingredients are already in place; the crucial arguments have been won. All that is left is the implementation. That will happen too, much like other initiatives in tune with their time, like universal education, the NHS or statutory maternity leave and pay.

I can envisage children playing with other children in their communities at the early excellence centre or after school club, at the bottom of their road or lane – engaging in cultural pursuits, safe and stimulated while their parents work. I can envisage parents being able to work sensible hours, with fathers as well as mothers able to work part-time and able to drop off and collect from school, nursery or play scheme. I can envisage workplaces with more productive and less stressed staff working sensible hours but still getting the job done. I can envisage schools open all year round, where parents go for information about the local baby-sitting exchange as well as for top quality integrated education and care for their children.

We are in the midst of making all of this happen. We are all finding new solutions. Some mistakes have been made along the way, but we are getting most of it right. I have seen fathers transform in my lifetime. I see mothers all around me making a crucial contribution in their working lives outside the home as well as to their children's lives. I see children making friends and playing out. I see groups of families helping each other to look after their children and making friendships and connections. I see people getting together to work in partnership to improve local childcare and early years services. I see a small under-funded charity doing its best to support its employees balance their work and family lives.

Utopian? Of course, but as Oscar Wilde said, a map of the world which doesn't contain utopia is not worth a second glance. Families need these visions to turn into reality – and as quickly as possible. In Gordon Brown's first budget speech he said that a generation of parents had waited for their government to give them a National Childcare Strategy. In many other high-income countries it is already in place, supported by other family-friendly policies. There, policy makers, employers and parents share a recognition that helping families achieve balance between the satisfactions and duties of work and home is a fundamentally important contribution to social cohesion and long-term economic progress and stability. In Britain at the end of the twentieth century I believe that we are closer to achieving that longed-for equilibrium than we know – a society that supports families that work ⊙

Colette Kelleher is a mother to a daughter aged nine and son aged six and is Director of Daycare Trust, the national charity that promotes quality affordable childcare for all.

Childcare as public good

Sue Slipman

I have spent my career returning to the issue of childcare. One of my first serious campaigns was for a college nursery. This was in the early 1970s. The first national Women's Liberation Conferences were demanding state supplied 24-hour nurseries among the four key demands that would pave the way to women's freedom. I was quite vague about children's needs, but I understood that support with childcare was critical if women were ever to break through the social and professional barriers created by biology and cemented in place by tradition. I remember that at the time mothers were less sanguine about abandoning their little darlings to institutional care than the child-free among us – but we were looking for quick fixes.

When I eventually had my son, childcare became very personal. It has been chief among the plates that have to be kept spinning on top of poles while other things in life and career demand more immediate attention. The issues surrounding children – their creation, support and care – remain the constant echoes in women's lives. We won that first campaign for a college nursery, but after a heady beginning progress has been frustratingly slow.

As Director of the National Council for One Parent Families (NCOPF) for ten years, I charted the sharply rising need for childcare provision against the slow progress. For many years, the only successes were work and welfare-to-work related. Tax relief for workplace nurseries came first. NCOPF was successful in winning the first concession of a childcare disregard on social security benefits for lone parents to return to work. Voluntary activity on the part of

Daycare Trust and others led to the setting up of childcare information centres. I was part of the advisory team for the Department of
Employment's introduction of out-of-school places. As director of a
training and enterprise council, in partnership with Kid Club's
Network, I supported the implementation of the programme at local
level in east London. At NCOPF we raised money for a patchwork of
provision whenever we spotted an opportunity and supported voluntary sector and employer partnership pioneering schemes like
York Childcare. Then there were the unsuccessful campaigns for tax
relief on childcare provision – I could go on.

I accepted early on that we were never going to achieve 24-hour
state run nurseries – nor were they desirable. As a parent I learned
that you need to combine different forms of childcare to meet your
child's – and your own – individual needs. In my case as a fairly isolated lone parent, I chose a childminder because I wanted my son to
have access to other children and a wider family group. Then I combined this first with a playgroup and then with a part-time nursery
place when he needed it. Later ages present different problems as you
combine school with after-school and holiday care. Then you struggle to get your child into the best holiday scheme you can find, only
for him to announce on day one that 'it's crap. I'm never going there
again'. Any working mother understands that childcare arrangements are a time consuming, ongoing management task requiring
skill to arrange and patience to sustain. Parental choice matters and
children's choices and preferences cannot be ignored.

Childcare provision has been a big, heavy stone rolled up a long,
steep hill. But the government now claims it has a childcare strategy.
I disagree. This does not mean I am overly critical of government; I
can live with a 'let a thousand flowers bloom' approach. This should,
at least, generate more childcare places and provide better access to
information about them. Lottery money will help produce them. I
have misgivings about putting the programme into local authorities
– but this stems from the original out-of-school programmes where,
to my chagrin, local authorities refused to open up the schools for
this purpose. My misgivings are mitigated by the necessary involvement of community and other partners in schemes. In general, government action and commitment is welcome – but it is not a strategy.

The fact is that government lacks clarity about what childcare is
for. Is it to support working parents? Is it to give disadvantaged chil-

dren a 'head start' in education and associated league tables by opening up nursery education and testing its impact? Is it primarily a private benefit? Should it be provided by the state, employers or by a combination of both?

Take the case of working parents. Government is willing through the Working Families Tax Credit to enable adults to take the welfare-to-work route and to keep low-income families in work – but other working parents only get help if their employers provide it. According to the recent survey by the Daycare Trust at present only 8 per cent of employers give any kind of childcare support to employees. Most of these employers responded to a business case based upon recruitment and retention of 'valuable' staff – giving preference to those with executive value who are in receipt of executive packages. Even for this group the benefit is tax-free to the employer, but taxed for the employee. This is, of course, reasonable if childcare is a private benefit like the company car (given to only certain grades) but it leaves a huge group in the middle with little or no support. It may be that this group can benefit from out-of-school, cheaper end provision, but this is bound to remain patchy for a considerable time to come.

The truth is that the provision of childcare is more than a private benefit for high income individuals and a social benefit for the poor. It is also a social and public good, increasingly critical to a society in transition. Changes in family structures, growth of one parent families and the lack of wider family resources make childcare an important factor in keeping our children safe and under reasonable social supervision. In deprived areas it links to strategies for tackling crime. For deprived children it is critical to developing early learning skills. Where business requires a flexible workforce it is a critical factor in making this work for both employers and employees. Increasingly, the need for good quality childcare runs through wide ranges of economic, social and employment policy as an indispensable thread. It is increasingly important in our socially divergent and atomised society to regard all children as *our* children – but this does not mean they become a sole responsibility of the state.

In many other areas of our lives we are getting used to products and services deemed to be in the public good being delivered through 'third way' solutions. I entirely accept that government cannot fund all childcare supply. I believe it can be supplied through provision within and partnerships between the private, statutory and voluntary sectors, but individuals must have the resources to buy. No one wants to pay for the Norland nannies of the rich, but at present that is all that employers are encouraged to do. We need the children of that big group of parents in lower to middle incomes to benefit, too. A step in the right direction would be for government to stop treating employer-provided childcare benefits the same as company cars. Government could encourage employers to provide childcare benefits to a wider group of employees by giving tax relief to recipients. This would give a clear signal that government recognises the social significance of childcare and regards it as a public good.

Placing childcare provision within the context of a public good pluralistically delivered (and financed) provides the strategic framework that government needs to give some backbone to its 'blooming flowers' approach. You can set targets to achieve a public good. You can monitor your progress towards your goal, testing what works, discarding what does not work and adjusting your policies. In this framework you can develop your strategies for provision hand in hand with strategies for standards setting and quality and the provision of information and guidance. Outside this strategic framework you merely place more plates on poles for parents to rotate. Given the alternatives, more plates are undoubtedly welcome but their manipulation will remain endlessly precarious for families and ultimately for society as a whole ☉

Sue Slipman is Director of Social Responsibility at Camelot.

Modest hopes or great expectations?

Peter Moss

The new interest – expressed by government, employers, trade unions and others – in the relationship between employment and caring is to be welcomed, as are the practical measures being taken in this field. But in confronting the work–family relationship we are not dealing with some new and simple problem that can be fixed once and for all by finding the 'right answer'. Rather we are dealing with an age-old issue that is ever-present across generations, albeit in different guises. In the circumstances we might be better off hoping for important, but modest, gains, rather than harbouring great expectations of a definitive solution.[1]

The current political context brings new opportunities and new risks. I want to focus on three topics:

- the need for action and analysis
- addressing production and reproduction
- family friendliness and gender equality – a Catch 22.

The need for action and analysis

Current interest in family-friendly policies – from government and social partners – is very welcome. We need to put policy ideas into action in order to learn. And our learning opens up great opportunities for doing things better. However, at a time when the key policy question seems to be 'what works?', it is worth remembering the comment of the Italian historian Carlo Ginsburg that the minority world of the affluent West lives in a culture where we are constantly

1 This article is based on a presentation made to a conference on family-friendly working, 'Great Expectations', organised by the TUC in July 1999.

being offered solutions before we have asked the critical questions.[2]

It seems to me that the challenge is twofold: how to avoid concentrating our attentions wholly on solutions ('what works?'), and how to make time and space to find and ask critical questions which may help us to make a hard-headed analysis of what is actually happening – thus, we hope, producing more effective measures.

A range of questions flow from this. How do we prevent the language of 'family friendliness', with its focus on solutions, from lulling us into a false sense of security? Can we resist the urge to 'get on and do' without enquiring what the problems really are and how they came about? Can we address the work–family relationship without understanding the nature and implications of change, for example the emergence of a new form of capitalism, new media and other technologies, new forms of family life and lifestyle, and so on?

The reason I ask all this is because at the same time as 'family friendliness' has been gaining a high profile, other developments have been going on in the employment sphere which may *undo all the good* that family-friendly policies have achieved. We run the risk that for every step we take forward with family-friendly policies, we will be dragged back two steps by other changes. In a recent study at the Thomas Coram Research Unit,[3] Julia Brannen and I identified three main trends in parental employment:

- *Polarisation:* employment has been rising rapidly among already advantaged mothers since the late 1980s, but has been stagnant or falling back amongst disadvantaged mothers. The 'Matthew principle' has been in operation – 'to him who hath shall be given'. The most obvious example has been the widening employment gap between mothers in two parent families and lone mothers, but the same process applies elsewhere, most notably in relation to educational qualifications. There are also more two-earner families and more no-earner families – with one earner families squeezed.
- *Intensification of work:* in the UK the working hours of mothers have been increasing and those of fathers (already the longest in the EU) have not decreased. Family working hours are edging up inexorably.
- *Concentration of work:* paid work is increasingly concentrated on men and women in the so-called 'prime working years', that is

2 Ginsburg C, 1989, *Ledtrdor, Esser om Konst, forbjuden kunskap och dold historia* [Threads, Essays on Art, Forbidden Knowledge and Hidden History], Hften fr Kritiska, Stockholm.
3 Brannen J and Moss P, 1998, 'The polarisation and intensification of parental employment in Britain: consequences for children, families and the community', *Community, Work and Family*, vol 1, no 3, pp229-247.

between 25 and 50, a period of life which also now coincides with childbearing and child-rearing (the average age at which UK women now have a first child was nearly 27 in 1996, and men are presumably on average somewhat older). We are facing the prospect of a lifetime divided into three parts – the first third in education, the second third working and the final third in some form of retirement. One consequence is the 'headless chicken syndrome' during the prime working years, with men and women facing an ever increasing workload and considerable financial pressures, trying to fit too much into a finite day. Another may be more women and men opting for not having children: the UK, together with Ireland and to a lesser extent the Netherlands, 'stand out as [European] countries in which childlessness has substantially increased. One in ten women born in the United Kingdom in 1940 were childless, compared with one in five born in the late 1950s.'[4]

There may also be other employment trends, less well-documented but nevertheless important for family life, that should concern us – for example, a more rapid pace of change in organisations, increasing insecurity, and workplaces increasingly characterised by short time-frames with people working on short-term projects, changing jobs or their jobs changing on them, and so on. The last point has led the sociologist Richard Sennett to argue, in his book *The Corrosion of Character: The personal consequences of work in the new capitalism*, that:

'It is the time dimension of the new capitalism, rather than hi-tech data transmission, global stock markets or free trade, that most directly affects people's emotional lives outside the workplace. Transposed to the family realm, "no long term" means keep moving, don't commit yourself and don't sacrifice.... This conflict between family and work poses some new questions about adult experience itself. How can long-term purposes be pursued in a short-term society? How can durable social relations be sustained? How can a human being develop a narrative of identity and life history in a society composed of episodes and fragments?'[5]

More specifically, a recent national survey concludes that:

4 Pearce D, Cantisani G and Laihonen A, 1999, 'Changes in fertility and family size in Europe', *PopuTrends*, 95 (Spring 1999), pp33-40.
5 Sennett R, 1998, *Corrosion of Character: The personal consequences of work in the new capitalism*, Norton, London, pp25-27.

'Job insecurity has spread throughout the 1990s, particularly amongst professional workers. And work has become more intense. More than 60 per cent of employees claim that the pace of work has increased over the last 5 years.... Job insecurity and work intensification are associated with poor general health and tense family relationships ... The root cause of job insecurity and work intensification lies with the downsizing and delayering pursued by senior managers in response to the market pressures exerted by their competitors and dominant stakeholders: and in the public sector, by the force of fiscal stringency.'[6]

In raising these issues, I am not suggesting we can, or should seek to, return to some non-existent golden age of workplace security. I am not denying that change brings great opportunities. I am not arguing that we can do nothing in the face of overwhelming odds – I have no doubt, for example, that policy initiatives taken over 30 years in Sweden have helped working parents in that country.

But as well as moving forward with family-friendly policies, we need to make progress in analysing what is actually going on – in the workplace, in family life and in the relationship between the two – and not assume that *action guarantees solutions*. Nor should we believe in final solutions to big problems. Times change, targets move, new issues emerge. Above all, we have to work for some improvement, to find some better trade-offs, but understand that we do so in the context of forces which do not share identical interests and values and between which there are tensions which have existed before we were born and will continue after we are dead – not least the forces of production and reproduction discussed next.

Addressing production and reproduction

As a society, we need to be clear about our purposes and what priorities we give them. In particular, how do we see the relationship between economic and social purposes, between production and reproduction, between the busy-ness of business and the commitment of caring, between the managerial striving for order, objectivity and certainty and the inherent complexity, subjectivity and messiness of human relationships and everyday life? At a time when business values are predominant in policy calculations, there is a

6 ESRC Centre for Business Research, 1999, *Job Insecurity and Work Intensification: Findings*, ESRC Centre for Business Research, University of Cambridge and Joseph Rowntree Foundation, Cambridge, p1.

risk that social values, family relationships and those who are not economically active may be subordinated to competitiveness and productivity. There are real dangers that the only show in town is the business case and everything has to be fitted into that framework.

Michael Fielding raises the issue of purpose and value in relation to the Labour government's approach to education policy, but his words could equally well apply to other governments and policy fields:

> 'The most puzzling concern continues to be whether the [Government's education] vision is primarily an economic one with the occasional bit of social adhesive stuck on to ensure the enterprise remains viable, or whether the vision is one in which economics is the servant of a wider and deeper human flourishing. The differences between the two are profound, but show no evidence of having been acknowledged or properly understood'.[7]

A major challenge facing Britain, if we are to become a healthier and more civilised society which values social as well as economic thriving, is how to develop a dialogue between the economic and the social policy worlds, between business and caring – so that, at the very least, different parties can understand and respect each other's perspectives.

Of course, in practice, I am posing a false dichotomy, since most of us are concerned with both the economic and the social, are producers as well as consumers, carers as well as workers; the issue is not just about new relationships between different parties, but finding new relationships between different parts of our own identities and lives. We need to find fora where different perspectives, different interests, different values, ideas and practices can be brought together, debated and negotiated.

Elsewhere I have suggested that one of many possibilities for such fora might be *early childhood centres*, but only if we reconceptualise them as public spaces in civil society where adults and children engage together in projects of social, cultural, economic and political significance, rather than (as now) as processing plants for producing 'child outputs'.[8] We also need to recognise that dialogue about issues such as production/reproduction and the work–life balance is a political process, involving the confrontation of differ-

7 Fielding M, 1999, 'Taking Education Seriously: Two years hard Labour', *Cambridge Journal of Education*, vol 29, no 2, pp173-182.
8 Dahlberg G, Moss P and Pence A, 1999, *Beyond Quality in Early Childhood Education and Care: Postmodern perspectives on the problem with quality*, Falmer Press, London.

ent values and perspectives, and requires us to think in terms such as a 'politics of childhood' and a 'politics of caring' which, in turn, will help to generate those critical questions I have referred to above.

Here, government has an important role to play, not least because it is the only institution with a general democratic mandate and an overview of, and interest in, many different interests and needs. At present, there seem to be at least three departments (in England) with an expressed interest in work–family issues: the DfEE, the Home Office and the DTI, which is responsible for implementing Parental Leave legislation. A fourth department should have an interest, but has so far shown little sign of this – the Department of Health, which is the government department responsible for children, as well as adults with disabilities. And other departments may also have an interest.

I would suggest that 'joined-up' government confronts a major challenge in the field of balancing work and family life, concerning the *relationship between production and reproduction* – and that attention needs to be paid to government's role in providing fora and other opportunities which bring together in dialogue different perspectives, interests, ideas and practices. We need to ask whether overall responsibility for this field should be given to one department or whether in fact some new agency is needed for this role?

I would also suggest that the experience of implementing parental leave as a statutory entitlement emphasises the problem and the need to consider how government undertakes its responsibilities. For, as the most potentially significant family-friendly measure of the last decade or more, parental leave has become reduced to an issue of employment regulation rather than an opportunity to explore the relationship between production and reproduction in all its complexity. We have been neither challenged to discuss the purposes of parental leave, nor the conditions which might enable these measures to be met. The consequence may well turn out to be that policy for parental leave becomes a token, rather than an effective, measure.

Family friendliness and gender equality: a Catch 22

Parental leave is much on my mind at present, not only because it is in the offing in the United Kingdom but because I am co-editing a book on the experience of parental leave in the rest of the European Union.[9] What comes across from analysis of this experience is a

9 Deven F and Moss P, eds, (forthcoming), *Parental Leave in Europe: Research and policy issues*, CBGS/NIDI, Brussels/The Hague.

Catch 22 situation. Parental leave is often introduced ostensibly as an equal opportunities measure, to promote gender equality (for example, the EU Directive which has required the UK to adopt parental leave is an equal opportunities measure). But without having gender equality in the first place, parental leave can very easily be ineffective or actually make things worse – because women are far more likely to take leave than men are, and this can reinforce traditional gender roles in the home and weaken women's position in the labour market. I think the same is true of other family-friendly measures – that if used, they are overwhelmingly used by women, and so may impede rather than promote gender equality.

The challenge is how to take forward family friendliness without taking back – or at least retarding – gender equality. Space permits no discussion: only the observation that the issue of men's roles and actions in the workplace and the family remains one of the critical work–family issues. Yet so far in the UK we have failed to make any headway. It simply does not seem to be an important issue for politicians, employers, trade unionists or any other powerful players in the work–family area. And we seem only able to talk about *fathers* in relation to some perceived crisis or problem, which demands some immediate solution – but again, in this way we come back to our desperation for short-term fixes to superficially defined problems. Yet unless there are substantial changes in the way fathers in particular and men in general work and care, then we cannot build new and more equal relationships between production and reproduction, between the economic and the social, between women and men, between those who are in the labour market and those who are not.

The danger of the language of 'family friendly' policies and 'working parents' is that it hides the possibility of conflicting interests and gendered work – and diverts our attention from the really 'wicked issues' in the work-family relationship, which are to do with deeper questions about the role of work in our lives, the priorities we attach to work time and care time, and the lack of real equality between men and women. If great expectations are to become great realities, then those wicked issues of time, gender and the valuation of care need to be squarely faced and worked upon ⊙

Peter Moss is Professor of Early Childhood Provision, Thomas Coram Research Unit, Institute of Education, University of London.

A children's crusade

Paul Gregg

'Labour is nothing if it's not a crusade', remarked Harold Wilson in the 1960s, but for New Labour it's a children's crusade. On no other issue has this government been as bold as in its promise to eliminate child poverty in a generation. There should be no hiding the immense challenge this represents or the resources it requires. The UK has by far the worst record on child poverty in Europe. One in three children – just under four and a half million – was living in relative poverty when Labour was elected.[1]

The scale and nature of the problem

Large families and those with young children (and indeed young parents) are more likely to be poor because the mother is much less likely to be working to supplement the partner's earnings or as the sole family earner. One in five children lives in a household where no one works and almost all of these children are poor. Another one in eight children lives in a household with only low paid[2] or part-time work. These normally go together where the mother is the sole earner. The UK has the worst record of children growing up in workless households of any developed nation. Estimates by the OECD for 1996 are represented in Figure 1.[3] While one in five UK households contains children with no adult in work, the norm in other developed nations is around half this, even though many of these countries have vastly higher unemployment rates and far lower employment. The nearest country to the UK was Ireland, and their recent dramatic improvement in employment levels will have no doubt

1 Ireland was the next worst in 1993 with around 27 per cent of children in poverty, although their recent economic boom is likely to have reduced this figure. Portugal, Spain and Italy have around one in four children in poverty. See Gregg P, Harkness S and Machin S, 1999, *Child Development and Family Income*, Joseph Rowntree Foundation, York.
2 Low pay, here, is defined as being among the lowest quarter of hourly wage rates in the working age population.
3 HM Treasury, 1999, *Tackling Poverty and Extending Opportunity: The modernisation of Britain's tax and benefit system*, No 4, TSO, London.

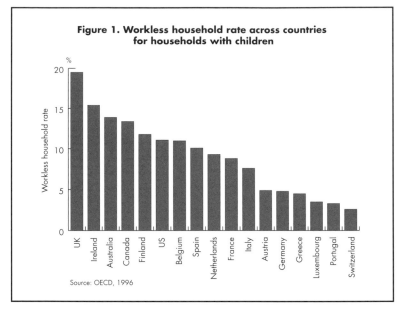

Figure 1. Workless household rate across countries for households with children

Source: OECD, 1996

widened this already large gap. In the UK, then, work has become steadily more polarised between 'work poor' households, with no earner, and 'work rich' households, with all adults working. The big losers in this process have been children.

In each of the past three decades there has been a progressive rise in the share of children living in households with no one earning. At the end of the 1960s one child out of 25 (just 4 per cent) was living in a household where no one worked. By 1979 it was one in twelve. This reduced further to one in six by 1990. While employment levels have collapsed in each recession, the subsequent recoveries have been sufficient for the recessions to contribute little overall to the growing number of workless households. Rather, the rise in workless households in general has then stemmed from a shift toward more single adult households and the way work has polarised across households in British society. Since 1979 the proportion of all working age households with no one in work has risen from 8 to 18 per cent. A fifth of this rise is due to smaller household size and the rest is due to the re distribution of work in Britain. Better educated women with children are working more than before and less educated older men far less. These groups do not live in the same households. Furthermore, only women with a working partner have increased their likelihood of working in the past twenty years.

It is easy to exaggerate the importance of lone parents in child poverty. While the number of lone parents has grown sharply and their employment rate is one of the lowest among developed nations, only one-third of children in poverty live with a non-working lone parent. Forty-six per cent live in households where someone works but earns too little to lift them out of poverty. This rise in working poverty has partly come about because of declining state support for children. There has been a steady erosion in the value of child support benefits relative to wages and a decline in the real value of Child Benefit.

The case for acting to reverse these unpleasant trends is made all the more compelling by research which suggests that deprivation damages children.[4] It is perhaps intuitive that children growing up in households facing acute or long-term financial deprivation do less well in life. But this new research has established beyond reasonable doubt that it is poverty that damages children and not just the lower education of parents or low innate ability of the children.

This research highlights four key supplementary findings. First, the effects of childhood deprivation last through to at least age 33, and manifest through low educational achievement, more unemployment and lower wages. Second, long periods of relative deprivation matter more than short bursts of low income. Third, the impact of childhood deprivation is evident in very young children, by 28 months, and these early years are very important. Fourth, childhood deprivation raises the likelihood of having children and having them young, including teenage pregnancy. Hence there is a strong intergenerational transmission of deprivation.

What is disheartening is how the educational system is failing to stem this process. Free universal education to age eighteen is provided to reduce the inequalities that family background has on children's educational achievement. However, such inequalities in child development continue to widen after entry into the education system. Our society's huge investment in education to limit such intergenerational transmission of deprivation is currently inadequate. The government is right in expecting more.

A child poverty strategy

A coherent strategy for attacking child poverty needs to consist of three elements:

4 Gregg et al, 1999 (note 1); see also note 3; Hills J, ed, 1999, *Persistent Poverty and Lifetime Inequality: The evidence*, Report No 5, Centre for Analysis of Social Exclusion, LSE, London.

1. A major increase in the income of households with children, especially those with younger and larger families.

2. A drive to reduce the number of children growing up in families with no one in work. Work in the household is vital to prevent families from just existing on welfare payments for long periods. Even if welfare payments are higher, they are unlikely ever to get a family far beyond the poverty line. And staying on these slightly higher incomes for long periods will still damage children. In 60 per cent of current workless households with children, no resident adult has worked in at least three years.

3. A diminution or elimination of the ways in which deprivation is transmitted into adult life. That means helping with early childhood health and development, reducing the impact of a poor background on educational underachievement and reducing the extent of unemployment among youths.

The government is acting on all these fronts but with finite resources choices have to be made. Should the government start by alleviating the most acute poverty: large families where no one works? Or, alternatively, should they go for areas where there is a potential to create virtuous circles or multiplier effects? Reducing working poverty, through the Working Families Tax Credit (WFTC) and the Child Tax Credit due in two years, will have a direct alleviation effect and, by improving work incentives, supports others to move into work. The Treasury estimates that the measures already in place or announced will lift 750,000 children out of poverty in this Parliament. This is a static estimate in that it assumes no change in the distribution of work.

Research I was involved with at the Institute of Fiscal Studies suggests it could reduce the number of workless households with children by around 130,000.[5] As many of these households have more than one child, which means that around 200,000 children will no longer be growing up in a household where no one works. And as most of these will also be moved out of poverty, I believe that around 1 million children will be lifted out of poverty through the government's programme by the end of 2002, as long as there is a reasonable macro-economic performance. Other initiatives on education and the like will have very long pay-back periods but should not be neglected. If successful, such interventions are like investments,

5 Gregg P, Johnson P and Reed H, 1999, *Entering Work and the British Tax and Benefit System*, Institute of Fiscal Studies, London.

reducing the future incidence of factors underlying poverty.

Even so, not all families with children will work in twenty years time and others will have only a few hours of low-paid work available. Many jobs available to those out of work are unstable. We frequently observe a 'low pay, no pay' cycle between such jobs and worklessness among those on the margins of the labour market. Canada, Australia and New Zealand have been moving toward creating integrated child support systems that cross the work divide. Hence a parent can at least guarantee that child support payments are available even with uncertainty over other incomes. These payments are then means tested slowly (in Canada) or partially at lower incomes and partially at high incomes (in Australia).

I believe that we should view children as a lifecycle event that increases need relative to income. This should be reflected in the tax system, the same as a drop in income is within a tax year. In this event, the lower income leads to a lower tax assessment and, if income dips far enough, a tax rebate. This lifetime perspective implies that having children entitles you to lower net tax contributions and, if income is low enough, net payments to the family. There are also very good reasons to make sure payments for child support go to the primary carer, which is normally (but not necessarily) the mother. This is because more money going into the household doesn't always mean it reaches the children. Research suggests the principal carer is generally more concerned about child welfare.

As assessment of need is best thought of as a 'family need' that does not match the individualistic income tax system, payments should be made as a regular refund from the Inland Revenue to the family rather than through the PAYE tax system. Of course, Child Benefit is such a payment but it does not reflect the families' income. In my view the child support payments in the new Working Families Tax Credit and in out-of-work benefits should be integrated with the proposed Child Tax Credit to create such a system. As much as can be afforded should go through the dense area of the earnings distribution and be affluence tested for richer families rather than aggressively means tested for poorer ones. This reduces the poverty trap and should help generate widespread support for keeping payments generous. However, some portion would be means tested as with WFTC currently to keep costs manageable.

This new system of Integrated Child Credits could be the main vehicle for the vital task of direct alleviation. It would preserve the newly improved work incentives provided by WFTC and offer greater income security around the risky transitions into and out of work.

In addition, a child poverty reduction programme should tackle intergenerational transmission. This should focus on getting the education system to work harder as an egalitarian force. Equality of opportunity necessitates that schools with children from deprived backgrounds should get more resources. Measures such as smaller infant class sizes and financial incentives for good teachers to work in our inner city schools would help. The Sure Start and Educational Maintenance Allowance initiatives top and tail this process, making education fight inequality from the cradle through to age eighteen at least. In our poorer neighbourhoods these programmes should be extended and integrated. Work on reducing teenage birth rates and tackling the disadvantages faced by those who leave local authority care must be supported.

These major reforms take time and, of course, resources. If the kind of extra resources put behind this project so far continue to materialise then this children's crusade should be a far greater success than its historical forebear ⊙

Paul Gregg is a Senior Research Fellow at the Centre for Market and Public Organisation at the University of Bristol.

New Labour, work and the family

Communitarianisms in conflict?

Stephen Driver & Luke Martell

New Labour has put the family at the core of its notion of the 'strong community' – stable family life is seen as the basis of a more dutiful and cohesive society. At the same time, social inclusion is seen to come about through paid work. On the surface, there appears to be a tension between the two approaches. Does the government's emphasis on paid work devalue unpaid work, especially caring for children? Or does this combination of communitarian agendas mark out a Third Way on the family for New Labour? In this article, we argue that the government's family and welfare policies are a mixed bag. But we believe that current tensions are being overstated and critics fail to give sufficient weight to the complementary aspects of Labour's welfare and family reforms.

Post-Thatcherism, the Third Way and the family

New Labour is a post-Thatcherite enterprise - both a reaction against, and a consolidation of, Thatcherism. As such, the Labour government marks an important break with post-war social democracy.[1] It is in this post-Thatcherite critique of the 'old left' and the 'new right' that New Labour has attempted to construct a Third Way.

The key to New Labour's embrace of family values lies in its dual critique of post-war social democracy and Thatcherite conservatism. Labour modernisers have cast the former as libertarians and social individualists whose neutrality on family forms had dire social consequences. The Thatcherites have been tarred as economic individualists whose only concern was the free market: an approach

1 Driver S and Martell L, 1998, *New Labour: Politics after Thatcherism*, Polity Press, Cambridge.

seen as destructive to community and families.

These caricatures distort the diversity and complexity of post-war politics. But they have served New Labour well. In particular, they have enabled Labour modernisers to construct a politics that prioritises responsibilities and obligations which individuals owe in the community. And the family, above all else, animates the notion of the dutiful community through parenthood. In policy terms, the family requires and underpins individual responsibility in the community.

Marriage, cohabitation, absent fathers, parenting and the like are now on the table and have explicitly become part of the government's agenda. By embracing the family – and by linking it with wider questions of 'welfare dependency' – New Labour has both reacted against Thatcherite individualism and taken on part of its conservative agenda. Its supposed advocacy of the 'traditional family' has brought accusations of 'prescriptive conservatism'. Others have criticised the government for not defining the traditional family enough.

New Labour's progressive and conservative agendas

Accusations of conservatism reflect partial truths. But they miss the mark. There are other more progressive agendas in play. New Labour's family policy is distinctive through its attempt to synthesise conservative and progressive agendas. This combination of agendas should not, as some critics argue, be thought of as incoherent, whatever tensions there may well be. It is this combination of agendas, pragmatically conceived, and not some grand transcendence of traditional political divides, that defines the Third Way.[2]

One progressive agenda focuses on women's growing independence and participation in the labour market. Alongside this, there is a more conservative agenda about the changing structure of the family, the growth of lone parenting and the perceived contribution this has to social problems such as crime and social exclusion. Rhetorically at least, this conservative agenda has received most attention. Tony Blair, Jack Straw and others are on record in favour of the married two parent family as the best environment to bring up children. There is generally the obligatory caveat that they don't want to knock lone parents but that two pairs of hands are better than one; that family income is usually higher; that children

2 2 Driver S and Martell L, [forthcoming], 'Left, Right and the Third Way', *Policy and Politics*.

respond better to having role models of both sexes; and that marriage is preferable to cohabitation, mostly because it involves more commitment. Without fathers boys are liable to turn out to be irresponsible themselves, more likely to commit crime and to father children in whose parenting they themselves will not participate.

At the level of rhetoric this conservative agenda has a symbolic significance. It sends a message that certain sorts of families are preferred and can demonise or demoralise others who feel alienated from, and unsupported by, the government. There is a cultural politics here, of validation and disapproval, with potential psychological, cultural and political effects. The Labour government's policies do often reflect this conservative rhetoric. A number involve advice and support to encourage and protect marriage as a preferred form of family relationship. The 1998 green paper *Supporting Families* proposes measures to improve couples' decision-making about getting married, and to enhance services that help prevent marriage breakdown. And while there are certainly also proposals to make divorce fairer and to support cohabiting couples, there is a definite emphasis on 'strengthening marriage', as the relevant chapter of the paper is titled.

For some, these plans amount to an attack on, and a discouragement to, full-time lone parenting. Such a view gained ground with the government's decision in 1997 to implement the previous Conservative government's reductions to lone parent benefits. Labour's argument that its welfare-to-work programme would cover lone parents was taken as further evidence that the government was putting undue pressure on lone parents to find work. While the New Deal for Lone Parents does not have the same elements of compulsion as other government New Deals, recent changes will expand the requirement to attend a job search interview to a wider range of people.

Yet against the charge of prescriptive conservatism it is important to acknowledge the progressive agendas in the government's family policy. *Supporting families* (note: families *not* the family) takes a largely pragmatic view on family forms: what works should be supported and in practice most families get by. Many of the government's proposals are about providing support in the form of finance, services and advice to families as they exist, whatever form they take –which should be judged on whether they actually work or not. The New

National Family and Parenting Institute, for instance, will provide services for all forms of family and parenting, as would the Sure Start programme, health visitors in a new expanded role and the childcare support under the new Family Tax Credit. Gordon Brown's budgets have not only marked a significant shift away from public policy support for married families with the abolition of the Married Couples Allowance, but Treasury policy has seen a shift in resources from childless families to families with dependent children. And there have been recent discussions in the Lord Chancellor's department about increased rights for cohabiting, including gay, couples.

None of this marks New Labour out as a government in the grip of an unyielding conservative agenda. Its more conservative agenda competes with, and is tempered by, progressive family policy that is interventionist but less prescriptive, more liberal and pluralist and that recognises the diversity of contemporary family forms.

This combination of agendas reflects wider debates *within* the Third Way about the characteristics of the contemporary social world and the kinds of social policy best suited to 'new times'. On one side are 'post-traditionalists', like Anthony Giddens, who argue that late modern society is marked by flux, diversity and change – and families need to be seen as changing with these times rather than as institutions counteracting them.[3] On the other side, we have the 'social moralists' – and Blair often appears rhetorically to fall into this camp – who place far greater emphasis on the family in its more traditional guise as providing the stability and moral glue in a modernising age.

Work and the family: communitarianisms in conflict?

Does this mixture of agendas create untenable conflicts and contradictions? Two communitarian approaches are clearly at work. The first focuses on excluded individuals, categorised as those unable to get access to the labour market. Paid work is the key to their inclusion. Welfare-to-work and the New Deal are key measures for achieving this. This is generally acknowledged to be the most significant discourse in Labour thinking and policy. Ruth Levitas calls it SID (a socially integrationist discourse).[4]

The second communitarianism is about shared community morality and adherence to the norms and roles of society. This is seen to come through strong families, which inculcate values, provide role models and supportive stable underpinnings for later life. All these

3 Giddens A, 1998, *The Third Way: The renewal of social democracy*, Polity Press, Cambridge; see also Wilkinson H, 1998, 'The Family Way: Navigating a third way in family policy', in Hargreaves I and Christie I, eds, *Tomorrow's Politics: The third way and beyond*, Demos, London.
4 4 Levitas R, 1998, *The Inclusive Society: Social exclusion and New Labour*, Macmillan, Basingstoke.

ensure conformity and community. Many social problems, irresponsible behaviour and lack of socialisation into shared values (teenage parenthood and so on) are blamed, at least in part, on lack of community integration through the family. The solution is strong families, preferably two parent families bound by marriage. This is part of what Ruth Levitas calls MUD (a moral underclass discourse).

Critics argue that the dominant communitarianism, which stresses paid work, appears, on the surface at least, to undermine the importance of the unpaid work that props up the modern family. The emphasis on the paid work devalues unpaid work and seeing paid work as the route to inclusion fails to provide routes for inclusion for unpaid parents and for carers. For Ruth Levitas:

> 'There is a profound contradiction between treating paid work as the defining factor in social inclusion, and recognising the value of unpaid work. How can Labour's claims to recognise the value of unpaid work be reconciled with their insistence on inclusion through paid work?'[5]

Childcare, flexible employment, working tax credits, benefit cuts and job advice requirements are geared to getting unpaid parents into the world of paid work, particularly lone mothers.[6] This does seem to devalue the importance of full-time parenting, and to prioritise paid work for them. For the critics, Labour must go one way or the other but cannot adhere to both the communitarianisms simultaneously. There are further tensions between Labour's calls for more responsiveness from employers to parenting needs, on one hand, and their emphasis in economic policy on more flexible labour markets, on the other. Proposals for parental leave could be a lot stronger.

The search for synergy

Nevertheless the picture is more rounded than some critics have painted. There may be more complementarities and opportunities. New Labour does value unpaid work but in terms that are not always economic and which focus on the inclusion of the child as much as the parent. The rhetoric values parenting and the family – as the basis for the development of moral values and responsibility, as a source of security and stability, and as a major contributor to children's opportunities in life.

5 See note 4, p145.
6 Although lone parents with very young children are not being pressured, nor are dependent spouses, and lone parents with older children are not being compelled into work.

Lack of economic opportunities and social exclusion are linked, by the government, to problems of parenting and family. Labour argues that family life is a key part of the explanation for why some people become part of an excluded underclass and for social problems: teenage parenthood and lone parenthood, crime, lower rates of educational attainment and irresponsible behaviour. But unpaid parenting, as such, is valued in non-economic terms to do with morality, responsibility, security and children's opportunities and inclusion. And it is valued for inclusion of the child as much as the parent.

Paid work can also enhance family life and have practical benefits for parenting. For some, full-time childcare, for all its joys, can also be tiring, boring and unfulfilling. The hours are long and demanding and can leave little space for the exercising of other capacities and needs, such as intellectual ones. As such, full-time childcare can make the parent less happy and fulfilled and, consequently, a worse parent. The opportunity to find periods away from childcare and develop other capacities can allow for better parenthood. Of course this is by no means the case for all parents, but it can be for many. In addition, paid work brings in money and can provide children with the role model of a parent with paid work status, both of which may be beneficial for the family and child. So paid work may not necessarily clash with unpaid parenting. In fact there are reasons to believe that it can enhance it, through providing resources, a working role model and a more rounded, happier parent.

Furthermore, if women are to be able to get into paid work with the help of increased childcare and flexible employment practices, then that is one more step towards men being able to play a greater parenting role. Increased male parenting is hardly a top priority for Labour. But there is a potential in Labour proposals for facilitating further male parenting. Certainly more progress towards this is needed. But if women partners find it easier to get into paid work because of training and advice, or childcare or tax credits, then that can give more of an opportunity for men to do less as a breadwinner and more as a caregiver. Of course, many may choose not to take it up. But policies to promote female employment at least provide a step towards it. More generally, flexible employment practices do not just make it easier for unpaid workers to get into paid work, as is often emphasised. They can also help men and women to play more of a parenting role, so benefiting unpaid parenting and the family.

Conclusion

New Labour's approach is a reaction to a number of factors: from social change in the family to perceived weaknesses in family policy, or lack of it, and to Thatcherism and social democracy. It is clear that the Labour government's policies on work and the family encompass a number of different ideological and policy agendas – traditional conservatism on the family, a desire to cut the welfare bill and welfare dependency, and a progressive view on women's employment opportunities, for example. These varying influences are evident in the diversity of ambitions of Labour's own proposals and in the two communitarian discourses which underpin their approach.

A key question remains unresolved. To what extent does Labour's emphasis on inclusion through paid work devalue family life and the committed parenting they wish to promote? There are tensions but we believe that these communitarianisms can co-exist. They need not undermine each other. In fact, they have the potential to be mutually supportive. The debate should keep a balanced sense of the possibilities and opportunities in finding a third way ⊙

Stephen Driver is a Senior Lecturer in Sociology and Social Policy at the Roehampton Institute London.

Luke Martell is a Senior Lecturer in Sociology at the University of Sussex. They are authors of New Labour: Politics after Thatcherism *(Polity Press).*

The sustainable family
Families, space and time

Ian Christie

The politics of *time* has been developing strongly over the past decade as changing work patterns and the stresses of a long hours culture have thrown up problems for families and organisations.[1] At the same time, a new politics of space has begun to make its way up the policy agenda, and is intimately related to the quality of family life, time and work. Our present working patterns and mobility have a major impact on family life and the environment – and if we want environmentally friendly families *we will need to fashion a far more family-friendly environment first.*

The politics of space

The new politics of space is, above all, about transport and housing. In both cases the rise of an affluent society has led to demands for access to space that cannot be met without serious clashes between *private wants* and *public goods*.

Firstly, take transport. The growth of car ownership and use has led to a big expansion in both road building and traffic congestion over recent years. The more cars we have, the more our lifestyles come to depend on them, and the more restricted and inefficient public transport becomes. The more we depend on cars, the more we want free access to the roads, but the more crowded the roads become.

The 1990s have seen us reach a crunch point. While many of us have come to depend on our cars, we also resist further road building because it is eroding our countryside and few remaining areas of urban tranquility. On the other hand, we also dislike the prospect of

1 Wilkinson H, 1997, *Time Out: The costs and benefits of paid parental leave*, Demos, London; *The Time Squeeze*, Demos Quarterly, issue 5, Demos, London.

new charges on car use to make us take public transport.[2] The need for serious action on greenhouse gas emissions and air pollution also means we *have* to find ways to curb car use.

Secondly, take housing. There has been a massive expansion of suburban and semi-rural living in recent decades, as households have moved away from cities. Increasingly, there is pressure on Green Belt areas in suburbs and the countryside, and fears of further 'sprawl' developments. Government forecasts suggest that some 4 million new households will need to be accommodated by 2016. The official policy is to house at least 60 per cent on brownfield (that is, already developed or vacant) sites in urban areas, and to avoid rural development on greenfield sites where possible. Although most people approve of this in theory, they also resist the idea that their neighbourhood could accept more house-building to meet the demand.[3]

Policy gridlock is upon us. In transport, people will not shift from their cars until public transport is improved, but government shows few signs of making the huge investments in transport services that might make a difference to car drivers at the margin. In housing, we know we need millions of new homes, but most people want to have them in the very suburban and rural areas where government and many local residents don't want them to go. *Public transport and urban living have to be made popular* if we are to resolve the current conundrum – albeit that this goes against the grain of economic and social change over the past half century.

Social exclusion is another key issue. Over the past few decades, 'aspirational' and affluent households have relied on private consumption and private space to deliver quality of life. Meanwhile, the excluded minority make do with ever scruffier, more harried and penny-pinched public services. Changes in work have reinforced these trends. As more employment has shifted to more highly qualified jobs, organisations have relocated to suburbs and rural areas or recruited from the aspirational and affluent ranks of people who live there.

These trends have a geographical dimension. The squeezing of the poorest households into communities that have few jobs, little mobility and low-quality personal and public spaces accompanies an expansion of private consumption by the affluent classes across space. Competition for 'positional' goods, such as nice homes in

2 See Christie I and Jarvis L, 'Rural spaces, urban jams', in Jowell R et al, eds, *British Social Attitudes 1999*, NCSR/Ashgate, Aldershot, 1999.
3 See note 2.

pleasant areas with good schools, and convenient access to roads and commuter services, pushes affluent and would-be affluent people ever further into suburbs and countryside, and increases the distances they travel.

Families, spatial sprawl and time squeeze

What does all this have to do with families? A great deal. It accounts for many of the problems of the 'time squeeze' on affluent households and increasingly on poorer ones too. Here are the connections.

- Cities suck in young single people and push out many affluent families, who choose suburban or country living.[4] They leave cities for homes with gardens, more space, less noise and pollution, less crime and better schools. This increases households' dependence on cars and commuting in areas that have less extensive public transport.

- Dislike of city life leads to more pressure for house building in suburbs and country areas. Most of this is for private ownership, reinforcing spatial sprawl of housing and putting more space between the affluent and the low income communities of cities. This heightens spatial social exclusion.

- Travel stress is the price paid by the affluent worker for spatial comfort. Longer commuting trips add to time squeezes and 'hurry sickness' for households.

- Those middle-class families remaining in cities often reject local schools as poor in quality and escort their children by car to 'good schools'. This reinforces the cultural divide, makes ownership of a second car more likely and intensifies the problems of 'sink' schools.[5]

- These trends create serious environmental problems. The 'school run' accounts for 20 per cent of rush hour traffic, and average journey length for school trips has risen steadily over the past two decades.[6] The school run exists because families imagine that there are growing risks to children's safety from traffic and strangers. The more we escort children by car, the more congestion and the more we feel the need to shield them from traffic; the school run also makes bus transport less effective. It is the perfect example of a self-reinforcing crisis – a mass of private choices causing a public problem.[7]

4 Champion T, 1997, 'The facts about the urban exodus', *Town and Country Planning*, March 1997.

5 The links between education and housing options in cities are the subject of a new research project by Comedia and Demos. This will look at how education and housing policy can be brought together to find ways to persuade more middle class families to stay in inner cities and to support local schools, and to improve the housing and school services for lower income households.

6 DETR, 1998, *A New Deal for Transport*, The Stationery Office, London.

7 Hillman M, ed,1993, *Children, Transport and the Quality of Life*, PSI, London; Hillman M, 1991, *One False Move: A study of children's independent mobility*, PSI, London.

- The school run, along with the contraction of child-friendly space (smaller gardens, the lack of green space on council estates, the scandalous sell-off of school playing fields), makes children less physically active. It reinforces car dependency, adds to the inaccurate perception that the street is a dangerous place and squeezes parents' available time. Remarkably, it can be shown to be one of the main factors leading women to take part-time jobs rather than full-time ones, and goes some way to explaining their continuing secondary role in paid work.[8]

- The absence of new social housing and the lack of a regional policy means that the economy of London and the South East is increasingly hostile to low income families, who face house price inflation and shortages of rented accommodation. This means that London's low-paid public service workers must look for homes outside the city, which increases their commuting time and costs. The time squeeze is thus being inflicted on low income workers too.

Car dependence and the problems of urban housing and education add to the core problem of finding time for ourselves as *family beings*. Such trends also reinforce social exclusion, segregating communities by income and mobility, and intensifying the disadvantages of low-income households. The time-squeezed affluent are anything but squeezed in their use of space; the 'time-rich' poor are *spatially hemmed in* to their 'excluded communities'; and low paid workers, living on the margins of the city economies and forced into commuting, are probably the most strained householders of all.

All these trends are potent sources of household stress. They must therefore play a part in promoting family *breakdown*, which has its own impact on the environment. A large proportion of the 4 million new households that we need to accommodate over the next generation will be divorced or separated adults, and lone elderly people who have lost a spouse and have family living far away. Family splits and the decline of the multi-generation household thus impose not only emotional and financial costs but spatial ones as well.

The limits of New Labour's approach
Given the direction of change over the past 50 years, any government wanting to deal with the politics of space faces a struggle so

8 Gershuny J, 1993, 'Escorting children: impact on parental lifestyle', Hillman, 1993 (note 7).

uphill that it is practically vertical. To reduce urban flight, policies must be designed with the needs of children and families in mind. It must make parents confident about entrusting children to public transport or walking to school. To reduce the number of new households, it needs to find ways to keep couples together and bring grandparents into family homes.

Government also needs to recognise that the supply of space for roads and suburban and rural housing is not indefinite. It will have to plan for a large-scale programme of *demand management* – actively seeking to change consumers' attitudes and behaviour for the public good.

On social exclusion and family life the government's spatial analysis and policy have been cogent, ambitious and more 'joined up' than ever. The New Deal for Communities and the action zones on health, education and employment reflect a determination to reconnect – spatially, culturally and economically – excluded neighbourhoods with the 'mainstream'.

The new politics of space – the impact of private choices on public goods such as the environment – must also be about managing and changing demand among the affluent and aspirational *majority*. Such an approach is a recipe for antagonising key voters, and risks accusations of nanny-statism, anti-car attitudes and social engineering. All these criticisms have been levelled at New Labour as it makes anxious steps into the minefield of environmental demand management.

The main policy statements so far are the Urban Task Force report on an 'urban renaissance' and the Integrated Transport Strategy.[9] The Urban Task Force study calls for a long-term programme of measures to make cities and large towns more attractive as places to live as well as work and play, and to make building on out-of-town greenfield sites more expensive. The transport strategy envisages new charges and other restraints on car use to encourage drivers on to public transport, which is to be improved through better regulation, more spending on services and better coordination between transport modes. The school run is to be discouraged by a mix of measures: better bus services, encouraging 'safe routes to school' projects and experiments with special pedestrian escorts for children.

The measures trailed in the Urban Task Force report and the transport white paper will make a difference if implemented and funded effectively. Making the inner cities more habitable for families of all

9 Urban Task Force, 1999, *Towards an Urban Renaissance*, DETR, London; DETR, 1998 (note 6).

classes is vital. The gradual improvement of public transport and safer routes to school will begin to make a difference to the school run. But there is little sign of the major investment in local bus and train services that will be transformative, nor of the congestion charging schemes that could help pay for it.

There are other limits to the government's vision. First, the settled preference of well-off and aspirational families for roomy homes in green, safe, tranquil areas where 'good schools' can be found is rock solid. Making the cities liveable for families as well as childless loft-dwellers and young in-comers means meeting families' key desires for quality of life – *good schools and a reassuring environment*. Second, the public transport system cannot be sufficiently mobile to reduce car use significantly. We need other approaches to reducing the time squeeze and the spatial sprawl.

Towards a family-friendly politics

Demand management needs to be based on carrots as well as sticks; and the carrots need to be offered before the sticks are wielded. We must provide people with attractive 'bridges' to more sustainable behaviour, not just make their quality of life worse while we try to find the money to improve the buses or build new homes in cities. There is no point in exhorting families to become more environmentally friendly unless the government first makes investments in rendering the environment more family friendly. Four areas stand out for possible policy innovations.

Transforming schools

The quality of education is central. If we want more mixed urban communities then we must put *much more investment into under-performing schools* so that middle-class families see them as a good choice for their children and so that low-income families have access to high-quality schools. Schools that integrate community functions– such as healthy living centres, cafés, sports facilities open to adults, adult education – can reduce travel times for parents and relieve time pressures. Using schools in this way improves the prospects of effective use of space and time for parents, children and other residents.[10]

To reinforce this, we need to ensure that new housing in cities makes effective links with educational services – dedicated public transport connections, well designed pedestrian and bicycle access

10 See Bentley T, 1998, *Learning Beyond the Classroom,* Routledge, London.

for children and adults, and proximity of homes to public services. This depends on far better connections being made between education and housing policy at central and local levels.[11]

An ecology of sharing

The problems of public space are related to the growth of private, individualised choices to consume alone rather than to share. This is most obvious in the use of cars rather than public transport, but it also is manifest in the growth of single-person households. It is time to realise that there are economies of scale and scope to be had from an ecology of sharing – something cities make possible and desirable to achieve equitable and sustainable use of resources.[12]

Encouraging new co-operative action by families and others is going to be an important source of innovation in the future. For example, car-pooling, car-sharing, parents' clubs for sharing the role of escorting children by foot or bicycle, and a revival of multi-generation homes (good for sharing childcare) all deserve *reward* via tax breaks or other incentives as a compensation for impending taxes on congestion and greenfield site development.

Family-friendly public space

If cities and big towns are to become attractive places for families to live then urban spaces have to become more secure, tranquil and reassuring for parents, children and elderly people. This does not simply mean tackling traffic. It means 'conspicuous care' – repopulating social housing estates, parks, high streets, public conveniences, public transport services and stations with trusted and visible police officers, attendants, wardens and the like.[13] This is both an investment in useful labour-intensive employment and a vital contribution to making people feel that their places are cared about and safe. It is also the reverse of the policy trends of the past two decades in the public sector.

The need for new New Towns as well as transformed inner cities

A programme of building high-quality social housing and private housing in the cities and large towns – preferably in mixed 'urban villages' with easy pedestrian and cycle access to schools and shops – is essential. But we have yet to have a meaningful debate about the 30 to 40 per cent of new housing that will not fit into the revitalised

11 Greenhalgh L, 1998, *Habitat, The Richness of Cities* working paper no 5, Comedia/Demos, London.
12 Levett R and Christie I, 1999, *Towards the ecopolis, The Richness of Cities* working paper no 12, Comedia/Demos, London.
13 Worpole K and Greenhalgh L, 1996, *The Freedom of the City*, Demos, London.

cities. Will it go into new suburbs or be tacked on to villages across the country? The scale of the need, the force of families' preference for suburban life and the focus of demand on the South-East suggests that we should think of *a new wave of New Towns*, centred perhaps on existing out-of-town retail centres or small towns and outer suburbs on rail commuter lines. Future New Towns could be built with *environmentally sustainable, family-friendly design of services* as a core principle, drawing on the many lessons of the past half-century of planning and development experience.

Future New Towns would cluster housing near multi-function school campuses and incorporate 'lifetime home design', allowing home space to be rearranged as families evolve;[14] they would be a twenty-first century version of the old ideal of 'garden cities', combining the best of the family-friendly suburbs and the density of services in the inner cities.[15] This strategy could be a powerful demonstration to the old cities of how to plan their spaces in the new century.

Conclusion

The time squeeze on families is directly linked to spatial sprawl and the collective effects of private lifestyle choices. Current policy proposals will have to go much further if we are to make families love the city and cut down on car use. If we want environmentally friendly families, we need to make our environment family-friendly first ⊙

Ian Christie is a Senior Associate of Demos and Comedia, and Associate Director of the Local Futures Group.

14 Brewerton J and Darton D, eds, 1997, *Designing Lifetime Homes*, Joseph Rowntree Foundation, York.
15 See Hall P and Ward C, 1998, *Sociable Cities*, Wiley, Chichester.

The new old age

Michael Young & Jean Stogdon

The main difference in being old is that we have a bit more leisure, which means a bit more choice about what we do with ourselves. We are no longer so subject to the tyrannies of the secular Protestant ethic that has dominated the twentieth century. We are given a precious last chance (if only we can avoid poverty) to cure ourselves of the pandemic hurry sickness before we subside into rest.

We even have a little time for an education wanted *not* because it will qualify us for a more monied and a more hectic life – almost alone, we can experience education for education's sake. This was the impetus behind the unsubsidised University of the Third Age[1] (U3A as it is generally called), which now has 393 local branches and 87,000 paid-up members, and the unsubsidised Open College of the Arts, which has brought almost all the arts within reach of people who love them. These same people often gave them up as teenagers in obedience to their elders who imagined themselves their betters and advised that they should prepare themselves for something well paid and more secure than the arts.

But life cannot be given over entirely to the delights of non-vocational education and to relief from the pressures of a competitive market for esteem. New pleasures are being combined with new duties, particularly because increasing numbers of grandparents are becoming even more involved with grandchildren than they were, and some are becoming active parents for a second time round.

The need is obvious. Marriage has become less popular, divorce more so. There are more single parents and, above all, more children

1 Started by Michael Young and his colleagues.

in distress because their parents have broken apart. Evidence is growing that, in these circumstances, grandparents are now doing what they did when parents were even more insecure in the course of evolution. Some geneticists consider that women, unlike men, have the menopause so that they can help in the survival of their descendants who are not their children but their grandchildren.

Evolving 'grandparenthood'

The most ample evidence for the growing modern practice comes not from Britain but, as so often when there is a new social trend, from the United States. There, the national census has been asking questions about grandparenthood since 1970, and a US Census Bureau special report was released in July 1999, when one of the authors (Jean Stogdon) was in Washington DC.

It showed that 4.7 million grandparents in the US live with their grandchildren, and this does not count millions more who are caring for grandchildren without actually living with them. Out of the 4.7 million, 3.7 million are raising them (as the American expression goes) in the grandparents' homes. One million others are living with their children partly because they want, and need, to play an active part in supporting their grandchildren. Climbing divorce rates, teenage pregnancies and drug use are cited as the main reasons for grandparents being in a role that, when they were themselves parents of young children, they would not have predicted for themselves.

As a result, in the past 30 years there has been a steady rise in the numbers of children who are living with their grandparents (see Figure 1).

Who are they? Two-thirds of grandparents living with their grandchildren are women. Grandparents with grandchildren in their homes are younger and healthier than grandparents who live in the

Figure 1. Number and percentage of children living with their grandparents, United States, 1970–97

Year	Numbers	Percentage of all children
1970	2.2 m	3.2%
1980	2.3 m	3.6%
1992	3.3 m	4.9%
1997	3.9 m	5.5%

Figure 2. Grandparent family types

Type of household	No of grandparents	Dominant racial group
Both grandparents, one or both parents	1,676,000	White (57%)
Both grandparents, no parents	824,000	White (63%)
Grandmother only, one or both parents	702,000	Black (45%)
Grandmother only, no parent	340,000	Black (54%)
Grandfather only	152,000	White (58%)

parents' homes. Grandparents with grandchildren in their homes are most often white, but single grandmothers who have grandchildren in their homes are most often black. The situation can be summed up as shown in Figure 2.

The three family types with incomes below the poverty level are single grandmother households with and without parents present and households with only the grandmother present.

Support for grandparents in the United States

The United States is fortunate to have a far more impressive array of support groups than Britain. There are between 600 and 700 active local grandparent groups which do all manner of things for their members, including representing them to the local authorities. In addition, there are strong grandparent lobbies at Washington and in individual states. The famous and politically powerful American Association of Retired Persons with more than 34 million members is taking an interest in its grandparent members, and more financial support is coming to those in poverty. The part played by grandparents is generally respected and acknowledged. They are seen as an indispensable resource for children who would otherwise be parentless. And acting as substitute parents is only the beginning of what they do.

Social workers in the USA also seem to have accepted the view (more than in Britain) that grandparents should be considered first (although they are of course not always suitable) as foster parents. The old myth – that if the parents have in some way failed it must be the fault of the grandparents in not bringing up their own children properly – has taken a long time a-dying in Britain, creating a sort of guilt by association that is quite unjustified.

For this reason, and no doubt also because of the strange neglect of the extended family over the whole of British social policy, many social workers have been unwilling to call on grandparents as foster parents, instead of giving them priority. In USA, kin placements are becoming increasingly common. In California and Illinois, for example, half of all children in foster care are placed with relatives. A recent report from the Child Welfare League of America, *Kinship Care: A natural bridge*, spells out the advantages for the children of being cared for by relatives (apart from avoiding the stigma of being a foster child):

- enabling children to live with persons whom they know and trust
- reducing the trauma children may experience when they are placed with persons who initially are unknown to them
- reinforcing children's sense of identity and self-esteem, which flows from knowing their family history and culture
- facilitating children's connections to their siblings
- encouraging families to consider and rely on their own family members as resources
- enhancing children's opportunities to stay connected to their own communities and promoting community responsibility for children and families, and
- strengthening the ability of families to give children the support they need.

British experience of grandparents as foster parents

There are British exceptions, of course. In Plymouth the city council social services department has taken an interest. David Pitcher, a social worker there, published a remarkable report in 1999 called *When Grandparents Care*. He interviewed grandparents whose their grandchildren had been placed with them when a case conference or court had found there was a risk of abuse if the child remained in the parental home.

It was not always easy going. The grandparents did not have as much energy for rough and tumble and dealing with schools as when they were younger. The grandchildren could be less respectful and want to buy more things, and drugs and violence in the streets were common concerns. Moreover, the child had no grandparent figure in reserve as they had before, and some of them worried about what would happen to them when the grandparent died.

But the comments were overwhelmingly favourable, around the theme of:

- '"Family is family", a tautology which is not at all one.'
- 'He's so lovely, the funny things he comes out with.'
- 'She can bring sunshine into the room.'
- 'They look a lot healthier and brighter, and they've put on weight.'
- 'He blossomed.'
- 'She's ours. She's part of us.'
- 'I've been blessed. Whatever price I've had to pay, it's been worth it.'
- 'It would be boring. I'd be sitting here twiddling my thumbs. They've kept me young.'
- 'We miss her even if she's out for a while.'
- 'It's when he says "I love you nanny" and throws his little arms around me.'

In Britain the first full study of grandparenting with a large representative sample has just been completed by Geoff Dench of the Institute of Community Studies in conjunction with the National Centre for Social Research. The study shows that the proportion of children living with grandparents is much lower in Britain than in United States. But in all sorts of other ways, British grandparents are doing a great deal for their grandchildren, especially when the parental family is, or has been, breaking up. Why are grandparents not paid something when they step in, sometime giving up work to make it possible, and why do they get nothing extra for grandchild care even when grandparents are on income support?

The extended family is making a comeback

What we are seeing is a revival in the importance of the extended family.[2] This is going on alongside a vital change in its structure. When the original Bethnal Green studies were done in the 1950s the extended family had a very large lateral extension Some people had many dozens of relatives living locally – married brothers and sisters

2 See also Wilkinson H, 1999, 'Celebrate the new family', *New Statesman*, 9 August.

and their nephews and nieces and all the in-laws. Children were surrounded by aunts and uncles and cousins of different degrees.

As fertility has continued to fall, and families have become smaller, the lateral has begun to give way to the vertical. More people live longer. There are more grandparents and more great-grandparents. The uncles and aunts have to some extent been replaced by the grandparents and when there are step-children, the numbers of grandparents a child possesses can be more than four. A new cross-generational extended family is coming into existence, as the vertical replaces the lateral.

This new kind of caring family has profound consequences for society in the next century. It looks as though alongside the more traditional family there will be growing numbers of grandparent–grandchild families which take over from the parents who are bearers of the children.

More parent–grandparent agreements will be made individually wherever they are both willing. Both parents will work and have freedom while they are relatively young and not take on parental responsibilities until the children who have been brought up by their grandparents have children themselves. Unfortunately, state policy in Britain lags well behind fundamental social changes of this kind.

But government can and should do more to facilitate and support the involvement of grandparents in family life. The Children Act of 1989 recognised that grandparents are 'family'. As a result, some children, who would otherwise be put in care or placed with foster-parents who are not relatives or already known to the children, have been put with grandparents as foster-parents. But the policy is patchy and many social workers are still suspicious of grandparents' parenting skills. This is really nonsense – with this issue the whole official policy needs recasting.

A good deal has at least been done to provide finance for childcare for working parents. But although grandparents often provide childcare their working sons and daughters, they cannot receive any allowance for all their work when they as grandparents are on income support. There are many ridiculous anomalies: why should grandparents be unable to get help with travel expenses to visit children in prison when a host of other relatives are eligible?

But the most important point to make about policy is about proximity. Grandparents cannot support parents effectively unless they live near each other. Housing policy has divided families, millions of them since the war, so that sons and daughters are rehoused all over the place without any consideration for kinship links. If some of the discrimination against grandparents were removed that would be the beginning of a family friendly government policy ⊙

Michael Young (Lord Young of Dartington) is a sociologist and the author, with Peter Willmott, of Family and Kinship in East London *and* The Rise of the Meritocracy.

Jean Stogdon is a former Manager in Camden Social Services, who is presently a Guardian Ad Litem, an independent childcare agent appointed in public law cases to give an assessment of a child's best interest.

Family and work balance

Who's responsible anyway?

Linda Tarr-Whelan

The political debate in the United States on the balance of family and work is finally shifting, with women in business and politics providing new leadership and energy. There is much at stake. More than one-third of American women workers identify the balancing act of reconciling workplace and home priorities as the key problem concerning work.[1] Today, women-led solutions are focused on economics, not 'women's issues'. No longer an issue on the margins, solving the problem of the family and work balance is in the mainstream. Family-friendly corporations are highlighted by the White House and appear on the front cover of *Business Week*, not simply in the columns of *Working Mother*.

The power of women's leadership

Women leaders, drawing on their own experience in balancing, have framed this set of problems in an inter-generational context. Family and work are the 'yin and yang' of women's lives. The economic and social consequences for working families and for communities are remarkably similar, regardless whether it is elderly persons or school-age children who need care. No longer can we assume that combining family and work is only a real issue for mothers of young children. Failing to create effective family support systems places workers and their families across the board at risk. That will dampen productivity for women and men who are torn between their roles as workers and family members – an unnecessary drag on economic vitality.

[1] Center for Policy Alternatives, 1996, *Women's Voices Poll*, CPA, Washington DC.

In April, 1997 100 women leaders gathered from all sectors for the White House Women's Economic Summit co-sponsored by the Center for Policy Alternatives (CPA) and chaired by First Lady Hillary Clinton. At the summit, they launched a women-led economic agenda that invests in women, families and communities. CPA's Blueprint for Action, since ratified in state capitols across the country, makes its case clearly. As we enter the twenty-first century, it is economically feasible and politically smart to invest in an infrastructure for family support. It is high time to remove the obstacles that prevent women and men from becoming fully engaged in the economy and the family.

The American ethic says that everyone works. With a long economic boom and welfare reform it is increasingly true that all parents work. In fact, according to the 1997 National Study of the Changing Workforce by the Families and Work Institute, 85 per cent of US wage and salaried workers live with family members and have day-to-day family responsibilities. Among married full-time employees, 75 per cent have partners who also work full-time. Almost half of all workers (46 per cent) are parents of children under eighteen.[2] In 1996, the National Alliance for Caregiving identified the typical caregiver of an elderly person as a 46 year old woman who works full time and spends eighteen hours per week caring for a family member.[3] It is not an either/or proposition: many Americans now work and care for families at both ends of the age spectrum.

Slow, slow progress

Progress has been painfully slow. I know this well. Thirty years ago my children were small, and I worked full-time as a nurse. Childcare was scarce and quality was a problem. Childcare workers earned poverty wages. After-school care was considered to be a frill. Elderly care was virtually non-existent. Flexible hours were not even on the horizon. Now, a generation later, our grandchildren are small, and our daughter faces all too many of the same hurdles.

In 1969, 38 per cent of married mothers worked for pay: in 1999, it was 68 per cent.[4] Over the same period, the number of women in the US workforce has more than doubled from 27,711,000 to 58,320,000.[5] Thirty years ago, women-owned businesses were both insignificant and invisible. Today, they are the fastest growing sector in each of the 50 states and contribute one-fifth of state business revenues.[6]

2 Bond JT, Galinsky E and Swanberg JE 1998, *The 1997 National Study of the Changing Workforce*, Families and Work Institute, New York.
3 National Alliance for Caregiving/American Association of Retired Persons, 1996, *Family Caregiving in the US: Findings from a National Survey*, NAC/AARP, Bethesda, Maryland.
4 US Council of Economic Advisors, 1999, *Families and the Labor Market, 1969-1999: Analyzing the 'Time Crunch'*, USCEA, Washington DC.
5 Figures from US Department of Labor, Bureau of Labor Statistics, 1999.
6 National Foundation for Women Business Owners, 1997, *Women-Owned Firms Increase in 50 Metro Areas*, NFWBO, Washington DC.

Then there was no discussion about family and work. The operative theory underpinning social policy was simple: men worked, and women raised families. Women, it was said, 'chose to work' or 'worked for pocket money'. While this was never the case for millions of women, it became the rationale for placing family life wholly in the realm of personal responsibility. In sum, for working women, the message from society at large was: 'Your children, your problem'.

Female entrepreneurs

Three decades later the atmosphere is finally changing. New policies are emerging. Women are transforming the workplace with their values, dynamism and economic clout. In the United States, women now account for 46 per cent of the workforce. Perhaps even more importantly, women entrepreneurs now own 36 per cent of all American businesses and, with women starting businesses at a much faster rate than men, that number is expected to exceed 50 per cent early in the new century. Women-owned enterprises employ one in four American workers, and these businesses are more likely to offer higher wages and benefits such as flexitime.[7]

As women's contributions to the economy have grown, more and more families have faced the challenges of balancing family and work. The 14 million households headed by women – with generally one-third of them in poverty – have had a particularly difficult time.[8] They were little helped by the marginalisation of the problem as a 'women's issue'. That line began to lose influence when a public furore broke out over the possibility of creating a 'mommy track' as a solution. Public debate began to move beyond the simple allocation of personal responsibility and began to focus on the benevolent employer or strong union model characterised by 'your children, your employer/union helping you'. Next we moved to a more inclusive way of encapsulating the issues: 'Your family, but it is your employers' problem, too'. Here the new subtext to the debate was that progressive family and work policies could boost productivity and profits.

Now, American women leaders, and some key male opinion formers, including President Clinton, argue for shared personal, public and private sector responsibility. Family care initiatives are essential ingredients for economic growth and the well-being of children, families and communities. The shorthand slogan of 'our fami-

7 National Foundation for Women Business Owners, 1999, *Key Facts About Women-Owned Businesses*, NFWBO, Washington DC.
8 Figures from US Department of Labor, Women's Bureau, September 1996.

lies, our economic future' brings in its train complex policy goals in terms of time and stress; healthier children, more independent elderly, increased worker productivity and decreased turnover, better bottom-lines and increased family security.

It has been a long journey in a society where messages about 'caring and compassion' are most likely to remain political rhetoric. We still have a long way to go. In the meantime, many families face a tightening 'time squeeze' and limited options.

Time is becoming as important as money

The 'time squeeze' or 'time crunch' is a pressing reality. We're long overdue for a correction. A recent study by the Council of Economic Advisors shows that American parents have 22 fewer hours per week to spend at home than they did in 1969, creating a 'parenting deficit'.[9] Societal changes are required to rebalance the scales in relation to caring and working for women and men.

The United Nations Development Programme reported in 1995 that women do two-thirds of all of the work of the world when both paid and unpaid work are calculated.[10] But women can't do it all. According to a series of recent polls, women's stress levels continue to increase dramatically.[11] More to do, less time to do it in; more time to commute and work, less time at home – these are the predisposing factors for major stress in families in affluent economies.

Family demographic trends add new and additional pressures. Single-parent families, usually headed by mothers, face tremendous odds in terms of both pay and time. A few years ago the emphasis was on the baby boomers becoming the 'sandwich generation' – working families caught between the needs of their children and parents. Increasingly, we are talking about four-generation families; the 'whopper generation' is providing care for their parents, children and grandchildren. We must now ask questions about how to close the caring and parenting gap while working the fast-paced 'flexible' whirl that US firms are promoting as the new work standard.

There are some hopeful signs that men are moving towards 'sharing the caring'. Survey research and a quick look at who is picking up the children after school shows that younger generations of American men are increasingly engaged in caring for both the young and the old. Forty-two per cent of men request family and medical leave, usually for the care of ill parents or for paternity leave.[12]

9 See note 4.
10 United Nations Development Programme, 1995, *World Economic and Social Survey*, UNDP, New York.
11 *Roper Reports Worldwide: Global Consumers 2000 Study*, 1999.
12 National Partnership for Women and Families, 1996, *A Workable Balance: Report to Congress on family and medical leave policies*, NPWF, Washington DC.

This popular US policy provides twelve weeks of unpaid leave to women or men to care for newborns, newly adopted children and to deal with health emergencies for spouses, parents and children. Groups are now campaigning to expand the programme to small employers and for family and medical leave to be paid by insurance tied to workers compensation or unemployment compensation programmes.

Commuting time adds to long working hours. The *Washington Post* recently ran a front-page story on families in the outer suburbs of Washington who rise every day at 4 am to get children to daycare and still arrive at work at 8 or 9 am. Single mothers moving from welfare to work were shown as they made use of three buses on the way to work and again at night to bring their children to childcare. Flexible working hours may be seen as one answer to the stress but such approaches are moving only gradually into the workplace. In 1997, 28 per cent of a full-time wage and salaried workers had flexible work schedules, up from 15 per cent in 1991.[13]

Women's leadership makes a difference

Women leaders in large corporations, in their own businesses, in unions, at the grassroots and in the public sphere are moving family and work balance to the top of the economic policy agenda. Several examples are from the state level, the center for innovative policy action. Here are some vignettes to illustrate the difference that a critical mass of women leaders can make.

In 1999 Maine Senator Susan Longley, and her women colleagues who make up 27 per cent of the state legislature and chair many of the key committees, led the passage of a massive public-private child-care programme in Maine as a central economic development initiative. Maine is a conservative state and previous efforts to expand childcare were often seen as 'too liberal'. Conservative legislators and the Maine Chamber and Business Alliance joined enthusiastically in this new approach. Senator Longley set the tone: 'Childcare is the third largest industry in our state and we haven't been treating it like a business. It's hugely important, both for the child and family and for the development of the state'.[14]

Under the sponsorship of the Center for Policy Alternatives, a bipartisan group of 32 state legislators from nine Western states (all but one of them women) met in June 1999 in Seattle, Washington. The

13 See note 4.
14 Wall Street Journal.

states they represent have a patchwork quilt of pilots, models and demonstrations – but few systems for family care. Their states mirror the US economy with a large and increasing proportion of workers employed in small business. The women now taking their place as legislative leaders will increase their state' competitiveness by creating community infrastructure investments for family care by implementing a multi-state simultaneous legislative strategy. The Western states have the highest percentage of women in the legislatures; women there hold an average of 30 per cent of all seats as contrasted with the US Congress where women are 12 per cent of the members.[15]

Women in senior corporate positions are changing the landscape too. The Families and Work Institute's Business Work–Life Study of 1998 looked at businesses with more than 100 employees. They found that firms where women held one-half or more of the top executive positions (only 20 per cent of the firms) family and work policies were vastly improved. For example, 82 per cent of such companies provide flex-time compared to 56 per cent of companies with no women in top management (30 per cent of the firms). There were similar differences for on-site or near-site childcare, dependent-care assistance plans and elderly care resource and referral programmes.

What needs to be done?

There is much to be done to create seamless family care supports. Preschool childcare is expensive: between the ages of three and five, childcare is the greatest expense after housing and food.[16] And it is not of good quality; nor are there enough facilities. Six out of seven childcare centres provide a service that is rated as mediocre to poor.[17] Childcare workers in the US make an average of $10,000 a year, almost one-third less than the poverty threshold for 1998, compounding the quality problem in a dynamic economy.[18]

Caring for school-age children is an equally large problem. Only North Carolina, Maryland, New Mexico and Nevada have extended day programmes in schools for 40 per cent or more of the children.[19] The demand for childcare will continue to be strong: almost two-thirds of women with children under six are in paid work and more than three-quarters of women with children aged between six and seventeen are in the workforce.[20]

Elderly care is an emerging public priority. An Alzheimer's Association study in 1996 showed that informal women caregivers

15 Center for Policy Alternatives, 1999, *Balancing Family and Work: Facts about Working Families*, CPA, Washington DC.
16 US Census Bureau, *Statistical Abstracts*, Table 711, 1997.
17 Children's Defense Fund, 1998, *Children in the States*, CDF, Washington DC.
18 See note 15.
19 See note 17.
20 AFL-CIO, 1999, *Bargaining for Child Care*, AFL-CIO, Washington DC.

are providing $130 billion of the $194 billion of unpaid care that elderly citizens need – often, at great personal and emotional cost. Two-thirds of these caregivers are employed.[21] In 1996, more than 7.1 million elderly who are disabled needed care.[22] The demographic trends are clear: the need will continue to grow. The hidden costs to business are mounting. MetLife in 1997 estimated that costs for absenteeism, lateness and lost productivity for workers who are also caring for elderly family members could be as much as $29 billion annually.[23]

Flexible working arrangements and hours – including telecommuting and flextime – still apply to only a handful of workers. Paid family and medical leave is still a dream. The current unpaid family leave is mandatory only for employees of firms with more than 50 employees.

What does the future offer? These messages stand out when we consider the potential benefits of changing the work–home balance:

- Sharing the challenges and joys of raising children is as important for men as it is for women. New neurological research makes it clear that the period of birth to three years of age is a critical formative period and high-quality loving care is essential. Caring for family members across the full lifespan is a mark of our humanity. Valuing the paid and unpaid work of caregiving is central. Giving care is valuable to the individuals who need it, to those who give it and to society as a whole.

- We must have *shared solutions* – personal, public and private sector responsibility – to rebalance family and work. As long as this balance is posed as a 'women's issue' we cannot be victorious. Women leaders — from corporate boardrooms, grassroots groups and floors of legislatures – will provide the answers and forge the policies. Women's political and economic muscle will move the debate. But in the end, it is the family and economic issues that will catch the support of the public and politicians. It is time to invest in a better balance for family and work balance. Who's responsible? We all are ☉

Ambassador Linda Tarr-Whelan is the President and CEO of the Center for Policy Alternatives, a 24-year-old progressive policy and leadership center located in Washington DC. She also serves as the US Representative to the United Nations Commission on the Status of Women.

21 See note 20.
22 Urban Institute, 1999, *Confronting the Challenges Presented by an Aging Population*, Urban Institute, Washington DC.
23 Metropolitan Life Insurance Company, 1997, *The Metlife Study of Employer Costs for Working Caregivers*, Metropolitan Life, New York.

From work ethic to ethical work

Ed Mayo

As organisations in society and the economy adapt to technological innovation and economic change, the market economy impinges more than ever on family life. Jobs are less predictable. Hours spent at work are reaching new peaks. Four in ten people take no real holiday at all. 'Kitchen table' firms are the fastest growing source of new jobs in the UK economy, according to the New Economics Foundation's recent report on micro-enterprise.

Are these simply new opportunities and new freedoms, around which we will choose new patterns of family and community? Or is it a conceit of free market economics that money could ever triumph over life? Should we rein in market forces or harness new approaches to rebuild and strengthen family and community in the new context?

The need for a new economics

The historic settlement between paid and unpaid work is unravelling. The truth is that it has always been possible to make economic growth and profits look good by eroding family life to promote market activity and by marginalising and disenfranchising those involved in the bulk of care. However, the extension of markets into all aspects of our lives has now corroded society's systems of care, nurturing and reproduction beyond critical thresholds.

It is time to challenge this thinking. An economics as if family mattered would expose it as a pathological value system, generating a wide range of social costs and risks that eventually come home to roost. This means pointing to the growth of 'defensive expenditures' in society, such as the £9 billion spent on criminal justice, consequent on the erosion of family life. Chilean economist Manfred Max Neef argues that industrialised countries have now passed the threshold beyond which defensive expenditures outstrip national income growth. This suggests that the 'reproductivity gap' for these countries is now greater than any productivity gap.

An economics as if family mattered also means presenting households in their true position as a source of wealth rather than a cost to business or government. For example, while methods vary, a wide variety of research presents a consistent picture that household production is a highly significant component of economic production. An illustration is the Index of Sustainable Economic Welfare, which we have helped to develop at the New Economics Foundation. This includes an estimate of the value of household labour as a contribution to economic welfare. International comparisons across the richest (G8) countries demonstrate that this has risen by half over the last twenty years. The sector is worth 22.75 per cent of G8 GDP, in comparison to 3.3 per cent for agriculture, 33.1 per cent for industry and 63.6 per cent for services.

Despite the increasing rigour of this kind of socio-economic analysis, statistics themselves do not make change. For example, the long-standing call for the appropriate valuation of all women's labour is now generating a deluge of time use surveys. But there remains a resistance to include informal household labour within core accounts. The authors of the UN System of National Accounts excuse this by stating that 'the location of the production boundary is a compromise but a deliberate one that takes account of most users.' Of course, as Marilyn Waring, author of *If Women Counted*, points out, it is hard to be a user of statistics if you are treated as invisible.[1]

If the first steps in building visibility for unpaid work are slow to come, the reason must be a question of power. Unpaid work underpins society. Ivan Illich pointed out that 'shadow work feeds the formal economy. Its unpaid performance is the condition for wages to be paid.' Balancing market and non-market life therefore requires us to rethink at a more fundamental level what we value in terms of work and why. It requires us to replace a work ethic with a sense of ethical work.

1 Waring M, 1989, *If Women Counted*, Macmillan, London.

Redefining work

Work is something of use or value to the person who does it, or for whom it is done. Many of the most important and fulfilling parts of our lives – such as caring, favours and parenting – fit within this description but are not predominantly organised as employment.

It is relatively easy to categorise family activities. These include childbearing and rearing responsibilities or the care and maintenance of others, including those in employment. You can call it work, but it is fun or fulfilling for many. When people are motivated by a need that inspires care, whether unpaid or paid work such as teaching or nursing, there can be a richness in the motivation – in effect, real wealth – because it is needs driven and sustaining of people and society.

This is ethical work. Fritjof Capra claims 'we can't be empowered by work that destroys the environment around us or creates systems of inequality. No matter how our work is organised, it cannot fully empower us unless we believe in its purpose.'[2] This would include both paid and unpaid forms of work, because the reality is far more complex than a simple division between paid and unpaid work.

In paid work, people are being rewarded in terms of money and status when they are often behaving very destructively. At the same time, those involved in unpaid work, whether care, parenting or volunteering, suffer low status, poor conditions and on many indicators face increasing stress and personal costs. The burden of this work continues to fall disproportionately on women whether or not they are in the labour market as well.

The labour market itself continues to discriminate against the time, skills and competencies involved in different forms of unpaid work. The lack of pay does matter. The financial opportunity costs of unpaid work generates tomorrow's social exclusion, as those involved lack the opportunity to build the assets and savings required for pensions or dealing with crises. While unpaid work can be a good way of getting by, new research from the Joseph Rowntree Foundation shows that, contrary to common perception, self-help is more open to the middle classes than unemployed households.[3]

The Protestant work ethic, beloved of New Labour, does not distinguish between meaningless or fulfilling work. A hallmark of modern economic development has been that it brings into markets work that used to be unpaid, along with assigning a low status to work

2 New Economics Foundation, 2000, *Brave New Economy* (CD-Rom), NEF, London. **3** Williams C and Windebank J, 1999, *A Helping Hand: Harnessing self-help to combat social exclusion*, Joseph Rowntree Foundation, York.

with no monetary return. In this process, unpaid work is not simply a residual, if significant activity, it is systematically devalued culturally and economically. The enclosure of work as employment means that the labour market exclusively defines how we organise and validate work within society (where those out of employment are dismissed as economically inactive). The results are all around us. We have two twin evils: mass unemployment on the one hand and a large amount of socially useful work in families and societies remaining undone on the other. It is hard to imagine a worse outcome.

Time economics – a new currency

A new agenda has to move us beyond the either/or of market and family, paid and unpaid work. A number of the building blocks are already in place. In research terms, there is an increasing rigour to quantitative analysis outside of the traditional domains of orthodox economics. There is also growing work to understand and model interactions between households and markets. A new generation of researchers will emerge for whom gender blind analysis is not simply bad research but unethical practice.

An example of one such tool is the social audit, an international approach that the New Economics Foundation has pioneered over recent years with ethical businesses. Social audit offers a method to account for and report on the social and ethical performance of an organisation.

In policy terms, we require a spectrum of policy support and recognition for different forms of work, from paid to unpaid. After all, paid work doesn't just happen. There are a wide range of rules and institutions that support the labour market: training, legal forms for business and employment, job agencies and other means of matching supply and demand, systems of reward, business support. In each case, we will need the same type of innovation to support unpaid work.

In the area of consumption, for example, there are huge opportunities for efficiency gains. British households hold opportunities for consumption on stock, whether cars or lawnmowers, that would keep villages in poor countries going for a year. The efficiency revolution here is driven by experiments such as co-housing and community composting, part of a growing new economy at community level.

Another example, pioneered by Dr Edgar Cahn in the United States and being developed by the New Economics Foundation, is time money. This is an alternative currency that credits the time people spend helping each other. While LETS focus on exchange, time money promotes gift relationships.

In the Peckham Hour Bank, for example, this means that participants earn credits for doing jobs – an hour of your time entitles you to an hour of someone else's time. Credits are deposited centrally in a bank and withdrawn when the participants need help themselves. The Health Centre in Rushey Green is using time money to galvanise patient self-help and support groups. In Watford, older people are revitalising local services like waste recycling, local transport and homework clubs for children using money to unlock time, knowledge and expertise.

Time money is therefore a hugely powerful potential approach to organising and promoting non-market activity. One way the government could support such an approach is to confirm that involvement in such emerging initiatives would be tax exempt, subject to suitable conditions. But a more proactive policy toolkit for time money would see government taking a more pump-priming role in supporting non-market activity through time money.

Time money illustrates the new work–life agenda because it recognises that unpaid work is based on reciprocity, as has been the case in most cultures over time. While still little more than a pioneering set of pilots into new models of work, it demonstrates that it is possible to innovate and develop new structured ways of developing self-esteem, access to goods, services and information, skills development or personal fulfilment in return for unpaid labour.

Another active area is education and support for parents, driven by thousands of grassroots initiatives and increasingly supported by government. Parent Link is a course run by and for parents through the Parent Network. The Family Caring Trust materials are also widely used by voluntary groups. The Parenting Forum has a database of organisations running support programmes in England and Wales. Children in Scotland has a similar role north of the border. Other forms of support for family learning include children's museums, libraries and out-of-school activities.

However, in community action and the 'devolution' of government responsibilities to the community there is often an unspoken assumption that there are under-employed people sitting around with time on their hands ready to take over. Such an approach does not begin to address the reproductive tax that women bear.

Therefore, real money has to play a role too. For some forms of unpaid work, such as caring and volunteering, one approach would be to pilot an extension of the working families tax credit to cover a wider set of people. This is what Colin Williams and Jan Windebank of the University of Leeds describe as an 'active citizens credit'.[4]

After all, if parents or grandparents on benefits who look after children could choose an hourly rate of payment to be imputed to them when considering their potential for other jobs, it would soon become apparent whether it was worthwhile to continue to penalise in relative terms those who do not choose employment.

On the paid side of the spectrum of work which links closely to family life, business support programmes too should better serve micro-enterprises. Two-thirds of businesses in the UK have no employees. Of these only around 5 per cent are 'growth' firms typically targeted by governments for support. Even the renowned programme of long-term bank finance for the Mittelstand in Germany systematically excludes and marginalises micro-entrepreneurs.

The goal of ethical work

A host of creative, pragmatic initiatives could be taken to orientate existing institutions to promote unpaid work in family and community. After a period of experimentation, we will know more of the scale of the challenge implicit in creating a new social settlement around unpaid work across gender, age and class.

For example, we are learning from a decade or more mainstream 'work–life' business policies. There have been significant steps forward, including the widening of best practice to include non-traditional families. But the greatest predictor of whether companies in the United States take up family friendly policies, for example, remains whether they have recently downsized. We still have a long way to go before business leaders and markets embrace the idea that there is more to life than 'busyness'.

Over time, we will need to redraw the systems and principles of taxation and welfare in order to reflect the work–life agenda, as well as other changes required for quality of life and sustainability. High on my list would be an insertion or citizen's income that could

4 See note 3.

develop out of the current interest in tax credits and the proposal for an active citizens credit.

This would replace all existing benefits and tax allowances. It would be a tax-free income paid by the state to every man, woman and child as a right of citizenship. It would be age-related, with more for elderly people and more for adults than for children. This would replace child benefit and pensions. There would be supplements for disability, housing need and other exceptional circumstances. This would provide insurance for all so that if they engage in unpaid work, they would have a basis on which to live. It would offer a more autonomous base for families in the face of economic change and insecurity.

But a citizens' income of £77 per week for pensioners, £55 per week for adults and £15 per week for children would cost £108 billion. While it would also allow administrative savings in government, a citizen's income is usually perceived to be off the political agenda as it would cost too much.

There is no doubt that it could not be financed through income tax, but would require funding through new taxes such as energy or land-rent taxation. A package such as this has been developed by James Robertson for the New Economics Foundation as a vision of a long-term programme of benefits and taxes reform.

There is plenty of scope in this field for creative policy and practical innovation that can support family life and build a better balance between non-market and market life to the benefit of both. If done correctly, these are likely to be progressive in terms of class and gender. But creative initiatives should not substitute for a deeper public debate about the political issues that underpin any system of work in terms of who gets power, status and reward for what. The time is ripe for a new economics and revaluation of the family too ☉

Ed Mayo is Director of the New Economics Foundation (NEF), an independent think tank working through practical innovation and policy development for a just, sustainable and human-scale economy.

An equal marriage?

The new partnership between parents and the state

Maureen Freely

According to Aristotle, the relationships between man and wife, and children and fathers are

> 'part of a household, and every household is part of a state; and the virtue of the part ought to be examined in relation to the virtue of the whole. This means that both women and children must be educated with an eye to the constitution – at least if it is true that it makes a difference to the soundness of a state that its children should be sound, and its women too. And it must make a difference; for women make up half the adult free population, and from children come those who will participate in the constitution.'[1]

Aristotle wrote those words three centuries ago. Nevertheless, we can still look at his writings on the proper management of households and see current debates on the family foreshadowed. Children learn how to be citizens in households. The state has a legitimate interest in the moral fibre of those who raise them. If children are not educated well, they will not be inculcated with the appropriate values, and when these morally defective children take over from their fathers, civilisation as we know it will founder.

All these themes are present in *Supporting Families*, the document that sets out New Labour thinking on the family. But that is not all there is. In significant ways, it represents a radical break with traditional family policy. New Labour uses the word 'parent' where

1 Aristotle, *The Politics*, edition published in 1981 by Penguin, Harmondsworth.

Aristotle would have used wife, mother or woman. And while the government still sees the family as the building block of society and the place where children receive their early moral education, it does not see it as a separate realm in which stay-at-home wives and mothers live out their lives as dependents of male breadwinners. In the world foreseen by this document, parents balance unpaid work at home as well as paid work outside. In principle, all parents are equals.

All parents are doing a difficult job: this is another new theme. The traditional view of childcare was that it was not a job at all. Today's family policies define childcare not just as a job, but as an economic issue. Government has a part to play in helping parents find good childcare, obtain work in flexible jobs, receive proper training and get extra help at times of crisis. The goal is to ensure that all children get the consistent, humane care they deserve.

In its effort to ensure that all children are receiving consistent, humane care, the document proposes a new definition of privacy. What adults do in the privacy of their own homes is their own business. But the way they raise their children has *public* consequences and concerns us all. Just as government has an obligation to parents, so parents also have an obligation to government. Government is offering a new contract: a partnership, in which parents and the state work together to create a new morality and a better, strong, more productive society.

This is an inspiring vision. Can it work? I believe that key issues need to be addressed before we know the answer. But first let me put my cards on the table. The new policies offer tremendous opportunities, for parents, their children, and for society. But they could also pose tremendous dangers.

New Labour, new morality?

Firstly, there is a danger that the new morality could become a more pernicious version of the old morality, in which parents continue as second class citizens, but without the protective shield of privacy.

Second, the terms in which the new morality is phrased are fuzzy, open to misinterpretation or even abuse. They need to be better defined and defended.

Third, the architects of the new family policies have yet to understand the enormity of the task they have undertaken. The neatness of the package suggests that some of them think that the problems of modern family life can be 'fixed'.

My own view is that the problems of modern family life cannot be fixed so long as we define them in the way we do today. We need a new framework for policy, in which the citizen-parent can actually operate. The new family policies need to be bold and to spell out a morality that is truly new.

Over the past year, Jack Straw and other members of the Ministerial Group on the Family have worked hard to bring middle England round to their new vision of the citizen-parent. More recently, Tony Blair gave the project a big push, and a great deal of publicity, by calling it a moral crusade. The word 'crusade' might be media-friendly, but it is also misleading. It implies moral truths to be imposed from above rather than generated by a national debate. In fact, the debate Blair and Straw have in mind is better described as a 'megalogue', which according to communitarian writer, Amitai Etzioni, is a moral dialogue involving an entire society during a time of transition.[2]

In Etzioni's view, politicians willing to engage with the big story of the moment can voice their concerns about what is going wrong with society, and express the core moral values that they support. Tony Blair, for example, used the uproar about the two pregnant twelve year olds to convey the same messages. First he asked why it was that our society had come to this, and then suggested that the way forward was for parents to work with government to create a society in which such tragedies did not happen.

If the nuances of his argument got lost, if most observers took his call for a moral regeneration as a threat of a crackdown, it is not his fault. But the problem with megalogues is that they are very hard to control and they do not lead inexorably to greater enlightenment. As such, they are not always moral-minded politicians' ally. They can inadvertently generate moral panic fuelled by the right wing press. Politicians who use tabloid scandals to promote the new morality run the risk of promoting the old morality by default.

Fuzzy thinking

There are other problems. Let's begin with the word 'parent'. The word sounds modern and gender-sensitive even though it has no gender at all. In the plural it implies not what mothers and fathers

2 Etzioni A, 1997, *The New Golden Rule: Community and morality in a democratic society*, Profile Books, London, pp106-110.

are in conflict about, but what they have in common. This is good, but it obscures the fact that mothers and fathers have *different* problems and interests, and these need to be acknowledged. For example, fathers have fewer rights than do mothers. Many have a hard time keeping contact with their children after separating from the mother. But many mothers suffer from violence at the hands of their partners and ex-partners. The only way to balance the rights of both parties is to be keenly aware of all the issues. This cannot happen if policies are always designed for 'parents' and never for 'mothers' and 'fathers'.

Supporting Families stresses the diversity of parents. We live in many types of families and come from many ethnic backgrounds. To use the word parent when describing this diverse group is to stress what parents from all backgrounds believe they have in common, and agree all parents must do. Certainly a new morality depends on such a consensus – but can we really say we have found it? It seems to me that we need a lot more debate before it is clear what all parents agree on, and where they agree to disagree. The consensus needs to rise out of this debate. It should not be assumed or imposed.

The word parent also implies a classless society in which all parents deserve and receive the same sort of support. This is a step in the right direction but, again, one step is not enough, because we do not live in a classless society. To be officially blind to class differences is to overlook the ways in which parents' needs can differ.

In reality, the new policies are far from blind to the needs and problems of parents from different backgrounds. Most policies are designed for under-privileged parents and parents with serious problems. These policies are generous, but also interventionist. The policies directed at functioning middle-class parents might be less generous, but they are also a good deal less heavy-handed. The danger is that there are two standards – one for the malfunctioning 'socially excluded' parent and another for the functioning middle-class parent.

Now we come to the word 'support'. The word implies wise, compassionate assistance. And this to a large degree is how it is interpreted by counsellors, educators, and public sector employees charged with implementation. In *Supporting Families*, the word support has a wide range of meanings. Parents can be supported with informal advice when they're having the first baby or with parenting orders after their teenager plays truant. They can be supported with financial assistance or with fines. No matter how much practitioners use funds to empower parents, the policies themselves as currently framed give parents more obligations than power.

All of which raises issues about the meaning of the word 'partnership'. If parents have little power and government has the right to intervene in family life with little accountability to parents, and with its own definition of what constitutes successful and 'problem' parenting, then this goes against an equal partnership. It raises questions about the government's new approach to family privacy. We might wonder when 'support' might become coercion. *Supporting Families* says that the state should only intervene in extreme circumstances, for example where the welfare of family members is at stake. But who decides what's normal and what's extreme?

Such definitions and policies need to be defined and developed not just by government, and experts, but by parents too. Parents need to play a part in forming the rules they are meant to live by, and shaping policies that define their lives.

Towards a new framework

In my view there's a simple reason why the new family policies slip back into the old conventions they are meant to replace. Citizen-parents are not given an equal role in this new partnership because, historically, people engaged in unpaid caring work have had no political role. Indeed, while new policies might depart from old thinking in significant ways, the concept of the family as the bedrock of society, the thing underneath that needs to be managed from above, remains unchallenged.

The weaknesses of this approach are self-evident. If you start from this vision of the family, even the most benevolent policies will be paternalistic in structure if not in spirit. They assume that parents are ill-equipped to run their own lives and need careful guidance and management. Government will see any resistance to policy from parents not as the sort of challenge that keeps a democracy democratic but as recalcitrance. They will rarely see parents as a source of creative energy or imagine policy from the parent's point of view.

But that's precisely what we need if we really want that new partnership and the new morality. We need a framework that starts from the parents' perspective – a framework that allows us to ask not just what parents need, but sees them as a source of ideas and creativity – and then builds on those strengths. What would the outcome look like? There can be no final answers without a well-ordered, democratic debate. But a good place to start would be to look at the smaller but innovative debates already taking place in the EU, in the UN and in academia on these issues.

Let's begin with the care theorists. They turn Aristotle on his head and tell the story from the point of view of the wife, the mother and the child. Carol Gilligan's 1982 classic, *In a Different Voice*, kick-started this debate. It challenged the dominant theory of moral development, in which boys were said to have a better understanding of the ethic of justice than girls. Gilligan argued that the girls' moral development proceeded along a different path because they began with a better understanding of what she called the 'ethic of care'. She then went on to suggest that a full account of moral development had to include both ethics, for both sexes.

Another key figure in the early debate was the political philosopher Jean Bethke Elshtain. She argued that the home was not necessarily a site of oppression, and that a world without a private domestic realm was likely to be a totalitarian one. Many of her peers denounced her as a maternal revivalist. They did the same when the philosopher Sara Ruddick suggest that mothering was not a biologically pre-programmed task performed by women, but a practice requiring intelligence and judgement.

These women's ideas challenge us to come up with a theory that puts 'women's work' in a larger context and allows us to look at the caring work that goes on in society, and fully explain the ways in which societies depend on it. Jean Tronto, the political philosopher, defines care as including not just traditional unpaid women's work, but also the work done by nurses, domestic servants, childcare workers, office cleaners, cooks, rubbish collectors, famine relief workers, environmentalists and the like.[3] She argues that we need a working definition of care so that we can 'use this concept to review our own daily activities and notice that care consumes a large part of our daily lives.'[4]

Tronto also argues that the present assumption that 'all men are created equal' only works well for rich, healthy, and autonomous adults, and works against the interests of all others. As a solution, she suggests that we think of equality as an ideal – something we

3 Tronto J, 1993, *Moral Boundaries: A political argument for an ethic of care*, Routledge, London, p145.
4 Note 3, p137.
5 Note 3, see ch 4 and 5.

work towards, instead of assuming it is already there.[5] Thus, the aim of good childcare is to bring a child to the point where he can become independent and autonomous. The aim of caring for the weak, the elderly, and the ill is to get them as close to that same ideal as is physically possible, while also giving them special protection that reflects the nature and degree of their dependence and vulnerability.[6] By discussing care as something that helps people achieve full citizenship, it finally becomes possible to make it clear how everyone in our society, even prime ministers and media moguls, depends on it. And once you've established the centrality of caring work, you can begin to argue for a better deal for life's carers.

This is where the care activists come in. The prototype of the care activist is Selma James, founder of the Wages for Housework Campaign. She and fellow campaigners have targeted the system of national accounts by which the United Nations calculates the relative wealth of all the countries in the world. These calculations determine which sorts of workers are addressed in economic and social policy, and which are treated as if they didn't even exist. Until two years ago, anyone who reared her own children, did domestic work, or produced her own food didn't count as a worker.[7]

Thanks to the campaign to have women's work acknowledged, most countries in the world (including this one) now keep track of the amount of unpaid work in what they call a 'satellite account'. This, they hope, will change the way governments allocate their resources and plan their economies. For women to be on the political map, what they do must first be visible.

Now that women's unpaid jobs are better reflected in the records, other care activists in the EU and the UN are campaigning to get the traditional work they do in schools and communities counted in the political process. Some writers call this work 'small democracy'. British political philosopher Ruth Lister calls it 'informal politics' and claims that it is often overlooked because it doesn't 'look' organised to traditionally organised politicians.[8]

But it is not enough, Lister says, to get official recognition for the informal political channels traditionally used by women. Their interests need to be better reflected in employment law, pension provision, and the structure of work. It has become increasingly clear to those working on behalf of disadvantaged working mothers, that it is not enough to address the problem in a piecemeal way, and that a

6 Note 3, p135.
7 Waring M, 1989, *If Women Counted*, Macmillan, London.
8 Lister R, 1997, *Citizenship: Feminist perspectives*, Macmillan, London, 146.

central problem from which all the other problems derive is the traditional definition of citizenship.

Every law and policy that touches on the workplace, is designed with an ideal citizen in mind. That citizen is presumed to be someone who can leave the running of his house and the care of his children to a wife. That citizen, in other words, is a traditional middle class man. But if we are to make sure that society is designed in such a way that all women and men can enjoy all the rights and privileges that only middle class men with full-time wives do now, then we have to redefine citizenship as well as the social rights that attach to it. A citizen must have the right to give care as well as to receive it.

To propose the obvious remedy – to change every bit of fine print in our culture so that it serves the needs of the citizen-with-no-wife – is to embark on a huge project. But for a modern society that wants to support parents, it is the only way. To do anything less is to abandon them to institutions and social conventions that make their work a great deal harder, and their chances of doing the best by their children a great deal lower. Parents cannot change these institutions and conventions on their own. If government has one responsibility towards parents, surely it must be to use its power to force these institutions to shift. The new policy makers need to ask not only what the family can do for them, but also what they can do for the family. Until they ask this question, there will be no 'partnership' between parents and the government. And no new morality ☉

Maureen Freely is the author of five novels and two works of non-fiction. She is also a journalist and teaches the writing Programme at the University of Warwick. She has four children, aged between six and twenty, and two stepchildren. Her new book,
The Parent Trap: Families, children and the new morality, *will be published by Virago in 2000.*

© *Maureen Freely 2000*

Bookmarks

Having None of It: Women, men and the future of work
Suzanne Franks

Quoting Erica Jong, Suzanne Franks points out that the nineties woman has above all won 'the right to be terminably exhausted'. Striking a justifiably pessimistic note, Franks goes on to explode the myth that modern women can choose to live their lives in many different ways. Women still, it appears, do the bulk of domestic work in the home, and despite superior educational attainment and equality of opportunity at entry level, are scarcely in evidence at the highest levels of industry. Drawing on a wealth of data, this frightening but necessary book charts the hidden obstacles facing women in their careers, revealing the operations behind the 'leaky pipeline' – a more apt metaphor than the 'glass ceiling', Franks thinks, to describe how so many women make a promising start in their careers but fade out along the way. She convincingly demonstrates that, even when the pressure of children and families are removed from the equation, there remains a range of barriers to women's progression. Skilfully researched and eloquently argued, *Having None of It* sounds a wake up call to anyone who thought that the age of equal opportunities had truly arrived.
(Granta, 1999)

Divided Labours: An evolutionary view of women at work
Kingsley Browne

The quote on the front of this book – 'women care less about money, status and power than do men – consistent with evolutionary theory, biological fact and psychological data' – seems designed to incense a feminist sensibility. The rest of this slim tome does the job neatly. Drawing on evolutionary psychology, Kingsley Browne's core proposition is that the metaphor of the 'glass ceiling' conveys the wrong impression. It should, he says, be reframed as the 'gossamer ceiling', a barrier that women 'see'; but that is not strong enough to hold back those who choose to cross it. In general, though, women rarely want to break through this ceiling, content as they are with their primary role as mothers, and carers. As the title implies, Kingsley Browne hides behind evolutionary science to peddle an all too familiar script – men are from Mars, women are from Venus. The main problem is that the author's personal contempt for feminist arguments shines through much of the writing and it is all too apparent which side of the faultline he stands on. This is a shame. There must surely be space in the third way to accommodate feminist perspectives and evolutionary theory. Sadly this small volume does not even begin that synthesis.

(Weidenfeld & Nicolson, 1998)

Farewell to the Family? Public policy and family breakdown in Britain and the USA

Patricia Morgan

Farewell to the Family aims to demonstrate the economic and social costs of the decline of the single-income nuclear family, a decline hastened, suggests the report, by anti-family tax and welfare policies. While much of the material is rigorously researched and convincing, it is somewhat marred by a polemicism verging on hysteria. If around one in five families are currently single parent, this seems little reason to state, as Patricia Morgan does in concluding, that we are on the verge of 'an unprecedented social experiment, considering that there has been no known human society built upon the mother–child unit'. And if, as Morgan shows, a mother is frequently better off on benefits than married to a wage-earner, then this surely says as much about exploitative wage levels as anything else.

Indeed, tax-breaks and benefits that support married couples may encourage more people to remain in traditional family situations. What they will not do is counteract the complexity of cultural and social forces that has led to people living their lives in more diverse ways, forces that *Farewell to the Family*'s thesis does not sufficiently take into account.

(Institute of Economic Affairs, 1999)

Working Fathers: New strategies for balancing work and family

James A Levine and Todd L Pittinsky

At a time when 'the new fatherhood' looks set to rise up the agenda in Britain, this racily written book from America provides a comprehensive review of the key trends in fatherhood and family life and maps the ramifications of these changes on employers and business. The book presents a wealth of original data to argue that there are significant shifts in father's involvement in the lives of their children. They go on to argue that father friendly employment practices do impact positively on the bottom line – enhancing employee satisfaction, improving productivity and mainstreaming the work-family debate. The book aims to shift the way we think about fatherhood and does so in an accessible way, offering lots of practical tips to fathers, mothers and employers. Success for today's fathers, we're told, is no longer just about being a good provider, it is about being there for your children and actively parenting them too.

(Harcourt Brace & Company, 1998)

The Corrosion of Character: The personal consequences of work in the new capitalism
Richard Sennett

Through vignettes of working life from modern America, Sennett's latest book shows how job market insecurity results in the inability to plan and develop ties of obligation and responsibility. He relentlessly reveals the consequences of the crumbling of routine, of the rise of short-term contracts and of job descriptions that obscure the actual value of what workers do, ultimately showing how the work ethic itself is undermined by insecurity. Few sociologists write so accessibly as Sennett, and all the quiet fury of a mature egalitarian informs a book that is at once written for general readers and yet moves effortlessly between observation, social theory and political jeremiad. Offering no policy advice and no specific recommendations, occasionally *The Corrosion of Character* only just steers away from nostalgic lament. Sennett ends his book with a slightly mawkish statement of hope that sooner or later a system of work so demoralising as the one he diagnoses cannot survive.

(WW Norton & Co, 1999)

The Great Disruption: Human nature and the reconstitution of social order
Francis Fukuyama

According to Fukuyama, the monogamous two-parent nuclear family is the biologically ordained norm, and represents the proper, best and only way to tame the promiscuous and irresponsible young male. Since the 1960s, the availability of contraception and the participation of women in the labour market have, he believes, conspired to undermine the traditional family unit, resulting in rising crime and falling trust. If, however, this explanation of the putative great moral collapse of the past 40 years were correct, then Fukuyama's hypothesis that things are now getting better would be impossible to explain. For contraception is no less available now, female labour market participation is still rising and biology presumably has not changed in 35 years. *The Great Disruption* will be welcomed in some quarters, though, particularly that segment of American culture that yearns for prophets of community, cohesion and moral order. For it offers a jeremiad of grand decline, a story of how people are corrupt, the customs disregarded, the youth wicked and order collapsing, combined with a story of how, with a little more effort to exert authority, order can prevail. If you like that kind of thing, you will like this book.

(Profile Books, 1999)

When Work Doesn't Work Anymore: Women, work and identity

Elizabeth Perle McKenna

Can you achieve great success and wealth by climbing the corporate ladder, gaining all the attendant satisfaction and self esteem, while also maintaining a fulfilling relationship with your children, partner, and inner self? It will come as little surprise to most of us that the answer is no. For McKenna this realisation, as it came to her in her thirties, was somewhat of a shock. Frustrated at the corporate culture that is incompatible with having a life outside work, she decided to put the world to rights with this book. Drawing on original interviews with hundreds of women, she argues that we must changes the rules that govern our professional lives in order that women, and men, can lead more fulfilling lives. Part lament on the voracious demands of modern careers, part manifesto for altering both the way we work and the value we place on the trappings of success, the book does contain some worthwhile discussion of the plight of the modern careerist who is faced with the Hobson's choice of a successful career or a meaningful personal life. Unfortunately, for all her optimistic talk of changing the way we work, McKenna is some way off presenting a realistic future alternative.

(Simon & Schuster, 1998)

Changing Britain: Families and households in the 1990s

edited by Susan McRae

Changing Britain brings together findings of the ESRC Economic and Household Change Programme, set up to look at the relationship between household living arrangements and broader demographic change in the UK. A range of authors discuss kinship, divorce, same-sex couple households and stepfamilies in the light of the latest statistical data and research findings. Susan McRae's introductory essay is particularly useful - her historical demonstration that in many ways late millennial family life is not so different from that of the distant past makes for illuminating reading. The book shows, however, that there are some profound and unprecedented demographic changes taking place; for example, it is predicted that by 2020 more than one in three households will be made up of people living alone – a prospect with radical implications for policy-makers and town planners. *Changing Britain* will be an invaluable tool for those seeking detailed information on home life in modern Britain.

(Oxford University Press, 1999)

Related publications from Demos

The Family in Question
Stein Ringen
ISBN 1 898309 69 8 £7.95
A radical analysis of the role of the
family in modern society. The author
argues that the family is a grossly
undervalued contributor to the
nation's wealth and quality of life,
and that raising children is a job families do for the good of society as a
whole. The author proposes new
approaches to child allowances and
argues for more democracy within
the family including votes for children. Stein Ringen is Professor of
Sociology and Social Policy at Oxford
University.

Family Learning: The foundation
of effective education
Titus Alexander
ISBN 1 898309 98 1 £7.95
Families are our most important and
influential places of learning yet
most public spending on education
goes to support formal institutions,
while public expenditure on families
goes mainly on coping with the consequences of stress and failure. The
author presents a long-term strategy
for developing family learning including strengthening family learning
support networks and partnerships
between schools and parents, transforming schools into community
centres for lifelong learning and
improving coordination of family services. Titus Alexander is an independent educator and author.

Freedom's Children: Work,
relationships and politics for
18-34 year olds in Britain today
Helen Wilkinson and Geoff Mulgan
ISBN 1 898309 27 2 £9.95
Drawing on data from the British
Household Panel Study and MORI
Socioconsult, this report details the
lifestyles and values of the 18-34 year
old generation. It looks at everything
from violence to political activism,
and argues that we urgently need to
achieve a new balance between
freedom and commitment to improve
the lives of this generation and of
generations to come. 'It is time that
the UK started looking harder at how
better to accommodate the needs and
aspirations of its young.' *Financial
Times*

The Parenting Deficit
Amitai Etzioni
ISBN 1 898309 20 5 £5.95
Argues that the movement first of
men, and more recently of women,
out of the home and into work has
left a serious deficit of parental care.
Proposes economic and social measures to improve the quality of parenting and to raise its status. Amitai
Etzioni is President of the American
Sociological Association and founder
of the Communitarian Network.

The Proposal: Giving marriage back to the people
Helen Wilkinson
ISBN 1 898309 28 0 £4.95
This report argues that marriage can be revived if the institution itself is brought up to date. Drawing on historical evidence and international examples, it shows just how much scope there is to remake marriage for the modern age and to endow the wedding ceremony with a new authenticity by giving people the freedom to write their own vows, choose their own location and decide who presides over the ceremony.
'Radical' *Independent*

Time Out: The costs and benefits of paid parental leave
Helen Wilkinson with others
ISBN 1 898309 58 2 £12.95
Parental leave gives parents time off work to spend with their children. This detailed study shows how a new scheme of parental leave could be introduced into the UK with substantial benefits for parents and children, and with manageable costs for business, employees and the government. It draws on new surveys with workers and employers, analysis of parental leave schemes around the world and detailed costings of a range of options.

The Time Squeeze
issue 5, £8
Rising working hours and greater pressures to juggle work and domestic responsibilities are contributing to a 'time squeeze'. This issue provides the most comprehensive analysis of the economics and politics of time in the 1990s, as well as an imaginative set of policy proposals for achieving a better balance between work and life. Authors include John Gershuny, Ray Pahl, Jeremy Rifkin and Theodore Zeldin. 'A series of intelligent attempts to assess the coming death of the clock. This event may turn out to be as influential as the "death of God".' *Independent on Sunday*

Demos publications are available from:

Central Books
99 Wallis Road
London E9 5LN
tel: 0181 986 5488
fax: 0181 533 5821
email: mo@centralbooks.com

Visit our website at **www.demos.co.uk** for a full list of publications, information on upcoming events and our current reserach programme, and worldwide links.

Become a Demos subscriber

The price of annual subscription is £50.00 for individuals and £100.00 for institutions.*

You will receive:

- a minimum of four books (rrp £5.95–£14.95) containing policy, argument and analysis
- two issues of *Demos Collection* (rrp £8)
- one third off all Demos publications
- discounted entrance to Demos events
- any four existing publications free of charge (institutional subscriptions only)

* Subscribers outside Europe, please add £25.00 for airmail charges; subscribers in Australasia, please add £30.00.

Payment method direct debit / cheque

To pay by credit card, please ring Demos on 0171 353 4479.

Name

Address

Postcode

Telephone

DEMOS

Originator number 626205

 DIRECT Debit

✂

Instruction to your Bank or Building Society to pay Direct Debits

1 Name and full postal address of your Bank or Building Society

To The Manager

Bank or Building Society

Address

Postcode

2 Name(s) of account holder(s)

3 Branch sort code

(from top right hand corner of your cheque card)

☐☐ – ☐☐ – ☐☐

4 Bank or Building Society account number

☐☐☐☐☐☐☐☐

5 Demos reference number (for office use only)

6 Instruction to your Bank or Building Society:
Please pay Demos Direct Debits from the account detailed on this Instruction subject to the safeguards assured by the Direct Debit Guarantee.

Signature(s)

Date

Please send completed form to: Demos Freepost, London EC4B 4HP

Banks and building societies may not accept Direct Debit Instructions from certain types of account